Politics as Worship

Modern Intellectual and Political History of the Middle East
Fred H. Lawson, *Series Editor*

Select Titles in Modern Intellectual and Political History of the Middle East

The Autocratic Parliament: Power and Legitimacy in Egypt, 1866–2011
    Irene Weipert-Fenner

Everyday Politics in the Libyan Arab Jamahiriya
    Matteo Capasso

Figures That Speak: The Vocabulary of Turkish Nationalism
    Matthew deTar

Iran's Experiment with Parliamentary Governance: The Second Majles, 1909–1911
    Mangol Bayat

Islam, Revival, and Reform: Redefining Tradition for the Twenty-First Century
    Natana J. DeLong-Bas, ed.

Killing Contention: Demobilization in Morocco during the Arab Spring
    Sammy Zeyad Badran

Sayyid Qutb: An Intellectual Biography
    Giedrė Šabasevičiūtė

Why Alliances Fail: Islamist and Leftist Coalitions in North Africa
    Matt Buehler

For a full list of titles in this series,
visit https://press.syr.edu/supressbook-series/modern
-intellectual-and-political-history-of-the-middle-east/.

POLITICS AS WORSHIP

*Righteous Activism and the
Egyptian Muslim Brothers*

Sumita Pahwa

Syracuse University Press

Copyright © 2023 by Syracuse University Press

Syracuse, New York 13244-5290

All Rights Reserved

First Edition 2023

23 24 25 26 27 28   6 5 4 3 2 1

∞ The paper used in this publication meets the minimum requirements of the American National Standard for Information Sciences—Permanence of Paper for Printed Library Materials, ANSI Z39.48-1992.

For a listing of books published and distributed by Syracuse University Press, visit https://press.syr.edu.

ISBN: 978-0-8156-3823-0 (hardcover)
978-0-8156-3824-7 (paperback)
978-0-8156-5699-9 (e-book)

Library of Congress Cataloging-in-Publication Data

Names: Pahwa, Sumita, author.
Title: Politics as worship : righteous activism and the Egyptian Muslim Brothers / Sumita Pahwa.
Description: First edition. | Syracuse, New York : Syracuse University Press, 2023. | Series: Modern intellectual and political history of the Middle East | Includes bibliographical references and index.
Identifiers: LCCN 2023018168 (print) | LCCN 2023018169 (ebook) | ISBN 9780815638230 (hardcover) | ISBN 9780815638247 (paperback) | ISBN 9780815656999 (ebook)
Subjects: LCSH: Jamʿīyat al-Ikhwān al-Muslimīn (Egypt)—History—20th century. | Jamʿīyat al-Ikhwān al-Muslimīn (Egypt)—History—21st century. | Islam and politics—Egypt—History—20th century. | Islam and politics—Egypt—History—21st century.
Classification: LCC BP10.J383 P34 2023 (print) | LCC BP10.J383 (ebook) | DDC 297.2/72096205—dc23/eng/20230508
LC record available at https://lccn.loc.gov/2023018168
LC ebook record available at https://lccn.loc.gov/2023018169

Manufactured in the United States of America

For Rohan and Mira

Contents

Acknowledgments *ix*

Introduction *1*

1. How to Act for Islam in the World 28
2. Cultivating Citizens and Representing Righteousness: Daʻwa *and* Tarbiya *through Electoral and Parliamentary Politics, 1984–1987* 47
3. God and Rule: *Political Empowerment and Applying Sharia* 75
4. Political Work and the Practical *Tarbiya* of Welfarism 112
5. *Shura, Sharia, Sharʻiyya*: *Applying Islam in Government* 153

Conclusion 203

Glossary 235

Bibliography 243

Index 261

Acknowledgments

Individuals, to paraphrase a more famous writer, write books, but not in circumstances of their own choosing: they must be sustained intellectually, financially, institutionally, and emotionally. The seed for this book was planted in an assignment for a class on Islam and the Middle East at the Institut Catholique in Paris, on a study-abroad year, where I first read about the Egyptian Muslim Brothers (MB) and became interested in debates on what drives Islamist movements. It continued its life as a dissertation project comparing the Muslim Brothers and the Indian Bharatiya Janata Party (BJP) in the Political Science Department at Johns Hopkins University, where I was lucky to have the opportunity and support to study widely and across disciplinary lines and, more unusually in the discipline, to learn about and embrace non-positivist research methodologies.

The intellectual and emotional generosity that academia depends on—particularly where other support structures may be weaker—were important in nurturing this project. I was lucky to find my people in scattered places during the dissertation process: Scott Hibbard shared ideas and advice on research in Egypt; Margaret Keck offered theoretical and methodological guidance and support in her writing seminar; and helpful and supportive feedback from my fellow graduate students, Daniel Levine, Rameez Abbas, and others, was critical in helping me figure out how to frame my project. Anna Gruben's friendship and care helped me get through difficult times. Reneé Marlin-Bennett came to the project later and helped me see the forest in the trees; her guidance and careful, constructive feedback were critical to its completion. I would not have finished the dissertation or written this book without her empathetic and intellectually generous support.

The grants and awards generally recounted in acknowledgments are not part of this research story. With no institutional research funding or the infrastructure of elite academic networks to move me along, and a project too underdeveloped to win any of the few external grants I qualified for as a non-US person, I relied on the paid work I was able to get in Egypt, and teaching work in the United States while researching and writing. I am grateful to Nadia Naqib and the American University in Cairo Press for offering me work that allowed me to capitalize on my language skills (and the fiscal advantages of doing work in English) to support myself as a freelance proofreader during research in 2005-7. Nadia Naqib and Wiam el-Tamami were true friends during my time in Cairo. I owe Joshua Stacher an immense debt for welcoming me to a community of researchers in Cairo and taking me to Kifaya protests, and for generously sharing contacts. Along with Josh, Hossam el-Hamalawy and Issandr el-Amrani taught me a great deal about Egyptian politics. Elijah Zarwan offered helpful and clear-eyed feedback on later versions of my argument. Maye Kassem offered friendship and an introduction to the world of academic political science in Egypt.

I relied on the expertise and knowledge of several Egyptian researchers in working through difficult translations and understanding scriptural reference, some of whom did paid translation work for this project, but do not wish to be named due to political sensitivities in Egypt today. EM, MF, and WT helped to translate almost half of my textual sources from chapters 2 and 3, though final word choices and responsibility for errors remain my own. I am also grateful for my parents Manju and Vijay Pahwa's unconditional love, and their unstinting support of me in pursuing my goals. Back in Baltimore, Timi Gerson and Carol Higgs were my "family," welcoming and supportive, and offering me a place to stay. My spouse, Steve Negus, whom I met in Cairo, shared stories and anecdotes from his reporting years about people whom I had learned about on paper and kept me grounded in the realities of the lives and events I was writing about. By taking on childcare when we welcomed our first child, he gave me the space and support I needed to write over summers and weekends, and he continued to support me and take on family work while I conducted research and writing in later years as well.

My colleagues during my visiting instructor years at Skidmore College from 2009 to 2011, particularly Kate Graney, were supportive and kind, and students in my Islam and Politics seminar helped me think through questions as I wrote. The Saratoga Springs Public Library café and its staff offered space, coffee, baked goods, and encouraging queries to help the writing process along. My sister Sonali's emotional support and encouragement, and guidance through the hidden curriculum of graduate school, were critical at this time, too.

The January 25 uprising happened in Egypt just as I was finishing my dissertation, and the world and the Muslim Brothers' place in it, were turned upside down. Returning to Egypt in 2012–14, I had the opportunity to revise my research completely and benefit from the briefly accessible political atmosphere and willingness of MB activists and politicians to speak more openly. I owe MA a tremendous debt for introducing me to student activists who were essential for my newer interviews, and I am grateful to the activists (who, sadly, would stay anonymous as the political atmosphere became repressive again in 2014) for their generosity in talking to me. NY, who worked for me as a research assistant, helped me find elusive and important documents, doggedly and creatively tracked down curricular texts, and offered translation assistance with a side of entertainingly snarky commentary. Samer al-Atrush generously shared his Azhari training to help me figure out confusing phrasings in hadith references. Colleagues in the profession helped me move on and rethink my research substantially after the PhD. Tariq Thachil pushed me to consider important theoretical framings that I had been reluctant to engage; Steven Brooke shared sources and ideas; Nathan Brown encouraged me to embrace imperfect data; Marie Vannetzel pushed me to work through important puzzles; and Beth Hurd, Jeremy Menchik, and Tamir Moustafa helped me reconsider how to conceptualize key questions about religion in the political process. The late Ellis Goldberg was generous in sharing his incredible depth and breadth of knowledge about Egypt, religion, and theory, always willing to help me think through sources and methods, and is a lasting inspiration to me.

At Scripps College, Lara Deeb offered mentorship and pragmatic advice on teaching and research, Mietek Boduszyński was my partner in crime for talking about Middle East politics and making our way in the profession, and my colleagues in the Politics Department offered friendship. Scripps start-up research funds allowed me to pay for some translations, and expand my research to Morocco. A one-semester, paid, pretenure sabbatical allowed me the time to write. Ursula Lindsey was generous with connections and help in Rabat, OR was a stellar research assistant, and SA helped translate interviews when I stumbled over Moroccan Arabic. I am thankful to reviewers for the Syracuse University Press for their thoughtful and constructive advice on how to strengthen the argument of the book and for being willing to stick through the revisions process that was delayed a full year by the pandemic, and to Aaron Rock-Singer for sharing his expert feedback in the late stages as well.

As all academics but the lucky few know, the path of intellectual production has as many people who pull one down as those who lift one up. I remain keenly aware of the many points at which I could have fallen off the path, whether through lack of support from a graduate institution, or the put-downs of those who suggested that my work did not belong in my field, or that I lacked the capacity to finish a PhD. The persistence that writing this book required was also fueled by a small desire to spite them.

This book is dedicated to my children, Rohan and Mira, who always reminded me of what really mattered in life. Rohan put up with constant political conversations and curfews as a preschooler in post-2011 Cairo, accepting *muzahirat* and Morsi as part of his life, and his affection sustained me through the stress of dissertation completion. Mira's jokes and incisive questions ("Is your book based on a true story, Mama?"), and her hugs, give me so much joy. It is also dedicated more broadly to *umm el-dunya. Illegitimi non carborundum.*

Politics as Worship

Introduction

> The word "change" is not in our vocabulary.
> —Mohammed Morsi, quoted by Nathan Brown (2012)

> Why do I work in politics? For God!
> —YS, Muslim Brotherhood student activist, interview in Cairo (September 2013)

The Egyptian Muslim Brotherhood (MB) has aimed to build Muslims who could be a "new spirit flowing in the heart of the community" through ethical cultivation (*tarbiya*) and self-reform (*islah al-nafs*) since its founding ninety years ago. Its founder, Hasan al-Banna, saw political and social activism as part of its religious mission, arguing that the righteous Muslim had an obligation to change the world ("Between Yesterday and Today"). Over the decades, the movement leadership experimented with various political strategies to supplement its grassroots preaching and organizing, including elite lobbying, radical separatism, and quietism, and it embraced electoral politics from the 1980s onward, insisting all the while that these changing strategies were driven by an unchanging religious method (*minhaj*). External observers broadly agreed that faith was central to the movement's mission and that it motivated its members, but they took it for granted as a background factor and rarely studied how its role and meaning changed through the movement's evolution.

Political scientists who study Islamist movements like the MB tend to locate the driving force of faith in their history and founding moments. They frame the religious wings of movements—those dedicated to education and preaching—as their least dynamic organizational elements and treat Islamist religious and political missions as separate and increasingly incompatible. Analysts of the movement's adaptation to competitive electoral politics emphasize institutional interests and incentives that drive change and treat Islamist ideology and religious goals as a drag on adaptation. In most analyses, the MB's religious discourse influences electoral politics by motivating pious activists, or signaling their upright reputation to pious voters, but is itself relatively unchanged by political use (Jamal, Masoud, and Nugent 2014; Brooke 2018; Wickham 2002). Where some argue that the goal of building better Muslims was increasingly sidelined as electoral power-seeking became the main driver of the MB's strategy, others contend that fundamental religious goals, especially the mission to establish an Islamic state, remained constant, and that politics was a tool to achieve these. Both explain change within the movement by focusing on how either pro-politics factions or the movement leadership are able to capitalize on political opportunities to pursue their different priorities. The dynamic "party wing" is destined to be at odds, in this view, with the conservative "organization." To the extent that Islamist ideas evolve, according to these scholars, they do so by losing influence in favor of more liberal, democratic ideals of political activism. And, when put to the test of generating policy, foundational Islamist ideologies useful for mobilizing opposition are weakened and discredited (Roy 1994; Bayat 1996).

Yet when the MB chose to form a political party, compete in free elections, and form a majority government, following Hosni Mubarak's overthrow in 2011, the anticipated reckoning between "movement men" and "electoral specialists" did not come to pass. For the MB, religious leaders and goals were not strategically separable from political ones. The *tanzim* leadership embraced electoral pragmatism and a formally separate party, and party men promised to apply sharia and serve as the voice of Islam in politics. While some factions broke off from the MB, the movement remained more united around its religious identity than expected, through multiple elections in 2011 and 2012 (Wickham 2013, 155–87). What does this tell us about the way the Islamist religious mission adapted to electoral politics, and what assumptions about religion's role in Islamist political mobilization must we revisit?

I argue that the MB's religious and electoral missions did not diverge fully after 2011 in part because religious goals and ideals of ethical cultivation had driven political work ever since the movement entered electoral politics in the 1980s. While the organization's division of labor between preaching and politics led to factional disagreements on the relative importance of each, it was based on a shared understanding of political work as ethical conduct, rather than merely a shared end goal of a religious state. Throughout the evolution of the movement, its leaders used religious principles and norms to evaluate political choices, guide political strategy, and define priorities for members' social activism and training. "Working for God" and building a righteous, Islamic society through ethical conduct and cultivation were powerful motives mobilizing activists for political work, and *tanzim* (organization) leaders adapted their vision for an Islamic state and their ethical cultivation (*tarbiya*) curricula in response to political experience. Analyzing internal movement debates on preaching, activism, and social reform triggered by electoral opportunities from the 1980s to the 2000s, I will show how key ideals of righteous action in MB thought—particularly ethical cultivation (*tarbiya*), commanding the right (*al-amr bi-l-maʿruf*), applying God's law (*tatbiq al-shariʿa*), and enacting collective religious obligation (*fard kifaya*)—were applied to new fields and forms of activism, and I will consider how these debates changed the movement's operational priorities as leaders increasingly saw electoral politics as a resource for social Islamization.

I suggest that religious framing and appeals to "Islamic" norms helped to justify innovation and political adaptation, and not simply to assert the conservative authority of *tanzim* leaders. I analyze how, and in what contexts, leaders invoked the religious mission in political decision-making; how they framed the value of campaigning, constituent outreach, and parliamentary work in terms of performing and cultivating good Muslimhood; how they used religious frames in the movement's political message; and how they sought to affirm the Brothers' identity as the most sincere and effective "workers for Islam" in Egypt through their political choices. I argue that while these strategic choices responded to electoral and institutional incentives, the religious frames that movement leaders used to justify them had a more long-term impact: they attached new meanings to religious frames of righteous action that became part of the movement's discursive tradition, to be repeated in future calls to action and incorporated into movement literature on collective religious obligations.

Framing new kinds of political and social work as important for the core mission of Islamization, I argue, helped the MB leadership change operational priorities and shift the "boundaries of justifiable action" for the movement while also increasing its commitment to the state and to politics (Schwedler 2006; Philbrick Yadav 2013). Where the literature on Islamist political learning has identified external interactions and electoral incentives as the main drivers of change, I contend that internal debates are important drivers as well, and that movement responses to electoral incentives have weighed the actions that different choices entailed in terms of norms of ethical conduct as well as their utility in achieving short-term political goals. I suggest that new definitions of what it means to serve the Islamic mission in the social and political sphere are markers of ideational change, like externally directed movement commitments to democratic and liberal political norms, and that the latter depend in part on the former, rather than on an increasing separation of political and religious missions.

Constructing Islamic Mobilization

An overarching claim in this book is that "Islamic" and "religious" ideals are not derived solely from authoritative texts or religious authorities, but are constructed substantially through practice. In the language of social science, religious discourse is a dependent, not an independent, variable in political mobilization. Following Asad's (1986) argument for treating Islam as a "discursive tradition," I approach Islamist political thought as concerned with deriving and applying norms for righteous action and individual and collective religious obligation from the Islamic tradition (1986). I also follow Vannetzel's (2016, 22–28) call to "sociologize, not essentialize" Islamist ideology, showing how it draws on, but is not reducible to, founding doctrines, and studying how it is mobilized in specific historical contexts.

Social and political action have been key to achieving the promise of Islam for the MB since its founding: movement materials make regular reference to the fact that Hasan al-Banna, its founder, insisted that Muslims were a "practical people," and that Sayyid Qutb, a later MB ideologue, declared that the "living Muslim [was] the word of God on Earth." Islamist leaders refer to the Islamic *minhaj* or "method" for achieving a more godly society, rather than laying out goals in a manifesto. The MB's core mission of *tarbiya* consists of educating people in the Islamic scriptural tradition, as well as—and more importantly—in a set of values and norms about the kind of ethical conduct that will allow them to live as good Muslims and achieve salvation. Drawing on Mahmood (2005) and Menchik (2016), I focus on how Islamists see ethical practice and cultivation as religious acts and define religious motivations in context-specific terms. When MB activists appeal to Islamic ideals to justify or encourage certain kinds of behaviors and policies, they make a case for what it means to act according to divine norms in specific social and personal circumstances. The intended outcomes of this behavior are usually broad—justice, and enacting God's will on earth—but rarely defined clearly enough to meet any scriptural or universally recognizable standard of being "Islamic." Thus, while activists and leaders cite and draw upon texts and doctrines, understanding how Islamist ideology influences movement strategy and activist behavior requires understanding how Islamist leaders and activists interpret its elements in practice, interaction, and debate.

For the MB, righteous action produces the ideal Islamic society through what Kandil (2015) calls a "trickle up" process: individual Muslims taught to act righteously serve as examples to others and cultivate righteousness in their families and peer groups, ultimately creating a more Islamic society that, in turn, allows individuals the support and resources needed to live more Muslim lives. Righteous actions serve many purposes: they are constitutive, in cultivating the good Muslim individual's capacity for ethical conduct; performative, in asserting piety in the public sphere; educational, in modeling good Islamic conduct to others and cultivating goodwill for the Islamic way among potential sympathizers; and only partly strategic, in building a more Islamic society. When the MB leadership calls on activists to spread God's message, it incorporates all of these forms of righteous action within its understanding of "preaching" and defines the application or rule of God's sharia as the ultimate result of spreading righteous action and of "working for God"—laws and political outcomes are tools in the process, not the end goals of it. This contextual and adaptive approach has allowed the MB to fold a variety of social and political projects into its *minhaj* or method for social Islamization, giving the impression of a vague and self-contradictory Islamic ideology (Schwedler 2006, 156). As Spiegel (2015) has argued in his work on Moroccan Islamist movements, the "purposeful ambiguity" of Islamist ideology and its ongoing, contextual reinterpretation often serves to broaden, rather than to dilute, its appeal.

Explaining Change: Movement Evolution and External Engagement

How electoral politics, or the experience of governing, changes the worldview or ideals of Islamist movements is the subject of multiple scholarly analyses (Bayat 2005; Schwedler 2006; Clark 2006; Ghobashy 2005). Schwedler (2006, 154–70) argues that debates about what kinds of adaptation to electoral incentives are justifiable or imaginable given "core" Islamic principles and objectives are key to cementing ideational change within Islamist movements. Both Schwedler and Clark (2006) show how core commitments to Muslim ideals and identity constrain Islamist movement adaptation to political incentives and democracy primarily by highlighting issues that movements define as "red lines" because of their grounding in scripture or as core political issues, such as family law or policy toward Israel. Ghobashy (2005) argues that electoral participation in the 1990s encouraged the MB leadership to find common ground between religious and democratic concepts, while Bayat (2005) argues that "internal contradictions" and "societal pressure" tend to push all Islamist movements that embrace politics to "marry Islam" with liberal principles. Wickham's (2013) magisterial work on the MB's evolution in electoral politics emphasizes the influence of a pro-politics "middle generation" in nudging the movement to adopt new positions on pluralism and freedom, and the conservative pull of the preaching wing as a constraint on innovation.

Meanwhile, scholars who focus on the MB as a religious and ideologically driven movement tend to treat it as a self-contained organization, shaped less by social and political outreach than by its leaders' ideas about religious cultivation, recruitment, and training, and their desire to keep the movement alive and disciplined in the face of repression (Lia 1998; Mitchell 1969; Zollner 2011; Arian 2014). Anani's study of the MB as an organization (2016) explains how the MB organization, or the *gamaʿa*, functions as a hospitable space in which to build a Brother's righteousness, with social networks and practices that socialize individuals in a distinct identity. Kandil's study (2015) also focuses on the movement's ideal of spiritual cultivation as an induction into a "pious vanguard" that remains wary of and resistant to the pull of worldly compromise and argues that the movement has projected its goals of social Islamization on to the electoral sphere rather than being changed by electoral engagement. Like Tammam (2011), he contends that change within the MB was mostly a result of a changing, more socially conservative, membership profile.

I find that, despite the distinction between "the *gamaʿa*" and "the world" in movement discourse, action in the wider world is incorporated into the movement's model of ethical cultivation as well as into its mission of social Islamization. When the movement leadership embraced electoral politics, it did initially treat politics as a task for a specialized cadre. However, it gradually included political work in its teachings on righteous praxis and performing good Muslimhood. Electoral politics and the public sphere, therefore, came to matter in building the identity of the Brother and in the movement's ideational production. Where Kandil (2015) argues that the MB has pursued, but never altered, its religious mission in the public sphere, and Wickham (2013) and Ghobashy (2002) suggest that growing electoral pragmatism made liberal and utilitarian political norms more important than religious ones in shaping the MB's political strategy, I find evidence that public political engagement did affect the movement's understanding of its religious mission, and that its framework for "righteous action" continued to shape both its response to electoral opportunities, and leaders' adaptation of the movement's everyday priorities for political work.

While movement leaders were primarily concerned with upholding the MB's identity and mission, Islamist ideational production was substantially shaped by interactions with political and religious rivals: cadres frequently participated in debates on the Islamic political project in non-Islamic newspapers, in parliament, in public seminars, and in campaigning, and their discourse invariably straddled "movement" and "public" spheres and discourses. I suggest that the line between the movement sphere and the public sphere that MB leaders have themselves strategically mobilized to emphasize their accountability to divine rather than political norms, and that non-Islamists and scholars alike have made to position Islamism as the "other" of secular politics and ideals, is often crossed and blurred in practice. These public spheres and discourses, in turn, do not resemble idealized secular spaces, but are also sites of debate on what kind of Islam can be both authentic and acceptable for modern social and cultural circumstances. Building on Arian's (2014) study of the MB's new outreach strategy in the 1970s and early 1980s, and similar analyses of Islamist mobilization in Lebanon, Iran, Jordan, and Yemen (Phibrick Yadav 2013; Schwedler 2006; Tabaar 2018), I will show how these public interactions and their reinterpretation by movement leaders helped to constitute the Islamic project that the MB formed in the electoral sphere.

MB leaders have regularly incorporated and mobilized nationalist and "civil religion" frames in their arguments, positioning themselves as better able to deliver good governance, social justice, economic welfare, and education than non-Islamist political authorities. While the MB has always claimed to apply unchanging divine norms, its ideologues have embraced modernist and developmentalist goals in constructing a contemporary Islamic project and have worked with neighborhood welfare networks, positioning themselves as agents of social reform that anybody, religious or otherwise, could benefit from, giving the impression of reducing their focus on spiritual cultivation (Binder 1988; Brooke 2017). Building on Wickham's (2002) and Vannetzel's (2016) arguments for how Islamist activists enact and reinforce their identities as moral social actors through welfare work, I show that MB leaders framed electoral and political work as stages in a project of social Islamization and functional for the broader goals of Islamic justice, as well as forms of righteous action in spreading God's message, "commanding the right," and contributing to an individual's ethical cultivation. I also demonstrate how these new understandings of righteous action were folded into movement ideology, and how leaders included lessons from political work into formal training given to new movement members, and I consider how this sacralization of political work has helped to sustain support for the movement, even in the absence of electoral incentives.

Finding Religion in the Political Process

A goal of this book is to reconceptualize how religion works in political processes, by bringing insights from work in anthropology and political theory to bear on the way comparativist social scientists understand Islamist mobilization. The question of how religious ideals, motivations, intellectual production, and institutions shape Islamist movements has been approached in very different ways in different disciplinary traditions. Classic studies of the MB, such as those by Mitchell (1969) and Lia (1998), and more recent studies, such as Zollner's (2009) book on Banna's successor, Hasan al-Hudaybi, have shown how movement ideologues interpreted religious obligations and framed strategies for Islamic activism in response to specific historical pressures. They have treated Islamist ideology as something established at a foundational juncture and adapted in crisis, thereafter serving as a fairly stable reference point for the mission and forms that Islamic activism should take for movement members. Social scientific studies of Islamist movements since the early 2000s have moved away from analyzing their ideology and religious motivations and sought instead to counter frames of religious determinism and Islamic exceptionalism by showing how movements developed flexibility in response to electoral incentives, and how resource mobilization aided their political expansion more than any unique religious legitimacy (Ghobashy 2005; Wickham 2002; Brown 2012; Brooke 2018). These studies have tended to focus either on religious institutions and networks, or on ideas as communicated by Islamists to voters. The former have concentrated empirically on the ways in which Islamist networks function and mobilize for new purposes to address the needs of changing constituencies over time, emphasizing the organizational capacity and reputations of Islamists more than their ideas (Brooke 2019; Wickham 2002). Studies of the political power of Islamist ideas center around their reception and interpretation by voters, asking how religious references, particularly to sharia, influence support for particular policies or boost the credibility of those championing them to deliver social and economic justice (Masoud 2014; Jamal, Masoud, and Nugent 2014). Some studies in this category seek to separate piety conceptually from practice in order to better study its effects on political behavior—for instance, by using personal belief reporting and worship practices to assess how pious voters and activists are motivated to act or respond to politics differently from less pious ones (Pepinsky, Liddle, and Mujani 2018; Masoud and Jamal 2012).

I propose to study religion's impact on politics not through individually located beliefs or specialized networks, but through frames and discourses that position some kinds of action as more Islamic than others. The religious norms that motivate pious citizens and activists are not, I argue, exogenous to political processes, but are produced in them, by authorities as well as challengers. Islamists actively seek to shape these norms as well as to mobilize them for their own projects. Defining mobilizational frames as "religious" when they change over time in different social contexts is a challenge: what religious voters recognize as sharia, for instance, in political rhetoric, may depend on how sharia is framed in political and social debate as much as on religious education. Religion, in Tabaar's (2018, 20–34) words, may work more as a "strategic construct" than an independent variable in politics, as religious and political elites compete to generate and diffuse what they see as the important lessons of the religious tradition for the present moment.

Scholars may question whether it is useful to take whatever Islamists frame as "religious" at face value, or whether ideals and motivations that cannot be conceptually separated from practice can be defined as such. I suggest that interpretations of actions as "Islamic" or righteous (*salih*) in MB discourse are not open ended. The key religious frames of righteous action that Islamists mobilize in politics are powerful in part because they are "authorized" and accredited as religious in a particular time and place (Philbrick Yadav 2013, 165). I show how these frames acquire religious meaning and authority—for instance, by acknowledging established religious hierarchies, citing scripture, and engaging with official religious discourse.

Understanding how and in what context Islamists cite religious concepts to advocate for particular forms of social and individual action is important in explaining why activists see different kinds of work as "godly" over time.

Where other political scientists have sought to explain what gives Islamists credibility in promising to apply God's rules, questioning the assumption that appeals to Islam work as a trump card in Arab politics, I challenge the assumption that religion offers a stable reference or source of goals for political actors to pursue. I draw on anthropological work by Talal Asad and Saba Mahmood in studying Islam as a "discursive tradition" and a "practical ethic," to show how political activists engage in religious meaning-making. I extend Asad's (1986) understanding of a "discursive tradition" to the tradition of Islamist political thought, showing how Islamist activists draw on movement traditions and scriptural ones to formulate arguments for what it means to act Islamically in modern politics. I follow Mahmood (2003, 2005) in aiming to understand how Islamic activists see their work as a form of ethical cultivation. Where she contrasts ethical cultivation that was aimed at forming pious subjectivities in *da'wa* movements with what she describes as more nationalist mobilizations of Islamic identity by political movements, I explore how political movements have also used ideals and methods of ethical cultivation to mobilize people for electoral work and framed political choices in terms of salvation, suggesting that a discourse of ethical cultivation and individual salvation bridged *da'wa* and political Islamist movements. Following another anthropologist, Hussein Ali Agrama (2010, 2012), I also show how concepts and rules drawn from Islamic law are contested in debates on specific contemporary applications.

I draw on work in political theory and religious studies on the way concepts in Islamic tradition are contested and applied differently in new political contexts. Following scholars like Ellen McLarney (2015), Andrew March (2013), Raymond Baker (2003), and Rachel Scott (2007), I consider how religious thinkers and ideologues debate how concepts with both religious and political meaning—such as sovereignty, citizenship, and codes of moral conduct—should apply in new social and political contexts, and how such debates result in new institutionalized interpretations of religious obligation.

Where these scholars focus on debates in the legal sphere (Agrama 2012), or among influential religious scholars and public intellectuals outside the MB (McLarney 2015; Baker 2003; Scott 2014), I study how debates within Islamist movements focus on interpreting religious obligations for activism and for electoral politics. While MB leaders did draw on some elite Islamist intellectual writings and debates and considered the intellectual Yusuf al-Qaradawi a fellow traveler and guide to the movement, they did not draw on external so much as internal religious authorities: public intellectual and legal debates on matters of sharia, therefore, trickled down minimally to the movement rank and file, who tended not to be familiar with these intellectuals. The *tarbiya* division of the movement and its guidance on ethical cultivation in *usra* (movement cell or "family") meetings was the most powerful source of intellectual influence on rank and file activists and distilled religious and political teachings for them. While MB debates on what kinds of activism were most Islamic acknowledged and referenced broader theological debates, they focused on internal priorities and on the political outcomes that activists should work toward, as well as what kinds of activism would aid collective salvation and the individual salvation of movement members. Given the movement's focus on religion-as-practice, interpretations of how to "apply God's law" or "command the right" that emerged from internal arguments about activist priorities, and from strategic interactions in the public sphere, existed alongside theological teachings in its curriculum of religious education.

Methodological and Theoretical Approach

I use an interpretive methodology grounded in social constructivism to focus on how the MB have enacted and expressed their religious identity, and understood "working for God" differently over time and in different contexts. A constructivist approach shows how norms motivate actors, both as nonmaterial utilities that actors are driven to pursue, and as commitments that shape actors' interpretations of a situation and desire to respond to it in a way that maintains the norm and the identity of the actor that is committed to it (Finnemore and Sikkink 1998). It is particularly appropriate for analyzing a movement that explicitly requires activists to apply their religious commitments to the particular contexts of their lives and societies, and that argues that acting righteously is both its own reward and the yardstick by which strategic choices must be measured. Understanding how Islamists interpret their actions as religiously meaningful, what Wedeen (2010, 258–62) describes as the historical constitution of agentive action, is important in explaining why Islamist activists choose to act as they do, or the "microfoundations" of collective action. To do so, I analyze movement texts, speeches, public communications, interviews, and internal training documents to reconstruct the authoritative discourse and everyday arguments that movement leaders use to interpret political opportunity and frame options for activism over time, and I examine how movement activists are socialized in these interpretations of righteous action. Following Wedeen (2010), Khanani (2014) and Spiegel (2015), I pay particular attention to the everyday language and recurring frames in movement leaders and activists' discourse on what it means to "work for God," what counts as proper Islamic practice, and what their own role is in creating a more Islamic society—what I dub "mission talk."

A constructivist tradition in social movement analysis emphasizes the "informal histories" that movements narrate about their past and their mission as important in maintaining their coherence, and understands ideational production as rooted in a "group culture" that develops through interaction (Fine 1995, 128–34). Constructivists emphasize "framing" as a key element of how movement activists interpret a situation as worthy of attention and action and identify an issue or political opportunity as one that can be approached through existing repertoires of contention (Snow and Benford 1988). Like all social movements, Islamist movements contain founding narratives and continue to produce what Somers (1994, 618–25) calls "ontological narratives" that define their identity in relation to others and frame activism as what they must do to uphold this identity through changing times and in different spaces. Analyzing the manner in which leaders argue that Brothers are obliged to act in different situations to uphold their identities and religious commitments helps to explain how the movement perceives and pursues its interests in politics.

A constructivist approach also also highlights how Islamist activists generate new understandings of what it means to work for God. Scholars of Islamist political mobilization have argued that Islamists are not "beholden to nonnegotiable ideological codes," but are political entrepreneurs in the electoral sphere like any other group (Ghobashy 2005, 376). I argue that they are ideational as well as political entrepreneurs, framing political choices in terms of moral vision and justifying norms of righteous action in terms of their ethical and their instrumental value, as appropriate and necessary responses to new challenges. This "strategic framing" is an ongoing effort for the MB, as it is for Islamists in other contexts—ideological change does not occur only in dramatic shifts at critical junctures (see, e.g., Tabaar 2018). Ideational or "moral entrepreneurs" are usually leaders and authorities within the movement who frame new events as requiring new strategies for action, or justify innovations as necessary to achieve the movement's older value commitments and goals. They must often consider how to frame their strategies so as to persuade external publics to see a situation in their terms and to win internal movement debates on tactics and goals (Zald 1996, 267–69). A constructivist approach to explaining ideational change, in this instance, requires analyzing discourse that proposes and justifies political innovations in religious terms and showing how new movement policies on activism and politics cite these new frames of what it means to work for Islam. Discursive and institutional change are both important outcomes of strategic framing and reframing processes, even if they are not always intended by activists. Religious frames and norms retain their currency by being used in new debates, and the new meanings and justifiable forms of activism that are attached to them can be used to mobilize in other ways once they are accepted and formalized in official movement positions and training materials, or "directive discourse" that tells activists what they must do.

I focus my analysis on speech acts as key data in analyzing the MB's discourse on its religious mission in politics. Speech acts such as a statement or column by an MB leader in an Islamist or mainstream newspaper, a speech in parliament, a stump speech, a campaign statement, or a document arguing for a new policy or position internally, that frame particular social and political strategies as forms of "righteous action," show how movement actors interpret political situations and conceive of potential responses to them (Kratochwil 1987, 303). They may be instrumental as well as expressive, strategically framing an argument to appeal to potential supporters or bystanders and preempt criticism (Williams 1995). Speech acts may also assert movement values and policies or signal movement intentions and commitments to internal and external audiences—what Onuf (2013) dubs "assertive" and "commissive" speech acts. The specific events and contexts in which speech acts occur are important in analyzing their strategic purpose for movement discourse. For instance, they may make the case for how a situation requires Brothers to act as Muslims and assert certain positions and strategies as the best way to advocate for God in the public realm, while also representing efforts by movement leaders to uphold or challenge movement hierarchies, or to compete with internal and external interlocutors for the right to speak for Islam.

Speech acts that are targeted to internal movement audiences, potential allies, or wider national publics may address different political concerns and cite or engage in different debates, invoking religious, nationalist, economic, and social registers of discourse that are aimed at persuading different constituencies. Understanding the intent of a speech act requires understanding the history of the movement's discourse on an issue, and the incentives faced by and position of the speaker in the movement. The frames and movement narratives I analyze are generally those with an established history in the movement, or that invoke old movement frames. Yet, because Islamist speech acts frame religious obligation in such a variety of ways across time and context, it remains important to reconstruct discourse from the bottom up, "from the text to the frame," rather than presuming that the master frames of the movement's foundational discourse, or the master frames prioritized by analysts, notably on questions of secularism and pluralism, drive movement debate (Johnston 1995, 219). I identify the most common mobilizing frames and definitions of righteous action in the writings of movement founder Hasan al-Banna—notably, *da'wa* (preaching), *tarbiya* (ethical cultivation), *islah* (righteous reform), working for sharia (God's law), *fard kifaya* (collective religious obligation), and *al-amr bi-l-ma'ruf* (commanding the right)—and examine how and why later movement writings framed new political strategies in terms of these key principles of righteous action. I use secondary sources and interviews to locate discourse in its institutional and historical context and to identify its intended audience, its position in an ongoing debate, and its likely purpose.

The speech acts I focus on have the common denominator of referencing key parts of the Islamist mission or method (*minhaj*), connecting the movement's historical commitments to present and future opportunities to act in order to serve God. These speech acts also show how Islamist ideas and "mission talk" are mobilized and reconstructed over time: as MB leaders and activists debate about how best to work for God in relation to different actors and fields, they draw on and remake core movement norms of what it means to act righteously. Indeed, speech acts show which frames are powerful within a movement tradition, or what currency they have within a broader "symbolic marketplace" of Islamic activist discourse, by how frequently activists mobilize them (Philbrick Yadav 2013, 144).

Constructivist theory emphasizes how identities are formed in relation to other actors and contexts, and how affirming identities and values in the process of mobilization can lead to different activist choices. A constructivist methodology, therefore, maps the social act of communication within particular social and discursive spheres, emphasizing the way speech acts signal a movement's position to others, whether to court sympathy and acceptance or to stake out opposition; it shows how the specific interlocutors or fields that movement actors choose to engage can change how they position themselves as "workers for Islam." In MB tradition, both the movement milieu and the broader sociopolitical field mattered for constituting the righteous and committed Muslim, for this tradition held that the individual could only flourish spiritually in a morally supportive community, and society could expand or restrict opportunities for righteousness. In choosing to enter electoral politics in the 1980s, the MB acquired new interlocutors to compete with and define themselves in relation to, and new narratives of social reform to engage. I trace these interactions in new public sites—parliament, electoral campaigning, debates in non-Islamist newspapers—to explore how the MB repositioned itself and remade its own identity as the premier champion of Islam in Egypt in these sites.

The debates and sites that the MB chose to engage in their electoral outreach tell us what political and discursive opportunities they perceived, which positions they believed would win them new supporters, and who they saw as potential allies or opponents. Speech acts in these sites also allowed movement leaders to explain how they intended to expand the movement's mission of social Islamization through politics to internal constituencies; therefore, they offer a useful measure of the movement's changing discursive strategy. In line with constructivist arguments that ideologies are generally formed in contestation with some "common sense," that the meaning of speech acts depends on the rules of the "speech situation" that they form part of, and that movement entrepreneurs frame their discourse to anticipate critique from interlocutors, I examine how MB leaders used different credentialing strategies to persuade new potential allies and competitors of the desirability of electoral Islamism and the forms that it could take (Billig 1995, 66, 77; Johnston 1995; Williams 1995, 128–29). I look at how this externally oriented discourse tapped movement texts and traditions, affirmed dominant public narratives about religion and citizenship, and repeated frames that had been successful in other contexts and consider what this tells us about what the movement considered justifiable adaptation (Schwartz-Shea and Yanow 2012, 85–87).

I analyze the speech acts represented in these texts in terms of theme, particularly focusing on what they frame as righteous action required of believers in the social and political sphere, through the themes of *tarbiya*, *daʻwa*, *islah*, *fard kifaya*, and commanding the right or working for God's rule. I also locate them in social and institutional contexts, assessing what can be gauged about their intended audience from the publication site, whom they frame as potential allies and opponents, what policies and debates they reference, and what norms they appeal to. In some instances, specific interlocutors or audiences are mentioned, and the speech act is aimed at persuasion, whereas others attempt to represent and forward a movement position to an undefined public. These interlocutors vary for different episodes: in the early to mid-1980s, MB leaders' mission talk focuses on persuading movement members that electoral politics could serve the mission without diluting it and on reassuring potential allies and state authorities concerned about the MB's political ambitions that it only sought moral leadership through electoral politics; in the mid to late 1980s, debates on why supporting sharia legislation mattered for the movement's mission engaged state Islamic authorities, rival Islamists, and legal scholars as well; by the mid-1990s to early 2000s, internal dissidents and state authorities were key audiences, as the MB sought to selectively accommodate calls for liberal moderation without accepting a separate political mission; and, by 2011, MB discourse targeted voters and rival Islamists more intensively.

I focus on time periods and episodes in which the movement actively reframed its mission in response to new political opportunities, and in which it debated strategic decisions, such as the choice to participate in elections or change training for political work, and I show which key principles of righteous action and religious obligation were reframed in each episode. The main episodes and debates I focus on for different chapters are: 1984–87, when the movement debated how election campaigning and entering parliament could promote its *da'wa* or preaching mission; 1985–90, when the MB leadership debated how a political program focused on the state and laws could allow the application of sharia and the empowerment (*tamkin*) of believers to command the right; 1995–2007, when the movement formally incorporated political work in its platform and internal training programs as a form of *tarbiya* or ethical cultivation, and a collective religious obligation (*fard kifaya*), amid internal dissent and external repression; and 2011–15, when the movement created a political party and won electoral majorities for the first time, combined activism and religious training for electoral and preaching work, and debated tensions between religious and political sources of legitimacy (*shar'iyya*) following a coup against the elected MB president.

Tracing movement discourse in separate episodes, I consider how frames of the religious mission, notably those emphasizing collective religious obligation, were attached to some strategies more successfully than others, such that these political strategies were normalized as part of the *da'wa* or *tarbiya* mission of the movement and not subject to continued justification after a period of time. I consider what the most commonly used religious frames and credentialing strategies of externally oriented assertive and commissive speech acts, compared with those of internally oriented and more directive speech acts, tell us about how discursive strategies translate into changed commitments. Following Schwedler (2006), I focus on new movement positions, both public and private, and ideational commitments as indicators of change.

I also consider which religious frames persisted in externally oriented discourse over time, as successful discursive strategies that were added to the movement's future repertoire (Billig 1995, 77). As constructivist theorists argue, appeals to established norms for new purposes are often important in keeping these norms alive (Finnemore and Sikkink 1998). A growing acceptance of tactics and positions that were once considered off-limits from an Islamic perspective forms one of the important outcomes of the process of ideational evolution—what Schwedler (2006, 150–51) terms a shift in the "boundaries of justifiable action"—and also enabled future innovation in what counted as "righteous action."

I analyze how new ideational commitments, or "webs of promises," constrained movement action by being incorporated into movement socialization, particularly training programs, and institutional practice, which constructivists refer to as the institutionalization of norms (Risse and Sikkink 1999). Ideas may be "embedded" not only in institutions but also in discourse patterns and collective identities, and the recurrence of new frames in "authorized" movement discourse over time is an important measure of institutionalization (Berman 2001; Philbrick Yadav 2013, 145). Where the literature on Islamist moderation emphasizes how strategic commitments to electoral and democratic norms are gradually formalized and accepted as necessary changes to a movement's mission, I will suggest that these new commitments may diversify a movement's identity narratives, changing operational priorities and the movement's own narratives of its mission without transforming it irrevocably.

How religious frames and norms influence the choices that Islamists make in the electoral sphere is difficult to assess in terms of positivist causality, as norms work to guide, inspire, and entrench mutual expectations about behavior rather than clearly determining outcomes (Kratochwil and Ruggie 1986, 767). The persistence of religious frames in Islamist political discourse, even in electoral contexts where movements would be better served without them, is an indicator of their continuing importance to movements. Analyzing which frames persist, and under what conditions, tells us about the kinds of political adaptation that are justifiable and, therefore, likely to stick for a movement. In assessing what impact strategic construction and interaction had on the movement's mission, I focus on the new projects and political values that come to be regularly associated with traditional movement frames of righteous action and the norms of righteous action that continued to be cited to justify operational choices. Following Wedeen (2010), Kratochwil and Ruggie (1986), and Swidler (1995), I assess the language that members use to make claims and to appeal for sympathy and understanding as important indicators of the moral economy of the group, and the meaning that public discourse is likely to have for those who participate in it. I also measure norm shift through movement position pieces and curricula that indicate authoritative and institutional support for new frames and incorporate them into movement socialization, canonizing some positions and downgrading others, while adding new meanings and resources to "authorized language." Training curricula and teaching materials are particularly important indicators, as they index the issues and forms of knowledge that are prioritized in training and promoting members.

Data Selection

Choosing representative texts and identifying critical debates and political episodes in the evolution of a movement that is historically secretive and has evolved in an authoritarian public sphere is a challenge, because political fears and incentives invariably influence the kinds of statements and publications that a movement like the MB is willing to make public. Accounting for differences in availability, I have used different kinds of materials for different time periods. Some similarities in forms of ideational production persisted over time and allow us to identify authoritative, founding movement discourse: Banna, the MB's founder, wrote a series of epistles (*rasa'il*) laying out the movement's values and mission, and these epistles were reprinted, studied and referred to by successive movement generations. The general guides who succeeded Banna similarly wrote columns and essays intended to be authoritative for movement members. These texts are available in the public realm, in print, and were often published in internal journals (e.g., *al-Daʿwa*) and public newspapers (e.g. *al-Shaʿb*) by the 1980s. I selected writings by MB leaders in the archives of the Centre d'études et de documentation économiques, juridiques, et sociales (CEDEJ) in Cairo, the archives of the al-Ahram Center in Cairo, and referred to books written by MB leaders available at the American University in Cairo library. I also obtained books and training manuals recommended by my movement interlocutors from Islamist bookstores in Cairo's Sayyida Zainab square, and from movement members directly. In some instances, I consulted texts recommended by movement members that were catalogued on the IkhwanWiki website set up after the 2011 uprising. I consulted some videos of speeches and accessed public statements via blogs and movement websites. The multiplication of satellite television channels and sites debating MB positions after the mid-2000s made it particularly difficult to know who within the movement spoke for what position, and I have tried to contextualize sources clearly to make a case for whose voice they represented (Mellor 2018).

I focus on written discourse, recognizing that it represents a partial view of a sprawling and complex movement's ideational production, because it has generally represented the viewpoint of movement authorities and signaled the movement's strategic intent and formal justifications for positions in the public sphere. Written documents on the movement's position on *tarbiya* and *daʿwa*, similarly, tended to be written and vetted by those in leadership positions and represent "directive discourse" (Onuf 2013). I selected documents authored by known leaders (rather than well-known independent Islamist thinkers considered MB fellow travelers), often those referred to me by interviewees, or cited in other texts, based on availability. I acknowledge the selection bias inherent in this approach and try to be clear about what each form of discourse can tell us: for instance, leadership discourse is more likely to explain movement strategies and interpretation of opportunities for collective action than many other kinds of texts (Johnston and Klandermans 1995, 17–18). Internal debates are difficult to capture for the pre-1990 period, becoming more visible and well documented thereafter, but evolution, references, and credentialing practices in official and public movement discourse offer a comprehensive enough view of mission talk to work with. I also refer to an established secondary literature documenting movement debates and evolution in the 1990s and use secondary data and interviews to place texts in the context of institutional rivalries and strategies. I pay particular attention to formal changes in movement positions on political work, such as statements put out in 1994 on pluralism, and to the introduction of formal movement curricula framing political work in terms of religious obligation, to mark definitive changes in movement positions.

For the period after 2011, I use written, visual, and verbal campaign discourse, in-person interviews, official movement statements, speeches reported in the media, self-evaluation statements put out by competing factions, and new curriculum materials. I also use semistructured interviews that I conducted with MB political leaders, asking them to describe the leadership's position on political adaptation and coalition-building under Mubarak, in 2005–6, and with several younger MB activists as well as movement leaders in 2012–14, on how the combination of political work and preaching functioned in everyday movement outreach. I use my personal observations and notes on speeches at MB election rallies and demonstrations in 2012, and on MB rallies at Raba'a al-'Adawiyya square in the summer of 2013, for the same period.

The two main kinds of discourse that I will analyze are directive (internally oriented, instructing members how to achieve the movement's mission), and commissive (making commitments either internally or to external publics). Directive discourse for the MB centers on how members should work to achieve the movement's mission. It emphasizes worship, ethical cultivation, and preaching (whether through religious outreach or modeling righteousness) as practical activities to be pursued daily; it also tells members what they must do in order to uphold the movement's mission at every step. This covers a wide range of texts written by movement leaders, and occasionally sympathetic religious scholars, on matters of movement practice as well as religious jurisprudence. For the purposes of this analysis, I will focus on writings that directly addressed the movement's mission and social obligations, and that were cited by later movement statements or by members I interviewed.

In addition to tracts and commentaries meant for internal education, some of which were included among materials discussed in weekly *usra* (family or cell) meetings, leaders also wrote articles in national newspapers and columns in more Islamist-leaning newspapers (such as *al-Shaʿb*) on political and social issues and on the movement's vision for social reform, and they published electoral tracts and promises in these newspapers. I treat these as forms of commissive discourse, aimed at signaling movement norms and commitments to external audiences.

The Plan of the Argument

Chapter 1 traces the evolution of the MB's *minhaj* or method of social Islamization in its first two generations, using historical texts from the movement's Fifth Conference, tracts written by Banna and his successors, and secondary historical sources. I show how the movement developed its understanding of *tarbiya* as a tool for *islah* or the righteous reform of individuals and societies, through practical experimentation in changing political contexts, starting with anticolonial activism, proceeding through state repression in the 1950s and 1960s and ending with the movement's renaissance in the 1970s. I concentrate in particular on how leaders framed the political sphere as a site in which religious obligations and rules could be enacted, starting with Banna's argument for the state as a form of both *daʿwa* and *hukm* or rule, and for *al-amr bi-l-maʿruf* or "commanding the right" as a collective religious obligation to apply God's teachings. I show how key concepts of righteous action and obeying God's will in everyday life were extended to arguments for how best to apply God's will in the world. I examine how MB thinkers framed the religious meanings of politics differently in changing strategic contexts, tracing how political work was framed as a religious obligation in anticolonial resistance, even as partisanship was deemed ungodly; how a repressive national state was framed as a violation of God's sovereignty (*hakimiyya*) by Sayyid Qutb; how Banna's successor, Hasan al-Hudaybi, reframed *hukm* or rule as God's judgment, separate from the state and its laws; and how political liberalization and a more religion-sympathetic political regime in the 1970s emboldened a younger MB leadership to emphasize *daʿwa* via mass media.

Chapter 2 analyzes how the MB's leadership interpreted and responded to new incentives for electoral participation from 1984 to 1987 by embracing electoral campaigning as *daʿwa*, and parliamentary work as an opportunity to draw support by modeling righteous action, and a way to act for God by being the voice of Islam in a sinful context. In tracing MB discourse on electoral work in internal position pieces and instructional texts, and public writings, speeches, and parliamentary and media debate, I demonstrate how leaders framed electoral and parliamentary work as an extension of the tradition of active piety that had long been the movement's messaging and recruiting approach and positioned themselves both internally and externally as responsible religious representatives who would use new arenas to cultivate mass righteousness without partisanship.

Chapter 3 examines the MB's public discourse on sharia application from 1985 to 1990 to show how its leadership increasingly embraced state law and institutions as tools for applying God's law, for commanding the right (*al-amr bi-l-maʿruf*) and for the empowerment (*tamkin*) of God's mission on earth. I analyze how MB leaders framed the application of sharia as achievable through *tamkin* or empowerment via the piecemeal pursuit of social and political influence that would allow Islamic activists and upright citizens to "command the right." The movement's public-facing discourse also framed sharia as a popular demand and resource for effective governance to anticipate critiques of theocratic potential, and Brothers in parliament framed state-led religious education as helpful in building ethical and productive citizens. I consider the way the MB normalized state-centered activism in its *tarbiya* program by emphasizing how the state could serve individual and collective spiritual advancement, rather than framing an Islamic state as a distant outcome of social Islamization. I then look at how these new framings of sharia application via the state and in the everyday lives of citizens ended up being incorporated in the MB's internal educational documents in the late 1980s, as a sign that these commissive frames changed the movement's official interpretation of its own mission.

Chapter 4 lays out the participation of the movement's "organization men" in a broader internal debate over how electoral work could be compatible or at odds with preaching and ethical cultivation in the mid-1990s to early 2000s, during which time the leadership made important commitments to political pluralism and freedoms by framing them as compatible with the Islamic project. Analyzing new training curricula for MB members written in the early 2000s, I consider how the educational wing of the movement framed public work as a religious duty, *shura* as a kind of worship, and political outreach as a jihad that increased the spiritual merits of the doer and the recipient and accepted these kinds of work as part of preparing society for Islamic rule. As politics, whether in the form of governance, constituent service, or legislation, was folded into *tarbiya* or spiritual cultivation, as a site in which members cultivated their own righteousness and as a tool with which to cultivate righteousness in others, organization men became important drivers of the movement's commitment to competitive electoral politics, even as leaders resisted efforts by young dissidents to form a separate party and build political coalitions, because they maintained that a unified religious and political *minhaj* was the sole path to salvation.

Chapter 5 focuses on the period from 2011 to 2013, when the MB formed the Freedom and Justice Party in the period of democratization that followed Hosni Mubarak's overthrow. Using movement and party statements, interviews with movement activists involved in party work, and a new movement training curriculum produced shortly after the party was formed, I analyze how the leadership framed power-seeking and a fuller commitment to electoral politics as a culmination of the MB's mission to establish sharia-driven rule on behalf of a pious majority, and how the movement's public discourse became more populist and majoritarian as it competed with newer Islamist parties to be the premier "voice of Islam" in Egypt. Movement activists and the MB's new training curriculum framed the social capital earned from religious and political outreach as convertible, to encourage all members to embrace political work, and framed political work as a collective religious obligation (*fard kifaya*) to argue that governing for the public good was an opportunity to earn religious merit. In electoral discourse, movement activists and party leaders framed the application of sharia in terms of providing good governance and justice to people, which would build their trust in the Islamic political project, but were driven by electoral outflanking to specify more concrete legal processes and provisions to limit violations of sharia as the members of the constituent assembly. I find that the movement leadership's effort to keep the missions of *tarbiya* and politics closely tied were challenged by organizational tensions between those who favored a clear separation of the two kinds of work and those who feared that political work would overtake *tarbiya* and *da'wa* as movement priorities.

Next, the chapter examines the tensions that emerged between religious and democratic framings of legitimacy (*shar'iyya*) for the MB as opposition to the rule of its elected president, Mohammed Morsi, increased in 2013, and after he was overthrown in a military coup. Using interviews, field research at rallies, speeches, and media statements, I trace how the movement leadership confronted its visible failure to persuade citizens of the value of an "Islamic" government in terms of ideas of legitimacy grounded in both its obligation to God and its support from a believing majority, and framed political opposition as opposition to God's will, eventually reconsidering the desirability of achieving collective religious salvation through democracy. As the MB leadership was split by mass arrests and exiles in 2014–15, competing faction leaders situated their different strategic responses to repression in terms of the movement's historical mission of working for Islam, citing Prophetic examples and Banna's writings on jihad to define alternative, nonelectoral paths for the Islamic project, whether by reverting to neighborhood outreach, or championing active resistance to "un-Islamic" rule, or mobilizing transnational support to frame the movement's repression as part of a global threat to Islam.

The conclusion assesses the effects of strategic reframing on the MB's key concepts of social Islamization and righteous action over its decades of electoral engagement, asking what different meanings persisted in the movement's internal, directive framing of the Islamic mission, and what adaptations were conditional. I find that movement discourse that framed political work as religiously creditable enabled and later limited the movement's institutional response to new political opportunities, and its commitment to the state as a resource for Islamization. Analyzing self-evaluation statements put out by two leading wings of the MB in 2017, I ask how their visions for future Islamic political projects frame the ideal of an Islamic state, and I consider what political pressures, transnational alliances, and internal dynamics, are likely to shift the Islamic political *minhaj* in the near term. Moreover, I compare the MB's reframing of its Islamic mission in politics with that of newer Egyptian Salafi parties, and of two Moroccan Islamist movements, the MUR/PJD and the Justice and Spirituality movement, which espoused similar values of righteous action and understandings of God's justice and sovereignty on earth, but chose different political strategies. I show how different interpretations of political participation as religiously ennobling or corrupting in different institutional contexts, and of the value of state resources and political influence for achieving an Islamically just society through political experience, changed these movements' assessment of political opportunities. Finally, I consider what lessons about Islamic mobilization from these cases—such as the importance of contingent leadership framing choices or identity-affirming choices in different political fields, or outcome-driven vs. identity-driven definitions of the Islamic political project—may apply to religious mobilization in politics more broadly.

I
How to Act for Islam in the World

From its foundation by a schoolteacher, Hasan al-Banna, in 1928, the Society of the Muslim Brothers (the MB) defined its mission as one of religious education for sociopolitical activism. The movement's ideology and founding discourse focused on interpreting and applying religious norms of righteous action to serve contemporary social needs. This chapter will first discuss how the movement's leadership framed the mission of *tarbiya*—or ethical cultivation—to build virtuous citizens who would work for God's justice as the foundation of its mission of social reform; then it will show how leaders framed the religious meanings of political work differently as they adapted to changing political situations from the 1950s through the 1970s, with a particular focus on how they positioned state-oriented politics as a tool or barrier to righteous action in the world. I explore how MB thinkers argued for direct action and political protest as religious obligations in anticolonial resistance, even as partisanship (*hizbiyya*) was ungodly; how a repressive national state was framed as a violation of God's sovereignty (*hakimiyya*) by Sayyid Qutb; how Banna's successor, Hasan al-Hudaybi, reframed *hukm* or rule as God's judgment, separate from the state and its laws; and how political liberalization and a political regime in the 1970s more sympathetic to religion emboldened a younger MB leadership to emphasize a more activist *da'wa* aimed at rallying public support via mass media.

Building spiritually and socially upright Muslim souls (*insha' al-nufus*) was a key part of the MB's founding mission. Banna's emphasis on cultivating the "virtuous citizen" was similar in purpose to projects by national educational authorities and Christian missionaries to train young people in the bodily and intellectual habits that would make them ideal modern and moral citizens and contributors to national renewal (Kramer 2015, 197–98, 205–7; Starrett 1998, 67–78). The "new Muslim man" was to be cultivated through practical education adapted for the needs of his time and would be the primary agent in building a new moral order or *nizam* (Kramer 2015). Education and preaching were therefore central tools in what Banna defined as the movement's *minhaj* or method of bringing about a just, autonomous Islamic society. Banna asserted that Islam had to be accepted as an all-embracing concept regulating all aspects of life and argued that politics was not a matter separate from faith, even if faith did not permit partisanship—rather, Islam was necessarily concerned with worldly justice and happiness (Lia 1998, 68–69).

Accordingly, the movement's ideational production in its founding period focused on interpreting and reconstructing key religious norms of action for contemporary social and political needs. Banna's *rasa'il* or epistles, recognized and still read as the founding texts of the movement, focus squarely on the cultural, social, and political effects of colonization and argue that religious revival is necessary for social revival. *Da'watuna* (Our Mission) and *Bayn amsu wa-l-yawm* (Between Yesterday and Today), in particular, are mobilizing tracts, aimed not merely at asserting religious expertise, but at persuading public audiences. They directly address the believers that the movement hopes to mobilize for its cause and are written with the assumption that readers are concerned with national revival and social reform; that they need to be persuaded to see the MB's model as "Islamic"; and that they must be persuaded to choose the "Islamic way" from among several alternatives (Wendell 1978). In urging believers to choose an "intense" faith over a "dormant" one, and defining Islam as the best hope for national unity and medicine for national revival, Banna presents social priorities as central to true belief and frames action as an important component of faith. In insisting that the correct practice of faith as laid out in the Quran and Sunna required believers to have fellow-feeling and to "work for mankind in God's way" (41), Banna also situates himself in an Islamic reformist tradition rooted in the nineteenth century that focused on "making norms socially immanent" and reforming both the self and society to be more moral (Salvatore 1998, 59–60, 83–84).

In addition to participating in what Asad (1986) terms the discursive tradition of Islam, by framing the requirements of the faith in terms of how they could be realized in present and future circumstances, Banna's reformist discourse emphasizes the social order in which Muslims live as a site in which to practice and achieve the goals of faith. Action and application separate the MB from more scholarly reformists for Banna, who critiques the former for confining their work to the intellectual realm rather than trying to bring up a new generation of virtuous youth that might transform society (Lia 1998, 56–57). The ideal modern Muslim subject, for Banna, applies God's teachings in his everyday life and acts to uphold Islam in an increasingly inhospitable political environment, because Muslims are a "practical people," and their faith must connect words with good deeds; early writings repeat the Quranic principle that God will not change the condition of a people until they change it themselves (Anani 2016, 58–61; Lia 1998: 83).

The concepts of *tarbiya* or ethical cultivation, *islah* or righteous reform, *da'wa* or missionizing/preaching, *furud al-kifaya* or collective religious obligations, *al-amr bi-l-ma'ruf* or commanding the right, and *hukm* or the rule of God, are central to the *minhaj* or method of Islamization laid out in Banna's tracts and to the movement's understanding of how people must be mobilized to work for Islam. *Tarbiya*, frequently translated as "education," is the linchpin of the method. Banna argues that faith and a correct understanding of religion are essential to the formation of moral citizens and national revival, and discharging religious obligations requires moral action and practical training through social outreach. In an early pamphlet, Banna makes the case that the fully Muslim personality that he seeks to cultivate must have a sense of moral obligation to the Muslim nation, to God, and to the welfare of fellow Muslims (Rosen 2008). In the movement's doctrine, moral action is both the outcome of sound ethical cultivation and part of the process of cultivation, and a moral community is necessary for an individual's spiritual advancement.

Action in the world is part and parcel of the movement's organizational mission, not supplementary to it. It was decided at the movement's Third Conference that members' promotion within the organization would depend on their fulfillment of moral, religious, and social duties, rather than simply their religious knowledge (Lia 1998, 103). The MB set up a nationwide network of informal schools and religious classes that focused on scriptural knowledge and memorization while seeking to foster in youth a civic responsibility to realize the values of Islamic social justice. In an address to the MB's Fifth Conference in 1939 (discussed in a document on the IkhwanWiki website that lays out the movement's historical understanding of *tarbiya*), Banna notes that *tarbiya* is not quite the same as acquiring intellectual and scriptural knowledge, though the latter is essential, too; the ethical cultivation of *tarbiya* produces sincere people who combine worship (*'ibada*) with practice (*mu'amala*) to achieve the victory of Islam (2023). Although religious expertise was valuable to cultivate in potential movement teachers for their own spiritual advancement and to compete with state-recognized Azhari preachers, the knowledge that Banna wished to cultivate through his broader *da'wa* was an activist knowledge, pushing the believer to take action (Kramer 2015, 205). Lia describes the religious training given to the first generation of MB preachers as including Quranic memorization and the writing of a thesis, while noting that preachers were required to show that they were willing to make sacrifices and Islamize their homes and lives before being promoted (Lia 1998, 163–65). Further, what distinguished an MB preacher was that he inspired and moved people's hearts where official preachers used words that appealed to their brains (166). As the MB experimented with more active and outreach-oriented models of ethical cultivation—particularly with rover scouts, camps, and rural outreach campaigns, practical, group-oriented *tarbiya* came to be more deeply entrenched in its everyday practice, with the *usra* (family) meeting system established for all members in 1943 (176).

The *risalat al-ta'lim* or "Letter of Instructions" written by Banna in 1938 that originally formed the basic training for members includes twenty principles (*usul*) of "our faith" (*'aqidatuna*) and ten pillars of practice followed by thirty-eight duties and offers an example of how the movement's "mission talk" combines directive speech acts aimed at instructing followers with a strategic construction of the Islamic way, aimed at countering external critiques. The twenty principles lay out the MB's broad definition of the comprehensiveness of Islam, asking followers to affirm that Islam is made up of true faith and correct worship, as well as justice, morals, government, and culture, and that science and faith are compatible. The ten pillars (*arkan*) focus on the qualities the movement seeks to cultivate in the righteous individual: understanding, sincerity, action, effort, sacrifice, brotherhood, trust, and obedience (Elsasser 2014). For Banna, *tarbiya* had to be a practical and social endeavor: members built their Islamic personality by applying God's law in their own lives (Lia 1998, 104). The movement came to define its distinctive mission in terms of its method of cultivation (*minhaj tarbawi*), which leaders and later commentators argued distinguished it from all other religious movements and from political parties and welfare groups in its focus on combining religious commitment with social reform (Ikhwanwiki 2023). If working for God meant working for the Muslim community, ethical cultivation was necessary for both: movement commentaries on Banna's concept of *tarbiya* note that he envisioned the renascent nation as a school for its citizens and a "workshop for men," as the movement was a school for young Muslims (2023).

Ethical cultivation and *da'wa* or preaching are similarly intertwined: Brothers are called on to impart the understanding of Islam, the ethical cultivation and moral guidance that they had receive from the movement, to those in their social circles, and training in *da'wa* is part of a member's own ethical cultivation (Lia 1998, 107; Rosen 2008). Movement commentaries and writings on historical ideology and preaching emphasize that *tarbiya* is the movement's message as well as its method, with Banna's *rasa'il* serving as both reminders to the movement about its mission and a way of communicating the mission to society. The *rasa'il*, commentators note, laid out the *fiqh* or jurisprudence of collective work: the mission was not simply to get all Muslims to be more devout, but to convince them that the MB's unique method was the best way to apply Islam on earth (Ikhwanwiki 2023).

The movement emphasizes practical application and examples as key to both *tarbiya* and *da'wa*. Therefore, its tracts and ideological materials focus on sound practice and method, presuming a foundation of adequate doctrinal and scriptural training. In the MB's method, cultivating the virtues of a good Muslim so that he would act righteously as required by the sharia is more important than mere textual knowledge (Houston 2018,

7–8). Prayer and Quranic recitations at MB meetings affirm and renew the preacher's faith and prepare him to act. The movement's educational program by 1940 sought to train Brothers to become "productive preachers" by promoting not only their religious knowledge but also their ability to argue for the ongoing relevance of Islamic thought in contemporary social and political debate. It included texts interpreting Islamic scripture from the point of view of the MB, as well as studies by scholars on the reformist tradition and histories of Islamic civilization, separate readings on the history of ethics, psychology, sociology, and pedagogy, and texts on countering the arguments of Christian missionaries (al-Ta'ruf 1940). Yet, by the late 1930s, group meetings, activities, camps, and battalion-based work formed an increasing part of the training process (Lia 1998, 166–77).

Movement history emphasizes overnight camps with fasting, prayer, and religious discussion as important ingredients in the training of full members of the MB, framing this as a more intense kind of *tarbiya* that promotes spiritual cultivation by bodily, social, and emotional means rather than an intellectual process of acquiring knowledge. Banna ultimately prioritized the inner strength and the moral fiber that individuals derived from Islam and, echoing his Sufi experience, favored embodied forms of learning (Lia 1998, 173–74; Kramer 2015, 208; Houston 2018, 4). Commentaries insist that the movement's methods derive from a Prophetic example: the Prophet and his companions had affirmed their own faith, incubated their commitment, and preserved the values of Islam in the face of military threat by living together and supporting each other morally, and present this *ma'iya* or companionship as a model for contemporary Islamization as well, because a lasting positive impact on people is difficult to achieve if one does not live among them (Ikhwanwiki 2023).

Social *islah* or reform depended on individual *islah* for the first MB generation, because moral, political, social, or economic revival was impossible without spiritual reform in people's hearts. The *islah* or moral reform of the individual depended on direct instruction and on a willingness to act righteously to reshape one's own behavior and to serve as an example to others. The movement's social activities were meant to serve as a method and example for broader social solidarity building: as people prayed and worked together, united in the Islamic brotherhood and "melted in the crucible of the *da'wa*," their acquaintance (*ta'ruf*), familiarity (*tafahum*), and solidarity (*takaful*) with each other would intensify, and they would be better able to apply themselves to the issues of all Muslims and find support in each other to resist influences that took them away from God (Ikhwanwiki 2023).

The social and political realm was an essential site of movement work, as it enabled individuals to cultivate themselves and to spread the mission of *tarbiya*, reforming the nation one soul at a time. Social work was part of the good Muslim's ethical cultivation, and all "self initiated productive work. . . . aimed at bettering the conditions of the Islamic community" was viewed as a kind of jihad (Lia 1998, 83). The goal of *tarbiya* was ultimately to ensure that the "spirit of Islam"—defined as piety, self-abnegation, cooperation for social welfare, commanding the right, and responsibility for the nation—was as widespread in society as possible (Ikhwanwiki 2023). While social reform or *islah* depended on *tarbiya*, which Banna defined primarily in terms of peer-to-peer cultivation, the MB also recognized state education as an influence that could be harnessed for proper ethical cultivation. In the 1940s, when the MB had good relations with political elites, Hasan al-Ashmawi, a Brother, was appointed education minister, and the MB leadership hoped it would have more influence over schools as the "moral guide" of the nationalist movement in supporting the Free Officers' uprising in 1952 (Kramer 2010, 69; Rosen 2008).

The State and Politics in the Early MB Mission

The movement defined the application (*tanfidh*) of its mission and the rule (*hukm*) of God in changing ways in its first decade. Banna argued in an address to a conference of students in 1938 that politics mattered for the religious mission because both Islam and politics were concerned with all the issues of the nation and of Muslims, and because the comprehensive and detailed rulings of the Quran had not been revealed in order for the faith to be limited to empty ritualistic motions (Wa'i 2001, 3–4). Banna's argument for why religion had a place in contemporary politics was frequently framed as a counterargument to those who would seek to separate religion from politics (Wa'i 1998, 20). *Hukm* represented what God commanded Muslims to do: Banna quoted the Quranic verse commanding believers "to rule among them by what God has revealed" (5:44) in arguing that government was one of the basic concerns of the faith and contended that the state could not be a soulless material formation, but must be constructed on the basis of the *da'wa* until it became a "state of the message" (Wa'i 2001, 21).

Yet the MB's early ideational production did not elaborate "Islamic" policies or norms of governance so much as it asserted the value of Islam in informing ideals of an effective and moral political order in an era of competing, and more globally influential, political ideologies. For the MB's founders, Islam offered an ethical foundation and set of guidelines for politics, not a blueprint. Banna's *rasa'il* made the case that Islam offered better solutions to most contemporary political challenges than any other ideology. MB university activists set up study groups to discuss the lessons that Islam offered for good economic and political systems (Lia 1998, 185, 213; Kramer 2015, 206). Banna encouraged political activism as part of the cultivation of a model Muslim citizen, because one could "never become a real Muslim if he is not political and has a view for the affairs of his people" (Lia 1998, 202). For Banna, *participating* in politics and holding rulers accountable were qualities and obligations required of the upright individual, but partisan *power-seeking* was undesirable, because the good Muslim's obligation was to cooperate with others and build a strong, united nation rather than to pursue personalized ambitions (203).

Banna framed the religious obligation of commanding the right (*al-amr bi-l-ma'ruf*) as a matter of using personal example and moral exhortation to educate and correct others (Kramer 2015, 202). Commentaries on *tarbiya* and social *islah* laid out the movement's sociopolitical project as one that depended on training many committed people to work for the *da'wa*; transforming its principles into a movement and its message into men; turning a method into a generation; moving from reciting slogans to practicing their meaning; and offering Muslims social, emotional, and practical support to achieve a national renaissance (Ikhwanwiki 2023). The idea of a Muslim government represented a distant, collective religious obligation more than a concrete operational objective in movement commentaries, which argued that there could be no Islamic laws or Islamic state, or liberated nations, and no return to caliphate and the moral guidance of the world, without properly cultivated Muslim subjects (2015).

While Banna believed that it was important to support anyone who worked for the victory of Islam and oppose anyone who did not work to reestablish its rule (*hukm*), he defined Islamic rule as a combination of nationalist principles (e.g., resisting foreign influence, asserting Islamic autonomy) and a message of social justice (e.g., ending lavish spending by elites, promoting local enterprise and health and literacy projects), rather than an institutional or policy vision, and favored constitutional rule with a ruler accountable to, and advised by, experts as a beneficial system even if it was not derived from Islam (Kramer 2015, 204; Lia 1998, 206–11). By the early 1940s, Banna had started to call for specific policies such as nationalizing the Suez Canal and ensuring that laws were Islamic, but the only political action that he termed *tanfidh* or applying the Islamic mission was direct action against British and palace authorities on the Palestine issue after the 1936 revolt, and paramilitary training to send fighters to Palestine (Lia 1998, 260–68).

After Banna's assassination, Hasan al-Hudaybi, his successor as general guide, initially promoted an even more cautious approach to state politics. Hudaybi reiterated that the movement's mission was *tarbiya* and training for *da'wa*, expanding institutional commitments to set up schools to train preachers, and emphasized the movement sphere and the relationships between members of an *usra* as the most important way to "implement the meaning of Islam" (Rosen 2008; Ikhwanwiki 2023). But competition from a more revolutionary flank kept alive debates about the relevance of the state for the movement's mission. Sayyid Qutb, a former literary critic who joined the MB in the 1950s and directed its *da'wa* work for a few years before being jailed by the Free Officer–led regime, argued that the power of the state and its repressive capacity made it an essential target of Islamic activism, because political authority that rejected God's sovereignty supported an ungodly society (Arian 2014, 31–32). His proposal for an Islamic vanguard that would snatch power by force from a repressive ruler who had established himself, Pharaoh-like, as a rival to God, defined the most urgent and useful Islamic activism as that which focused on the state rather than on converting more Muslims to the MB's view of Islam (Goldberg 1991, 15–18). Qutb's arguments that the *da'wa*-based mission had failed because of its inability to account for the importance of state power, and that real Islam could not be actualized without appropriating political power for committed Muslims, were persuasive to movement members witnessing firsthand the effects of state repression on the movement's ability to function in the 1960s (Arian 2014, 13–32). Qutb's remarks in an address to an MB student conference that "the living Muslim is the word of God on earth," and that youth must be fighters willing to give their lives over to God, was documented in movement history as a more militant revival of Banna's *fikr haraki* or "activist thought" (Ikhwanwiki 2023).

After Qutb's death by hanging in 1966, and the mass arrests of MB activists that followed, the MB leadership under Hudaybi walked a fine line between acknowledging the popularity of a more political vision within the movement and signaling caution to Nasser's regime in order to protect the movement from further repression. Hudaybi's writings in this period, notably in the text *Du'at la Quda't* (Preachers, Not Judges), recognized that action and governance were both important for belief, but did not prioritize founding an Islamic state, asserting that *amal* (work or action) for Islam included any act of piety, such as prayer or pilgrimage (Zollner 2009, 83–84). By arguing that establishing a religious state formed a collective obligation (*fard al-kifaya*) for the Muslim community rather than an individual obligation (*fard al-'ayn*) for the believer, Hudaybi upheld the idea of righteous rule as something believers should be accountable for, while lowering the stakes of righteous rule from something that was a condition of belief (Qutb's argument) to something that was desirable without being a basis for *takfir* or declaring someone to be non-Muslim (Zollner 2009, 123–25). In engaging the debate of what kind of state was properly Islamic, and what responsibility believers had for bringing it about, Hudaybi did, however, incorporate political activism more explicitly into movement discourse about righteous action, even though he asserted its importance more than detailing its operational requirements. He distinguished righteous actions required of rulers or the public authority (*sulta 'amma*), such as jihad, commanding the right, consultation (*shura*) and caring for the poor, from righteous actions required by individual Muslims (Zollner

2009, 125–28). Individual righteous action centered on commanding the right and forbidding the evil (*al-amr bi-l-ma'ruf wa nahy 'an al-munkar*) in one's everyday life, by (following a well-known hadith) hand, then by words, and then in one's heart (130–38).

Hudaybi's writings emphasized moral *action* more than the achievement of specific *outcomes*: individual Muslims were religiously obliged to reject injustice and forbid and change the wrong and, specifically, to resist unjust rulers who violated God's law. However, the MB's directive discourse under Hudaybi did not define the particular kinds of injustice and action that Muslims must resist (Zollner 2009, 130–33). Hudaybi broadly asserted the superiority of Islamic *hukm* or rule, which, he argued, was based on God's law, over its "natural" and "political" alternatives, which were based on human greed, and emphasized that a caliphate was necessary for truly Muslim community to flourish, but was careful to describe Islamic rule in terms of the personal qualities of a righteous leader and the manner in which he was to be chosen, rather than in terms of the policies he might pursue (Zollner 2009, 119–20).

Despite arguing that the only righteous rule was that which applied God's law, Hudaybi also distinguished between making God the judge of all of life (*tahkim*)—an important individual obligation for Muslims—and the application (*tanfidh*) of this law by the state. He stated that each Muslim was obliged to follow the commands of religion in his or her own life, no matter what the state did, and rejected the idea that sharia could operate as a kind of *qanun* or state law, tacked onto existing institutions, because it represented a system that transcended these institutions (Zollner 2009, 118). God's law was meant to guide people in moral action, not serve as an end in and of itself. The believing community was obligated to recognize what was permitted and restricted by God and to defend the faith, and the ruler owed it to the community to abide by God's law. The imam or leader of the community was selected by the *ahl al-hal wa-l-'aqd* or those who could "loose and bind," who were required to have some level of religious knowledge (126–27). This framing of the requirement to act for an Islamic state therefore emphasized righteous action without a predefined goal and prioritized the righteous individual as an agent in bringing about a godly society, over the state.

Hudaybi reframed the idea of the sovereignty of God (*hakimiyat allah*) that Qutb had emphasized in arguing that ungodly rule was tantamount to apostasy, to suggest that the absolute requirements for obeying God's sovereignty applied to individual worship (*'ibada*), instead of to practical and worldly interactions (*mu'amalat*), for which God's commands required interpretation (Zollner 2009, 61, 101–3). In his book *Dusturna* (Our Constitution), Hudaybi focused on the detailed practical commands and regulations that the Quran contained for people's daily lives and relationships as the best way for Muslims to apply the sharia in their lives, and the best path by which believers could transform their communities (Rosen 2008). The political order reflecting God's will that Muslims had a duty to bring about was an order defined primarily, for Hudaybi, by its justice, peace, freedom, and security, not by specific legislation (Zollner 2009, 106–7).

Citing the Quranic verse (5:44) that called on believers to judge by what God had revealed, Hudaybi deferred to classical thought on deriving the principles of rule from the goals of sharia and discussed the many ways of reconciling subordination to God's law with the needs of governance, yet he did not describe Islamic governance, other than to argue that it must be personified in the office of a righteous ruler who would protect the faith, and by contrasting it with immoral rule (Zollner 2009, 110–19).

A Revival of Activism in the 1970s

Where the MB's organizational structure had been in a shambles in the 1960s due to the arrest of most of its leadership, the release of MB leaders in 1971 as part of a rapprochement offered by Anwar al-Sadat, Nasser's successor after his death, allowed the organization to rebuild cautiously. Through the 1970s, the MB revived its *da'wa* mission in a more liberalized public sphere and in competition and cooperation with newer, student-led, and more militant Islamist organizations. As student networks were becoming more politicized, and political debate and participation were encouraged under Sadat's liberalizing initiative of the 1970s that sought to promote religious values and to sideline leftism, the MB's renewed *da'wa* also embraced public outreach and political questions once more.

Hudaybi and his deputies, Umar al-Tilmissany and Mustafa Mashour, faced a fragmented and competitive Islamist field upon their release from prison: new student and youth groups unaffiliated with the MB, but who had adopted its goal of increasing religious cultivation, had mushroomed. Their university discussion groups had become influential, and they ran regular Islamic summer camps. Further, the new state leadership actively wooed these student groups, funding their summer camps and deploying its own preachers to win their hearts and minds (Arian 2014, 58–85). The new Sadat government was keen to co-opt the growing public enthusiasm for Islamic revival: Sadat's protégé and later speaker of parliament, Sufi Abu Talib, offered aid and advice to Islamist student groups as the vice president of Cairo University in the mid-1970s; Islamist intellectual Kamal Abou el-Magd was appointed secretary-general of the Arab Socialist Union's youth organization in 1971; and state media promoted loyalist preachers such as Shaykh Mitwalli al-Sha'arawi and Mustafa Mahmoud as popular religious guides (80–82).

This more hospitable political environment produced a flourishing Islamist ideational marketplace on the campuses of Cairo University and provincial universities in the early 1970s. Arian's study of this period describes student union committees on religion and society that turned into formal Islamic youth groups, the largest of which was the Gama'a Islamiyya, all of whom engaged the political issues of the day through campus debates with leftists, wall newspapers, and pamphlets arguing over religiously permissible behavior and contrasting contemporary political elites with those in Islamic history (2014, 116–18). The Gama'a Islamiyya, in particular, co-opted and revived elements of the historical MB model and discourse: it adopted an MB-style mission statement echoing Banna's twenty principles, a similar organizational hierarchy, and a curriculum aimed at preparing youth to face the "enemies of God" (129–30). Where the MB's mission had historically been embedded in its own organizational practices, it now found the *da'wa* mission adopted and reshaped by a variety of actors, leading to an identity crisis within the movement as it found its position as the premier Islamic movement in Egypt challenged (85–95, 154–55). This crisis also revived debates about what to prioritize in the mission and in organizational rebuilding, and on what it meant to work for Islam.

Mustafa Mashour, a one-time member of the movement's secret apparatus, argued for rebuilding a disciplined movement hierarchy and prioritizing the education of a committed cadre, insisting that there was no activism without organization, while other leaders favored a strategy of ideational outreach and diffusion to spread Banna's message, through what Arian (2014, 96–99) terms a "publishing house with a speaker's bureau model," to cultivate the movement's norms in youth without imposing organizational discipline on them. Umar al-Tilmissany, who succeeded Hudaybi as general guide in 1972, argued that both priorities could be pursued together: he pushed for rebuilding the guidance bureau and some of the movement infrastructure while limiting official recruitment and prioritizing outreach through schools, workplaces and mosques to maintain a low public profile (Arian 2014, 100). He championed a "mission of public advocacy that focused its efforts on society at large" while using the MB's organizational resources, such as its most committed activists, and its name recognition, to ensure that the "spirit of the message" was honored (107).

This rebuilding process took place in part by incorporating newer student Islamic networks into the MB's organizational and activist structure and by expanding the spheres in which the MB spread its message and the audiences to whom it appealed. By 1974, Tilmissany was eager to reconstitute the MB by gradually exposing student activists from the Gama'a Islamiyya to its ideas and writings and rearing them "in the intellectual side of the MB before the organizational structure came" (Arian 2014, 158–61). MB leaders and activists participated in the Islamic summer camps set up by university students, where they encouraged attendees to practice idealized Islamic norms in everyday interactions and to bond in their everyday prayer and physical activities, and distributed copies of Banna's writings that removed references to the MB's organizational structure (131, 156, 164).

The MB saw student camps and conferences as useful sites in which to spread their message and to counter regime messaging about them.

The movement also chose to continue its *daʿwa* via the media. Arian (2014, 176) notes that the movement's *al-Daʿwa* monthly journal, resurrected in 1976, was instrumental to this reconstitution, as its "more direct line to Egyptian society" and as a combined publishing and organizational headquarters. The focus on *daʿwa* as the unifying framework for the movement's work was important in establishing continuity with the historical mission for members (192). The decision to rely on public, mediated discourse to spread the MB message to a new generation did, however, change its ideational production: the journal framed the movement's mission with reference to current events and injustices as much as in terms of individual ethical cultivation; targeted a mass audience; engaged a variety of issues including gender and family norms, US-Israel relations, popular culture, and the movement's own history; and published more frequently than had older Islamic publications (Arian 2014, 177–82; Mellor 2017, 148–50).

The movement's discourse in the mediated public sphere, directed at external as well as movement audiences, was strategic, assertive, and commissive. Strategically, the journal offered a rare, independent platform open to the movement in a state-dominated media landscape, and Arian's interlocutors note that one of the main goals of the journal at this time was to reconstruct the movement's image in a positive light to counter the negative messaging of the regime (Arian 2014, 182). Columns in *al-Daʿwa* allowed movement leaders to publicize their mission to a wider audience that did not have personal contact with Brothers, making the case for why cultivating righteousness and enabling righteous action by individuals could be an effective response to social and political problems, and positioning the MB's religious interpretations and authority as more authentically attuned to the Prophetic legacy and concerned with the public good than its rivals. In a series of columns on *daʿwa* in the late 1970s, titled "Min fiqh al-daʿwa" (The Jurisprudence of Preaching) the movement's soon-to-be deputy general guide Mustafa Mashour framed its mission in traditional trickle-up terms as one centered on *tarbiya* and patient outreach, grounded in deep faith, precise orientation, and continuous action, with a solid understanding of Islamic history and doctrine as its foundation

(Arian 2014, 188–90). His columns reiterated Banna's argument that a call to faith and action would ultimately result in unity and the construction of a sound Muslim society and urged preachers to follow the sequence of *taʿrif* (acquaintance with the movement's message), *takwin* (formation and cultivation), and *tanfidh* (implementation) in cultivating new adherents and building a positive role model for the kind of Islam they wished to preach (190).

These columns also positioned the MB as a more credible defender of Islam than the state, even under the leadership of the ostentatiously pious new president, Sadat. They accused establishment preachers of having failed to present Islam correctly to the people by refusing to address the genuine moral problems of the day generated by economic and political injustices (Arian 2014, 188). MB leaders presented their own mission as more attuned to and better positioned to address the everyday manifestations of injustice in society and framed commitment to Islam, in both individuals and constitutions, as a force for accountability and legal equality (201). Mashour argued that the gap between an ideal society and the corrupt Sadat era required action, while challenging the idea—popular in more militant Islamist student networks—that working for Islam required armed force: he reminded readers that a passive assertion of faith was as valid a form of resistance as armed jihad, and that the path of sacrifice and patient *daʿwa* would lead to an eventual Islamic government. Yusuf al-Qaradawi, a former Brother and leading intellectual guide to the MB, similarly wrote in *al-Daʿwa* that a better understanding of the faith and an effort to cultivate a broader *daʿwa* culture were as liberatory as any kind of jihad (190–91).

Rejecting a violent, revolutionary strategy was both a pragmatic maneuver for a movement fearing further repression and a calculated effort to reassert the primacy of the MB's *minhaj* over those of newer, more revolutionary Islamist groups. The leadership used writings in *al-Daʿwa* to suggest that the Brothers were no strangers to armed combat and repression, emphasizing the sacrifices and suffering that the Brothers had undergone at the hands of Nasser's regime and in fighting for Palestine (Arian 2014, 193–97). Columns compared the MB's own history with that of the

Egyptian people's suffering under an unjust regime, to show the movement's commitment to winning redress for injustices and to gain popular sympathy (198–99).

In addition to competing with militant and politicized new Islamist student groups, the MB was drawn into more strategic debates on the uses of politics when President Sadat proposed a slew of political and constitutional reforms—notably, electoral reform to allow multiparty parliamentary elections—and started the Camp David peace process with Israel. Sadat's 1976 announcement that he would encourage multiparty elections while implementing a parties law that denied legal status to parties that mentioned sharia in their platforms offered conflicting incentives to Islamist movements. The Gama'a Islamiyya immediately rejected elections, but the MB responded pragmatically by inaugurating a new political bureau under the auspices of the Guidance Council, led by Umar al-Tilmissany, to explore electoral options, even as the movement's leadership insisted that *tarbiya* and *da'wa* remained the basic tools of the movement's work (Arian 2014, 168).

Tilmissany used columns in *al-Da'wa* to critique Sadat's policies and failure to follow through on promises for reform to deliver "true democratic rule" and the rule of law (Arian 2014, 199). By acknowledging that incremental policy changes mattered in building a more just society, the MB leadership reaffirmed its traditional argument that the Islamic *minhaj* must adapt to the concerns of the day, while also trying to counter the Sadat regime's efforts to co-opt Islamic politics. Editorials in *al-Da'wa* pointing out shortfalls in policy and governance offered counterproposals for measures to achieve more effective reform and argued for the interests and rights of all Egyptians, while pushing the government to recognize the Islamic values that should govern Muslim societies and to set a good example for citizens with their own moral conduct. Editorials similarly lauded the regime's initiative in the late 1970s to declare sharia the source of legislation as evidence that the MB's mission of infusing an Islamic ethos into society was making headway (Arian 2014, 200–201). In opposing Sadat's policies, the Brothers who wrote in *al-Da'wa* increasingly positioned themselves as the voice of justice and of the people speaking up to hold rulers accountable to the people. Sadat's contradictory statement that there must be no religion in politics even as he championed sharia in legislation inspired the MB leadership to renew its traditional complaint that the Egyptian state's defense of religion was insincere and manipulative and to join Islamist student groups in calling on the state to honor Egypt's Islamic identity by applying Islamic values rather than only championing ritual worship (138).

Sadat's project of generating a sharia-based legal code to bring the constitution in line with the principles of sharia, supervised by Sufi Abu Talib and a committee of Azhari clerics from the late 1970s onward, drew MB leaders further into arguments about the state's accountability to popular religious values and prompted them to propose their own committee to follow through on the government's faltering sharia proposal (Lombardi 2001, 139–48; Arian 2014, 202–3). *Al-Daʿwa* critiqued the government's half-hearted constitutional reform initiative to designate sharia a the main source of legislation while seeking to keep religion out of the political process as a sign of insincerity, reviving its argument that a constitution that was based on foreign sources, traditions, and principles rather than on "the religion of this nation" was bound to fail (Arian 2014, 202). In addition to criticizing the government for failing to uphold its duty to govern justly and according to God's law, leaders writing in *al-Daʿwa* also framed their mission as the defense of Egypt "against the designs of those who would deny the will of the people to live as devout Muslims, free from foreign or domestic subordination," and tied the situation of Egypt to that of the oppression of Muslims worldwide, including in Palestine (204–5).

The movement leadership's decision to allow its publications to become an oppositional voice, even as it limited its political message to one of principled exhortation, made it difficult to avoid clashes with the regime. When MB leaders resisted regime efforts at cooptation, notably Sadat's offer to legalize the movement in exchange for making it accountable to the Ministry of Social Affairs, and his offer of a government post to Umar al-Tilmissany, Sadat accused the movement of collaborating with Egypt's enemies and inciting its youth, and sought to ban its publications (Arian 2014, 173–74, 146). Yet the MB leadership continued to affirm a mission of gradual reform and outreach through "the word," even after a renewed ban on its activities following Sadat's assassination by a more militant Islamist group in 1981 (204, 216). And, as the political bureau and advocates of pragmatic political engagement became embedded in the movement organization, institutional politics became a more acceptable option in the movement's repertoire.

Conclusion

Scholars of the MB's entry into parliamentary and syndicate politics in the 1980s and 1990s have recognized the importance of student activism in the 1970s in pushing Islamism in a more political direction. A particularly influential argument points to the formation of an Islamist "middle generation" through student politics that was more comfortable with the pluralist and competitive values of electoral politics, as a key driver of the MB's shift to electoral politics (Wickham 2004, 2013). As this chapter has shown, a more pragmatic approach to political and public engagement also grew out of the MB's organizational rebuilding process and was debated as part of its religious *minhaj*. Divisions between leaders who prioritized organizational rebuilding and discipline and were skeptical of activism and those who sought more public outreach were significant from the 1970s onward (Arian 2014, 220–28). Yet those who prioritized outreach framed it as a more effective way to pursue the movement's *da'wa* rather than as an alternative to the religious *da'wa*. In the following chapter, I will show how debates around the value of political participation continued to use the discourse of religious mission for new operational goals.

2

Cultivating Citizens and Representing Righteousness

Da'wa *and* Tarbiya *through Electoral and Parliamentary Politics, 1984–1987*

How did the MB embrace electoral campaigning and parliamentary representation as extensions of religious work despite its deep-rooted opposition to political partisanship and given public skepticism of their political ambitions? The decision of Sadat's successor, Hosni Mubarak, to permit multiparty legislative elections in 1984 and to allow nonparty candidates to contest seats, offered the movement new political opportunities to expand its influence, but it also challenged the movement tenet that *da'wa* or preaching must remain the primary operational priority, and that all other kinds of work were secondary to it. In this chapter, using public writings, speeches, parliamentary and media debate, and internally directed instructional texts and position pieces to trace the movement leadership's discourse on electoral politics from 1984 to 1987, I will show how the MB leadership responded to external and internal resistance to politicization by framing new political work in terms of older traditions of active piety and positioned themselves internally and externally as actors committed to religion first and foremost, who would use new political arenas to cultivate public righteousness without partisanship. Examining the incentives offered by elections, electoral coalitions, and legislative agendas in turn, and the political strategies the MB adopted in response to them and its leadership's framing of these strategies, I find that the leadership positioned political work as an expansion, not a downgrading, of *da'wa*, to both rally internal support for electoral politics as a resource for the core religious mission and to allay external concerns about electoral politics as a play for Islamist hegemony.

This chapter begins by analyzing how internally directed statements and writings by MB leaders in the early 1980s justified a decision to contest parliamentary elections by framing campaigning and parliamentary performance as practices of *da'wa* and *tarbiya*, enabling activists to cultivate themselves by acting ethically as candidates and representatives in new public spaces, educating others in good Islamic conduct, and building support for the Islamic cause by modeling righteous political action and guiding voters in how to practice it. The chapter then focuses on how MB leaders framed their work strategically to external skeptics, in the run-up to elections in 1984, as a form of *nasiha* or moral advice aimed at supporting existing state commitments to religion and reinforcing rather than weakening national religious unity, while framing political participation internally as a way to protect and expand religious freedom by resisting state exclusion and allowing believers to exercise their moral agency in advocating for godly rule. It discusses how, once elected, MB leaders framed their political role both in terms of advocacy for sharia and an extension of *da'wa* via exemplary behavior and exhortation from the new pulpit of parliament, using the instruments of political representation to spread Islamic activist ethics, such as truth-telling, modeling righteousness, and holding rulers accountable to religion, rather than achieving specific legislative goals, in 1985–86. The chapter concludes with an assessment of how both campaign and internal directive discourse in 1987 framed electoral work, voting and encouraging others to vote, and mobilizing pious citizens to hold rulers accountable to Islam, as forms of *tarbiya* and *da'wa*, cementing the ideal of political work as moral, not instrumental, practice in movement literature, and as a key tool for achieving the religious mission of the MB instead of distracting from it.

Electoral Liberalization and Dilemmas of Participation, 1983–1984

President Anwar al-Sadat's announcement of a decision to permit multiple political parties and encourage parliamentary elections before his assassination in 1981 was the culmination of a broader state accommodation with a "moderate" Islamism in the 1970s that extended to the Muslim Brothers more freedom to speak, write, and organize even as the Egyptian regime monitored and repressed militant Islamic *gama'at* more closely (Lombardi 2001, 137–39). The MB leadership cautiously embraced these new opportunities, focusing on the possibility that a formal withdrawal of state repression could allow the *da'wa* mission to survive and expand, instead of enabling a political entente with the regime or a new political project. When Hosni Mubarak became president following Sadat's assassination, MB leaders encouraged all Muslims to rally behind the government, both because it needed support in a time of crisis, and because of its commitment to reform (2001, 154). Yet they framed this new stage as one in which movement rights and goals were not transformed, but restored.

In articles and open letters addressed to the new president in the newly relegalized MB flagship publication *al-Da'wa* in 1981, general guide Umar al-Tilmissany affirmed movement members' moral and political rights as Muslims and citizens to express themselves in the public sphere and to organize legally as equal members in the nation and as preachers (Kenany 1993, 67–69). He also framed the movement's public mission in both internally and externally oriented writing as fundamentally religious, deserving of political acceptance for its universally shared, rather than divisive, goals: strengthening bonds between Muslims and promoting love between then, while spreading acquaintance (*ta'rif*) with good Muslim practices and beliefs in order to counter harmful and more extremist versions (129–31). In editorials written to challenge framings of the MB as intolerant and extremist in the Arab press, following Sadat's assassination, Tilmissany emphasized the MB's *da'wa* as one of liberation through knowledge and awareness, aimed at guiding youth to spread God's message and being patient in pursuit of its fruits, rather than one of *ta'ssub* or chauvinism (129–31).

While this framing was explicitly meant to reassure state actors, it reflected and affirmed older movement positions and was repeated in internal communications on electoral participation as well. The MB's historical ambivalence to political work was rooted in Banna's suspicion of public work that was guided by personal ambition rather than God's will.

As shown in his letters and petitions to political leaders, educational officials, and Azhari leaders, Banna believed that, while political, social, and economic reform was central to the well-being of believers, and the decay of Muslim societies could be traced to a collapse of religious rule, moral education was a more reliable path to a Muslim society than partisan politics (Lia 1998, 28, 67–69). He argued that all political action and work must be motivated, like any righteous action, by a desire to serve God and unite the *umma* and to generate virtuous leaders, but that *hizbiyya* or partyism cultivated and served personal ambitions and divided the *umma*, and elections did not generate the most qualified workers (69–70, 249–51).

In a series of responses to readers' letters in *al-Da'wa* that asked about the movement's potential rethinking of its strategy and accommodations with the regime after Sadat's passing, Tilmissany emphasized continuities with the historical mission and invoked Banna's arguments for treating politics as an extension of the *da'wa*: the Brothers would spread God's word in all spheres, whether or not the law enabled or recognized it (Kenany 1993, 75–86). Like Banna, who had asserted that the movement must embrace multiple forms to spread the *da'wa* to the ears of those able to change society, and who had argued, during the MB's Sixth Conference in 1941, that parliament could serve as a pulpit (*minbar*) from which to spread God's word and clarify the MB's vision of reform, Tilmissany also framed the MB's public mission as guided by religious goals, to nudge rulers on a godly path and counter those who refused to apply God's will, and emphasized the utility of politics for the *da'wa* above all (Rady 1990, 20–23; Kenany 1993, 78–86). Tilmissany stated that the goals of working for government on an Islamic basis, regardless of its form—of gathering people to command the right (*amr bi-l-ma'ruf*) and bringing up youth on an Islamic basis until God's vision was embedded in the entire *umma* and rule was for God alone—continued to guide the MB's public work, and that it would always resist the "idol" of socialist and un-Islamic government (Kenany 1993, 76, 79–86). Echoing Banna's caution about allowing partisanship and political ambition to overtake religious motivations, Tilmissany emphasized political work as a kind of ethical praxis rather than an accommodation with dominant political norms: he insisted that the MB would remain committed to righteous practice in working for truth and justice as for *tarbiya* and *islah* and would never engage in opportunism, personal vendettas, or destructive protests (76).

Contesting Elections: Campaigning as *Tarbiya* and *Daʿwa*

When Mubarak passed a law in 1983 to allow multiparty elections to parliament the following year, the MB leadership faced an opportunity to expand their social influence that also triggered substantial internal and external opposition in quick succession. To reach the 8 percent threshold required for being seated in parliament, per the new list-based proportional representation electoral rules, and to get around restrictions on independent candidates, movement leaders formed an alliance of convenience with the historically nationalist Wafd party, giving rise to dissension within both conservative MB and secular Wafdist ranks around the ideological shifts that the alliance might represent (Ibrahim and Awad 1996, 77–78). MB leaders produced a flurry of public statements, including in Islamic publications that were aimed at movement members and the wider Islamic social sector and that framed the decision to compete in elections as an assertion of Islamic norms against secular hegemony instead of an accommodation with it; as an extension of the *daʿwa* and a form of *tarbiya* to the public by different means, and as a path to allowing moral political practice that could cultivate stronger Islamic ethics in activists and their audiences, with party collaboration serving to rally more support for the Islamic cause rather than increasing partisanship.

The MB leadership appealed to traditional religious authority by citing and printing writings in their newspapers by established religious scholars on the permissibility of participating in non-Islamic institutions like parliaments. In one text, leaders cited a religious scholar who countered Sayyid Qutb's objection to participation in elections as a form of cooperation with godless state authority that violated religious tenets, by arguing that political participation with the intent of working for the rule of God's law, as Turkish Islamists had done, was righteous, and that those who lobbied for religious rights were in the employ of God and the people (Rady 1990, 29–30). The movement's magazine, *al-Ikhwan al-Muslimin*, also featured an interview with a scholar in the faculty of Islamic law at

Cairo University who argued that parliamentary participation was religiously acceptable for the Brothers, as it allowed them to represent the highest ideas in parliament and to show the nation that government could and should be judged by the highest scales (31).

MB leaders and their allies also framed the decision to participate in elections as a pragmatic adaptation for *da'wa* under new circumstances. Shaykh Salah Abu Ismail, a Wafd party member who had once been a member of the MB, argued in an article in the MB-run newspaper *Liwa' al-Islam* that preachers of Islam must always choose the best available path to exalt God's work and apply his sharia, and that, given current restrictions on free expression in religious institutions like mosques and on *nasiha* (advice to rulers), parliamentary work must be added to teaching, study meetings, and publications as a form of *da'wa*. Rather than being responsible for ungodly legislation, which, as a parliamentary minority, they could not be, Ismail argued that Brothers could serve God by acting righteously to refuse legislation where God required it and could push back against "secularists, masons, atheists, and communists" who might permit what God had forbidden (Rady 1990, 39–42). The MB leadership insisted that their mission would not be swayed by popular majorities, and that their goal in parliament was not to subject God's law to majority approval, for the Prophet himself had, after all, been ill treated by the majority of the population in his time (Kenany 1993, 122). Tilmissany also argued in the pages of *al-Da'wa* that participating in politics was an obligation to those who wished to spread God's word to counter the political and cultural remnants of colonialism in the Muslim world, and an extension and exercise of its right to religious freedom. As long as God's book was not applied by God's followers on God's earth, he asserted, nobody could tell God's missionaries that this was not their business (116).

Godly work in the public sphere was a kind of jihad, Tilmissany declared, and the MB could fulfill the *umma*'s collective religious obligation to call for the right and forbid the evil by standing up to existing public authorities, offering them advice, and censuring injustice, so that those in power could fulfill their religious obligations (Kenany 1993, 118–20). Similarly, in Tilmissany's framing, ethical and exemplary behavior in parliament could help MB representatives enact and embody piety that could serve as an example to others and teach them what Islam looked like, in practice: even as an opposition in parliament, Brothers could model ethical and serious opposition for future generations, show that their critiques of the regime were grounded in Islamic awareness, and work for Islam by advising and redirecting government leaders, with the interests (*masalih*) of the people at heart, rather than resorting to slander (93–94, 124).

MB leaders who supported and joined in the parliamentary campaign effort emphasized how participation in elections and in parliament supported Banna's conception of the *da'wa*. Citing an argument from Banna's writings, repeated by other MB thinkers in subsequent generations, parliamentarian Mohsen Rady argued that parliament was the best pulpit available to allow the *da'wa* to reach as many hearts and ears as possible and presented parliament as a natural site for expanding the *da'wa* from the *muhit sha'bi* or popular sphere to the *muhit rasmi* or official public sphere (Rady 1990, 20). Deputy general guide Mustafa Mashour similarly made the case that while the traditional "vertical" approach to *da'wa*—the cultivation of Muslim society by starting with individuals and families—remained important, it was time to also embrace a "horizontal" approach, by spreading the *da'wa* and raising the spiritual level of fellow Muslims via *tarbiya* in whatever social spaces Muslims found themselves. Where the ideal Muslim individual and family would remain the building block of the MB's vision, Mashour stated, it was also important to cultivate a wider sympathetic public of upright Muslims (*muslimin salihin*) that would support and love the Islamic mission (Mashour 1989, 44).

Similarly, Tilmissany and Mashour both emphasized the didactic purpose of election campaigning, framing it as a kind of *tarbiya*. The goal of electoral participation, for Tilmissany, was not only to do God's will but also to nurture "religious spirit in the souls of people" so that public opinion would become a force for Islam (Kenany 1993, 124). Mashour asserted that faith was always the spring from which any religious activism must flow, and political *da'wa* was aimed at diagnosing and prescribing cures for the diseases affecting the faith of Muslim societies and helping them correct themselves (30, 101).

Tilmissany echoed the framing of parliament as a pulpit (*minbar*) in interviews with the non-Islamist press as well, arguing that parliament was one tool among many in spreading the MB's ideas to the public and for pushing the government to recognize that people must submit to God rather than to money.[1] In an interview with *al-Siyasah* in March 1984, he insisted that electoral work would be an extension of religiously motivated ethical practice because, while others might form political parties in the pursuit of power, Brothers were guided by the unchanging goal of protecting the rights of Muslims and awaited God's reward, not any worldly one (Ibrahim and Awad 1996, 139). Both Mashour and Tilmissany highlighted the religious nature of the mission of popular electoral representation. Timissany exhorted MB activists to remember their religious obligations as they appealed to Muslim sentiments, instead of being swayed by human wishes, and to be patient and steadfast when faced with repression and the forces of evil (Kenany 1993, 122). Mashour argued that applying God's sharia had turned into a mass demand that could not be ignored, and that the MB, in entering electoral politics, were responding to, as well as cultivating, the desire of young Muslims to change the corrupt status quo through a return to religion (Mashour 1989, 130).

The MB's most visible rethinking of the religious meaning of electoral politics came in the form of an exploratory initiative to form a political party in 1984. While maintaining a rhetorical commitment to the longstanding movement position that the "party of God" was the only legitimate political faction, a new movement committee to produce a party manifesto, headed by a leader of the founding generation of the MB, proposed two alternative party projects, in consultation with Islamist parties in other countries, that acknowledged the utility of parties for the Islamic mission (Awadi 2004, 83–84). The committee produced manifestoes for two potential parties that would champion the missions of *tarbiya* (cultivation), *hidaya* (guidance) and *islah* (reform) in the political sphere, which focused both on religious guidance and public welfare, freedom and security, as the end goals of Islamic politics. The proposed Shura (Consultation) Party's manifesto included a call "to establish the Islamic Egyptian state" that combined "being a state of guidance, guided by the

---

1. "Umar al-Tilmissany yaqul: al-Ikhwan al-Muslimin laysu intihaziyin," *al-Ahrar*, May 7, 1984.

light of Islam and committed to its rules, and being a welfare state that provides services to its citizens and works to ensure freedom and security." The manifesto of the alternative Islah (Reform) Party stated that its aim was to "reform the affairs of the Egyptian state so it becomes able to provide its citizens with services and work to ensure freedom and security, and makes available to its citizens all necessary needs" (83–84).

Other MB statements cautiously accepted political professionalization and pluralism as compatible with an Islamic social and political order. Mashour argued that pluralism was compatible with Islamic work both on principle and as a pragmatic tool to achieve Islamic goals: a division of labor between those focused on *da'wa* and those who worked on commanding the right was permissible for the Islamic mission, and political pluralism was acceptable just as disagreement among Muslims on how best to work for Islamic goals under changing circumstances was (Mashour 1989, 98–100). Tilmissany and Mashour contended that parties formed on the basic principle of accepting and working for Islam were legitimate, because they would work for the good, unlike parties formed around human ideologies that would divide Muslims, and cited the scholar Yusuf al-Qaradawi in arguing that multiple parties that recognized Islam as faith and law were actually valuable in guarding against tyranny (Mashour 1989, 94; Kenany 1993, 129; Wa'i 2001, 101). Framing legitimate political parties as similar to schools of interpretation (*madhahib*) in Islamic law, MB leaders argued that parties defined by different programs and strategies, not based on personalities or sectarian identities, could help generate the best ideas on how to achieve godly goals, just as multiple channels of expression and consultation were useful in generating the best solution for a given problem (Wa'i 2001, 106). This religiously bounded and cautious acceptance of political pluralism also helped the MB justify allying with political parties to pursue its goals.

Working with Others for a Pious Nation: Framing the Electoral *Da'wa* for External Audiences

When the MB chose to ally with the historically nationalist Wafd party (of which two prominent Brothers, Muhammad Abdel-Quddus and Salah

Abu Ismail, had been members), it faced public skepticism about its intentions, as well as concerns from secularists within the Wafd, who were worried about losing the party to leaders more sympathetic to religion. MB rank-and-file members were similarly worried that the alliance under the Wafd's banner would cede ideological space to secularism. In response, MB leaders and sympathetic Wafd leaders strategically framed their shared campaign in terms of freedom of conscience and working for the good or interest (*masalih*) of the nation and countering accusations of theocratic intent by framing the collective obligation to work for the divinely defined good in terms of citizenship and agency. In commissive discourse aimed at both external and internal audiences, MB and Wafd leaders emphasized, too, how little the alliance would change either side's preexisting ethical commitments, and how their parliamentary program would uphold rather than threaten the sectarian unity of the nation and existing national commitments to religion. To an interviewer with the state-run press, Tilmissany insisted that both sides would cooperate in the national interest without trying to change each other (Ibrahim and Awad 1996, 139). In other interviews with the state media, MB leaders like Tilmissany emphasized that they aimed to uphold state commitments to Islam—notably, article 2 of the constitution—and did not wish to monopolize the right to represent religion in Egypt.[2] Wafd leaders similarly made press statements affirming their support for constitutional provisions to respect sharia and a vision of sharia focused on promoting the national good, while indicating they would resist further legislation to apply its tenets (Ibrahim and Awad 1996, 118–22, 126).[3] In internal communications and in campaign operations, the MB maintained a clear distinction between their work and that of their ally: Tilmissany's internal statements assured cadres that the alliance was purely electoral, aimed at winning seats in parliament to work for movement goals (Wa'i 2001, 162). The two groups did not coordinate candidate

---

2. "Al-Sheikh al-Tilmissany: Al-'ilmaniyyah laysat al-ilhad," *Rose el-Youssef*, May 14, 1984; "Umar al-Tilmissany yaqul: al-Ikhwan al-Muslimin laysu intihaziyin," *al-Ahrar*, May 7, 1984.

3. "Hiwar ma' al-duktur Wahid Rafa'at," *Akher Sa'a*, March 21, 1984; Fathi Radwan, "Al-'ilmaniyyah wa tahaluf al-Wafd wa-l-Ikhwan," *al-Sha'b*, March 20, 1984.

choices, preferring to split up seats, and campaigned largely separately, with Brothers participating in only nine out of a total of twenty-six Wafd-led election rallies (Ibrahim and Awad 1996, 160–63, 169).

Outside political pressure, whether from the state or other political forces, did not encourage the MB to fully embrace politicization, but rather accepted its political presence conditionally, which pushed the MB leadership to emphasize its nonpartisan goals all the more in public discourse. In externally oriented discourse, MB leaders emphasized the unifying, nationalist nature of their electoral *da'wa*. A joint election manifesto put out by the MB and the Wafd contained a section on freedom followed by a section on sharia that declared a commitment to Islam in the realm of religion (*din*) and worldly politics (*dawla*), while affirming a parallel commitment to Christian-Muslim unity, an old Wafdist slogan. The manifesto framed religious cultivation and defense of morality as national goals, extending the traditional MB commitment to raising religious awareness and improving religious education to include churches as well as mosques, and calling for reforming the media of all that violated Egyptian, rather than just Islamic, culture and morality (Ibrahim and Awad 1996, 173). Tilmissany framed the alliance with the Wafd as an alliance for the public good, as the Wafd and the MB were two popular forces working for the *salih* (righteousness or good) of "this Muslim country" and promised that an Islamic vision of politics on the model of the Prophet's "enlightened Medina" upheld Christian rights to freedom of conscience more effectively than secular laws.[4] Evoking the older MB mission of uniting the *umma* behind God, Tilmissany called on all those who were "true in deed and word" to "join in undertaking the work of God most high" to unite all efforts to protect the nation (Kenany 1993, 54).

In other public discourse, MB leaders emphasized that ethical representation and fighting for people's rights was important for both religion and citizenship. Tilmissany promised that the Wafd-MB alliance's candidates would live up to high standards of virtue in carrying out their

---

4. "Umar al-Tilmissany yaqul: Al-Ikhwan al-Muslimin laysu intihaziyin," *al-Ahrar*, May 7, 1984.

obligations to the people, whether by holding ministers accountable, or not missing any parliamentary session, and generally acting with wisdom and dignity.[5] He also argued that holding rulers accountable had always been a religious duty in Islam, in that religious tradition required Muslims to speak out when a ruler overstepped the bounds of sharia (Kenany 1993, 68). In response to state media and secular Wafdist leaders, who warned that bringing "reactionary" Islamists to parliament would restrict the rights of those who did not share their beliefs and undermine Nasser's mission of national liberation, MB leaders framed themselves as defenders of individual rights and freedoms, and of the people against a repressive regime. Tilmissany vowed that the Islamic mission in parliament would return dignity to the nation and rule to the people, in contrast with the humiliation and misery they had faced under Nasserist rule, where the decline of individual rights and freedoms had produced a wider national decline (65–66). Responding to a column in the state-run *al-Ahram* warning of the risk of an MB political presence to the development of Egyptian democracy, an MB columnist writing in the Islamist-sympathetic *al-Sha'b* contrasted the MB's peaceful and lawful *da'wa* and social and student mobilization with the government's unlawful methods of repression against Islamic activists.[6] MB candidates also emphasized individual rights and freedoms as closely tied to religious freedom in their campaign discourse: free expression in mosques, freedom of *da'wa*, and freedom to publish for religious groups were recurrent themes in MB campaign rallies and speeches in 1984, while statements on the inadequate conformity of state laws with God's law were secondary (Ibrahim and Awad 1996, 164–65).

MB leader Muhammad Abdel-Quddus also challenged regime depictions of the MB as threats to national unity by emphasizing that the Wafd and the MB were true "sons of the nation" who shared a commitment to ending emergency rule, cementing freedoms and respect for human

---

5. Umar al-Tilmissany, "Al-tahaluf al-Wafd wa-l-ikhwan bi-la musawamat wa la shurut," *al-Wafd*, May 10, 1984.

6. Muhammad Yahya, "Al-haraka al-islamiyya wa qadiya fi sahifat al-Ahram," *al-Sha'b*, June 19, 1984.

rights, and opposing the Camp David accords with Israel.[7] Secular intellectuals like Louis Awad and Farag Foda resigned from the Wafd party in protest after accusing their pro-alliance party colleagues of enabling steps toward religious establishment by aiding the Islamist presence in parliament. However, the party president, Fouad Serageddin, argued at election rallies that the alliance was necessary to reveal "the true and free face of the popular will" against the repression and media manipulation of the ruling party.[8] Other Wafdist leaders supported the MB assertion that its vision of state support for Islam was a continuation of a long-standing commitment by the Egyptian state to support religious education and mosques, and that a religiously led state of the kind called for in Islam supported citizens' religious freedoms, unlike Christianity, with its more theocratic tendencies, and that the MB's enlightened interpretations of Islam would weaken the influence of extremists.[9]

Mobilizing Voices for God's Law in Parliament, 1985–1986

When MB and Wafdist candidates were seated in the People's Assembly following modest electoral successes in 1984, the issue of how to bring legislation into compliance with the principles of sharia, in accordance with revisions to article 2 of the constitution, was placed on the legislative agenda, by a Supreme Constitutional Court decision to decline lawsuits challenging legislation as noncompliant with sharia and to refer them back to parliament. In championing sharia as a reference and goal for legislation, MB representatives framed the work that must be done to bring about a sharia-governed social order in terms of empowering citizens to hold their representatives accountable. Moreover, the MB construed this effort as a religious obligation that must be achieved collectively, building on the discourse of popular empowerment through religion and parliament as a

---

7. Muhammad Abdel-Quddus, "Awlad al-balad," *al-Wafd*, June 14, 1984.
8. "Wa min al-intima' ma' qatl," *al-Ahrar*, January 30, 1984; "Al-mu'araka al-intikhabiyya mutahawilat ila mahzala," *al-Wafd*, May 17, 1984.
9. Radwan, "Al-'ilmaniyya"; Abdel Azim Ramadan, "Al-Wafd wal-l-Ikhwan al-Muslimin: lam kul hada al-zub'ah?" *al-Wafd*, March 22, 1984.

minbar to educate citizens on active faith that had permeated the group's election campaigning. Pushing back against state efforts to counter the "politicization" of sharia compliance, to focus on textual compliance, and to limit responsibility for ensuring moral legislation to the loyalist Azhari establishment, MB parliamentary leaders used their questioning power in parliament to push the regime to "return" responsibility for sharia application to the representatives of a pious nation, arguing that more political and religious freedom was needed to allow scholars of religion to carry out their obligations correctly on behalf of the nation.

As previously discussed, the MB's historical position on sharia was that it represented both a fixed religious obligation for all pious Muslims to respect and follow in their own lives, and the end point of the movement's project of *da'wa*, as those who had been properly cultivated in Islamic faith and ethics would call for sharia in government. They had not, however, been at the forefront of initiatives to legislate sharia in Egypt, but rather reacted to government efforts to expand and carefully control the expansion of sharia in Egyptian laws. MB leaders had supported Sadat's initiative to review all Egyptian legislation for sharia compliance in the late 1970s, and, when his successor abruptly shelved it in 1982, deputizing Azhari leaders to explain why it was no longer necessary, MB leaders joined other political and press voices in debating what it meant to establish more sharia-guided society and legislation (Peters 1988, 245–47). When the Supreme Constitutional Court and the Court of Cassation finally declined lawsuits challenging legislation for violating the newly amended constitutional article 2 in 1985 and directed parliament to take up sharia compliance instead, the MB joined other Islamist activists and Azhari reformists in pressing the regime to revive the shelved Islamic legislation agenda and present it to the People's Assembly (Dupret 2000, 74; Lombardi 2001, 155–56; Brown 1997, 372). Given that the MB had long maintained that God's law applied to all spheres of human conduct and life and had argued that a reason to be represented in parliament was so that they could stand up for and work to implement God's law, they eagerly embraced this new opportunity to discuss what a sharia-compliant, sharia-driven legislation might look like.

But several institutional incentives and movement priorities stopped the movement from proposing its own legislation or policies. As a minority opposition caucus, the MB knew it was pointless to generate precise legislation that had no chance of passing (Rady 1990, 13). Further, the MB's Wafdist allies in parliament voiced their support for a nonstatist approach to sharia application, citing Tilmissany's argument that Islamic reform needed religious awareness, improved morality, and social consultation.[10] Just as important, according to one prominent MB parliamentarian, new MB members of parliament had little experience with legislation and were forging their agenda by trial and error, developing what they saw as "Islamic" campaigns responding to issues affecting the social and moral welfare of Egyptians, such as protecting mosques, working for human rights, or protesting immoral films, rather than considering what legislation they might pass.[11] In several statements and reports in the Islamic and general press, the MB framed their role in working for sharia in parliament as that of serving as the voice of a believing public that wanted to be governed by God's law and mobilizing citizens and parliamentarians for the kind of righteous activism that was necessary to bring about a sharia-governed society. Preemptively countering arguments that advocates for sharia sought a monopoly on religious authority, MB leaders like Muhammad Abdel-Quddus argued that the movement sought to introduce more sharia in Egyptian public life by guiding people and offering them positive examples.[12] Exiled MB leader and legal scholar Tawfiq al-Shawy similarly asserted that applying sharia was a collective religious obligation (*fard kifaya*) for Muslims that required righteous action and deliberation from all kinds of secular and religious experts, whether judges, secular intellectuals, or others, who must be persuaded to work for sharia as a way of working for the public good and respecting people's faith.[13]

In addition to speaking up for God's law in all social spheres, the MB argued in both internally and externally directed discourse that their

---

10. Hassanein Kroum, "Yakhty' man yaqul an al-Wafd 'ilmani," *al-Ahrar*, April 8, 1985.

11. Interview, MN, Cairo, October 18, 2005.

12. Muhammad Abdel-Quddus, "Al-Ikhwan al-muslimin wa tatbiq al-shari'a," *al-Wafd*, June 28, 1984.

13. Tawfiq al-Shawy, "Sayyadat al-shari'a al-islamiyya wa sayyadat al-qanun fi Misr," *al-Sha'b*, October 15, 1985.

mission in building support for sharia in parliament was aimed at amplifying the voice of the believing majority of voters and enabling them to do their duty as citizen-believers in holding their governments accountable to God's law and to the constitution. In a speech in parliament, Umar al-Tilmissany responded to a government representative's argument that *da'wa* and moral preparation were sufficient for applying sharia, by countering that popular action was also necessary to ensure its application. Defining the *islah* or reform necessary to apply God's law as something that must start with cultivating "daring, ambitious youth, youth who would fight for their country, religion, and nation," Tilmissany urged parliament to pass laws that would help expose children to the right values, while reducing the environments of immorality that society and the media exposed them to.[14] Another MB parliamentarian, Mokhtar Noh, argued that the Islamic solution—a term he used interchangeably with sharia—was a collective responsibility (*fard kifaya*), requiring action from all contemporary Muslims, not just men of religion, to ensure that the principles of sharia guided constitutions, laws, and lives, and that existing laws did not violate them, also emphasizing that Islam had historically required rulers to respect the dignity of their subjects.[15] Tawfiq al-Shawy similarly underscored righteous representation as a pathway to applying sharia when he insisted that parliament was a place where human beings could and must apply the principles of sharia to work out the details of legislation so as to achieve the purpose of the constitutional provision to make sharia the basis of law in Egypt.[16]

In framing their goal of sharia application as a popular demand that could be achieved via parliament, MB leaders affirmed a core *da'wa* goal and pointed to similar statements by Azhari scholars who argued that the people needed sharia to solve social problems, for more mainstream

14. "Maglis al-Shaab: Ittifaq al-mu'arada wa-l-aghlabiyya 'ala dirasa al-muta'niya li-l-shari'a al-islamiyya," *al-Ahram*, February 12, 1985.

15. Mokhtar Noh, "Al-Islam: Ghany bi-hal al-mushkilat jami'an," *al-Akhbar*, August 24, 1985.

16. Tawfiq al-Shawy, "Mabda' hakimiyyat al-shari'a al-islamiyya wa shar'iyyah qawanin fi-l-tashri' al-Misri," *al-Sha'b*, October 22, 1985.

normative credentialing, even though Azhari leaders rejected political activism as desirable for this end.[17] In the popular press, MB leaders and sympathizers cited surveys that claimed to show that 90 percent of Egyptians favored the application of sharia, criticizing the speaker of parliament's contention that sharia should take a backseat to more pressing economic reform priorities by insisting that sharia application was essential for the reform and improvement of people's lives.[18] The MB and their allies countered state religious officials' warnings about making sharia a partisan issue by arguing that their call was intended to restore national unity around the issue. The Islamist sympathetic editor of *al-Sha'b* repeated the MB's call for *islah* through greater religious freedom by pressing the government to free up mosques and religious trusts to cultivate good Muslims and to spread the *da'wa* without restriction, while restoring full autonomy to al-Azhar.[19] The head of the Wafd party echoed the MB's framing of sharia as a national, uncontroversial demand that "all of us, rulers and subjects, agree on" and urged the regime to restore the authority and independence of the Azhari leadership from the state, with an independent board of religious scholars guiding the government in its legal decision-making.[20]

MB leaders cited support from more mainstream non-Islamist allies to frame their call to apply sharia as moderate and nationalist in contrast with the demands of conservative Salafi Islamists and members of the Azhari Scholars Front. Whereas a representative of the latter group contended, in a conference on sharia application, that the harshest criminal penalties of the *hudud* were a solution to preventing shocking crimes, MB

---

17. Tawfiq al-Shawy, "Sayyadat al-shari'a al-islamiyya wa sayyadat al-qanun fi Misr," *al-Sha'b*, October 15, 1985; "Al-Amin al-'am li-l-majlis al-'ali li shu'yun al-islamiyya: Tatbiq al-shari'a matlab dini wa sha'bi," *al-Sha'b*, October 16, 1984.

18. Ahmed al-Sioufi, ""Bayan al-hukuma tajahil tatbiq al-shari'a al-islamiyya wa lam yuhaddad dawr al-Azhar, wa lam yash'ar ila al-qadaya al-islamiyya," *al-Sha'b*, October 2, 1984.

19. Al-Amin al-'am li-l-majlis al-'ali li shuyun al-islamiyya: Tatbiq al-shari'a matlab dini wa sha'bi," *al-Sha'b*, October 16, 1984.

20. "Ra'is al-Wafd yada'w ila iqama mujtama' islami sahih," *al-Wafd*, March 7, 1985.

allies argued that the best way to help Egyptian law move closer to sharia was to allow al-Azhar the autonomy to fulfill its responsibilities.[21] In 1985, preachers from a conservative mosque organized a "green march," calling for the immediate application of sharia-based laws, in protest against a statement issued by a government committee for religious affairs arguing that sharia reform must wait (Peters 1988, 247). State authorities rebuked activists for seeking to "rush" the application of God's law through protests rather than trusting official religious authorities to do the right thing.[22] MB leaders used the opportunity to frame their own position as the responsible one, in line with national norms, and asserted that a truly nationalist approach to sharia required the inclusion of parliament, as citizens' representatives, in the process of deciding how to apply sharia.[23]

Activating Righteous Voters in the 1987 Parliamentary Campaign

By the next parliamentary election in 1987, the MB political leadership was less focused on reassuring internal and external skeptics about the intent and impact of their electoral participation and more focused on presenting their own work in parliament as an enactment of piety and a way of encouraging a believing public to develop its pious citizenship through voting and consultation practices. The five legal opposition parties in Egypt had held a joint conference in 1987 declaring their support for free elections and for a political party for the MB, should it want to form one.[24] While the MB severed its alliance with the Wafd party over

---

21. "Fi muhadirat 'an tatbiq al-shari'a al-islamiyya, al-muhandis Ibrahim Shukry: Innahum yumtihanun al-insan fi qism al-shurta wa yuman'un tatbiq al-shari'a al-islamiyya," *al-Sha'b*, June 12, 1984.

22. "Fadilat al-imam al-kabir: Tatbiq al-shari'a laysa bi sha'rat talassuq 'ala al-murakkabat: Wa 'ala kull fard 'an yatbuq al-shari'a fi manziluhu qabl al-dawla," *al-Akhbar*, July 13, 1985.

23. Tawfiq al-Shawy, "Mabda' hakimiyya al-shari'a al-islamiyya wa shar'iyyah qawaneen fi-l-tashri' al-Misri," *al-Sha'b*, October 22, 1985.

24. Ahmed Rizk, "Al-ijtima' alladi lam mutahadiruhi al-mala'ika," *al-'Itisam*, March 1987.

the latter's refusal to champion sharia application more enthusiastically in parliament, when electoral rules changed once again, enabling independents to contest elections, it found a more sympathetic ally for the 1987 campaign in the populist Hizb al-'Amal (Labor Party), which had rebranded itself the Islamic Labor Party after an internal struggle between socialist and Islamist factions (Singer 1990). The Labor Party offered the MB the additional benefit of regular column space in its legal newspaper, the *Jaridat al-Sha'b* (hereafter *al-Sha'b*), whose Islamist-sympathetic editors promoted Islam as part of the Egyptian "national personality" and embraced the idea of Islamic politics beyond a cautious *da'wa*-centered approach.[25] The MB formed an "Islamic alliance" to contest the 1987 election with the Labor Party and smaller Ahrar Party, dividing candidates in a 40–20–20 arrangement that favored MB members (Ghobashy 2005, 379). The movement's wariness about *hizbiyya* or partyism had similarly declined as cadres were won over to the utility of electoral participation for the movement; following Tilmissany's death in May 1986, the new general guide, Hamid Abul Nasr, ran for parliament himself, along with Banna's son and the son of Hasan al-Hudaybi, the second general guide (Meijer 1997, 6).

As the movement became more comfortable with electoral politics as a form of *da'wa*, its leaders and parliamentary representatives expanded their religious framing of electoral work beyond the imagery of parliament as a pulpit from which to spread God's message. Internally and externally oriented discourse about politics increasingly emphasized that voting and electoral accountability offered citizens both opportunities and responsibilities for righteous action and *tarbiya*. Echoing movement norms about *tarbiya* as a shared exercise in which activists cultivated their own piety by teaching and modeling righteous practice to others, MB leaders increasingly cast deputies' work in parliament to uphold righteousness in government, their ability to guide citizens, and citizens' own use of the vote, as religious acts that enabled *tarbiya* via practice. Where the initial language

---

25. Interview, AM, Cairo, November 22, 2005; interview, MH, Cairo, November 17, 2005.

of political *da'wa* had been didactic, MB discourse on elections by 1987 was more focused on the rights and freedoms of citizen-believers. MB leaders also used the language of righteous citizenship (*muwatina salima*) and the Islamic solution (*al-hal al-islami*) to emphasize their contention that the practical benefits of righteous Islamic representation could draw in and persuade a wider public of the credibility of the Islamic mission.

The MB's new general guide kicked off the 1987 election campaign with an open letter to president Hosni Mubarak in the *al-Sha'b* newspaper, which urged the government to act righteously and support the Islamic mission because it represented a popular demand.[26] Using a strikingly rights-oriented framing, Abul Nasr argued that Islamizing the political process required removing restrictions on individual freedoms and restoring the rights that sharia and the constitution had granted to the children of the nation. The state, he continued, was delegated by the people to implement the sharia compliance required by article 2 of the constitution, and this religious path responded to the spirit of the people and expressed its will (*tajawuban ma'a ruh al-sha'b al-misri wa ta'abiran an iradatuhu*). In election campaign speeches with Islamic Alliance partners, MB leaders similarly framed their mission as one aimed at "accomplishing the hopes and wishes of the public," supporting the rights and freedoms of all citizens, removing contradictions between the faith of the people and the laws that governed them.[27] Abul Nasr's letter appealed to Egyptian leaders to see their role as representatives and stewards of Islam both domestically and globally, by asserting that it was a religious and national duty to speak up against attacks on Muslims in Palestine and Afghanistan, and that this was an obligation for the people of the Egyptian nation rather than merely of al-Azhar.

The alliance's election manifesto also presented believing voters as active agents of the Islamic mission, calling on the entire nation and all decent people to participate in their political future and work for positive

---

26. Hamid Abul Nasr, "Risala min al-Ikhwan al-Muslimin li-l-ra'is Hosni Mubarak," *al-Sha'b*, February 17, 1987.

27. "Ru'sa' al-'Amal wa-l-Ikhwan wa-l-Ahrar: Nata'awunu min ajl al-shari'a wa-l-hurriya wa-l-'adl al-ijtima'ai," *al-Sha'b*, March 3, 1987.

change and promising them an awakening (*sahwa*, a broad term for the Islamic intellectual reform movement) to lift them out of their despair.[28] The manifesto exhorted citizens to vote conscientiously, for upright representatives, and to participate in politics as a religious obligation (*fard dini*) as well as a national duty, stating that true change would not occur until individuals exercised their political right and religious-national duty to choose a representative in whose sincerity and program they had faith. The manifesto appealed to the "youth" of the nation to lead to a "better tomorrow for our country, under the canopy of justice based on the heavenly law." It also promised political freedoms and accountability as a key part of the reform (*islah*) necessary for a more Islamic society: constitutional revisions to implement a truly multiparty system and make the executive truly answerable to the legislature, a repeal of emergency laws and laws that limited due process and individual rights, term limits for the president, electoral reforms, and reforms to promote judicial independence were all listed as goals in the social reform process. It described the *islah* process as one that depended on moral stewardship from economic and political elites: owners were stewards (*mustakhalifun*) of their property and, as such, were required to use it for their own good and the good of the people, according to the perspectives (*tawjih*) and obligations (*mafrud*) of Islam. Similarly, the manifesto stated, government must use education to strengthen religious values and allow al-Azhar more freedom to carry out its work of religious stewardship.

MB electoral tracts urged the "distinguished voter" to see civic obligations as infused with religious purpose as well, reminding them that the nation's hopes rested on their vote and exhorting them to support the "new believing spirit" that had carried moral, selfless exemplars to parliament, who would carry out a program that served the nation and pleased God.[29] In these tracts, leaders presented citizens as a righteous collective, not just as individuals to be preached to: Guindi framed the Islamic way as the "will (*irada*) of the people, and as the "true hope filling the

---

28. "Al-barnamij al-intikhabi li-qa'imat al-tahaluf hizb al-Amal," *al-Ahrar*, March 23, 1987.

29. Anwar al-Guindi, "Manshur intikhabi rakm 1," *al-Sha'b*, March 24, 1987.

collective hearts of the members of the nation."³⁰ MB leaders painted voting as a moral as well as a utilitarian choice, with religious and practical consequences for the public good. Guindi's tract warned citizen-believers to build their lives and societies on the *minhaj* of the Quran, to free themselves from the forces of darkness, and to vote to return the nation to the path of God, while also framing Islam as a political project that could be assessed positively from among a range of options. After trying foreign political paths—both Eastern and Western—that had not freed them from hunger or fear or led them to safety and security, Guindi urged voters to consider the *minhaj* of Islam, to help the nation overcome its economic problems and divisions, by the divine path.

Frames presenting voting as a religious act were repeated in Islamically oriented publications as well. The journal *al-'Itisam* carried a statement by the board of religious scholars that advised the Gami'yya al-Shar'iyya charitable association, with which many Brothers were closely associated, and that also exhorted the Egyptian people to "make sure your candidate is right with God" (*ishtarit rabbak 'ala murashahak*) and to help those who promised to apply God's will and to abandon those who were ignorant of God's law, or prevented its application, all as part of their religious obligation to abide by Islam's teachings.³¹ Writing in *al-Sha'b*, Mustafa Mashour commended those who had voted for having participated constructively in solving the nation's problems, saying they would be rewarded for supporting God's law and the truth, while encouraging all citizens, as masters of their own will (*sahib irada*), to participate in choosing rulers and holding them accountable and insisting that the political awareness of the popular masses (*jamahir al-sha'b*) was important in setting the nation on the right path.³²

MB deputies and leaders grouped civil liberties and religious liberties together in their advocacy for more popular freedoms, arguing that the

---

30. "Ru'sa' al-'Amal wa-l-Ikhwan wa-l-Ahrar: Nata'awunu min ajl al-shari'a wa-l-hurriya wa-l-'adl al-ijtima'ai," *al-Sha'b*, March 3, 1987.

31. Abd al-Latif Mushtahry, "Bayan kubar al-'ulama' al-Gami'yya al-Shar'iyya hawl intikhabat majlis al-sha'b al-misri al-rahina," *al-'Itisam*, April 1987.

32. Mustafa Mashour, "Kharij al-majlis," *al-Sha'b*, May 5, 1987.

liberation of political prisoners and limits on the interference of security forces in university elections were Islamic priorities and suggesting that the government's denial of freedom of opinion and religious expression allowed corruption of various kinds to spread.[33]

Active *Tarbiya* in Parliament: Cultivating Piety through Consultation and Testimony, 1987–1988

MB leaders regularly cited Banna's framing of Islam as a comprehensive religion governing all kinds of practices and not just prayer to argue that their expanding participation in electoral politics was as Islamic as praying or going to work and to suggest that politics included many kinds of religious acts.[34] In addition to framing electoral politics as a site where the MB could spread *da'wa* and *tarbiya*, by the late 1980s leaders also framed it as a set of relations through which citizens, preachers, and rulers could work together for a more Islamic society and enact righteousness through public work and consultation (*shura*).

Rising MB political leaders presented one of the MB's main missions in parliament as enacting and cultivating their own piety through their political actions, while conducting *da'wa* via the moral example they set—for example, by standing up for Islam and their pious constituents and working for the public good. Rising leader Essam el-Erian affirmed the movement's commitment to setting an example as a kind of *da'wa* when he declared that Islamic Alliance deputies would follow "Islamic norms" of behavior in parliament, with no place for name-calling, and would work to benefit the country by monitoring corruption and promoting economic production.[35] Mahdi Akef, another senior MB leader and a future general guide, asserted in a speech in parliament that applying God's will in society must start with applying it through righteous conduct (*suluk*),

---

33. "Fi awwal hadith li-l-murshid al-'am li-l-Ikhwan al-Muslimin ba'd al-intikhabat: tatbiq al-shari'a al-islamiyya yakun bi-l-tadrij," *Oktobar*, April 19, 1987.

34. Interview, EE, Cairo, November 24, 2005.

35. "Zu'ama al-mu'arada fi Maglis al-Sha'b: kayf yuqawadhha al-islamiyyun?," *al-Nur*, April 29, 1987.

good ethics (*khalq*), and serious work (*jiddiya*) in government, after which it could extend to the people (Wa'i 2001, 155–56). Mustafa Mashour similarly argued that when Islamist deputies in parliament questioned the government and called it to account before both God and people for its actions, they were not only raising the awareness of their constituents but also modeling public morality, as an act of *tarbiya* (Rady 1990, 26).

The practice of holding rulers accountable was also presented by MB leaders as a form of *shura* or consultation that was a religiously righteous practice in and of itself, as well as a pathway to achieving a more Islamic society. In a speech during a parliamentary debate on sharia, Mamoun el-Hodeiby contended that achieving the social conditions to allow God's ideals to flourish in Egypt required consultation of the kind embodied in the parliamentary process, and he posited *shura* between rulers and advisers as similarly essential in allowing rulers to fulfill their responsibilities to both God and people.[36] Echoing the MB's new acceptance of pluralism as a matter of different pathways or jurisprudential approaches to working for God's will, Hodeiby also argued that *shura* and its modern form, democracy, was an essential part of working out how to apply God's will in contemporary circumstances and to harness differences of opinion to produce a just social order. In a framing that acknowledged both liberal norms and Islamic goals, Hodeiby stated that this kind of positive, godly consultation required freedom for all political parties that respected Islam, freedom of publication for newspapers, and impartial elections, all of which would permit the formation and expression of enlightened public opinion and protect the dignity and rights of the citizen (presumed to be a believer), enabling them to exercise their duties to society and nation and to cultivate a desire for good, serious work.

MB leaders were careful, however, to affirm in both internally and externally oriented media that the *shura* they encouraged must work for religiously defined goals. Mustafa Mashour, writing in the Islamist magazine *Liwa' al-Islam*, argued that, in addition to using the pulpit of

---

36. "Munaqasha hawl tatbiq al-shari'a al-islamiyya, tashtarik fiha al-aghlabiyya wa-l-mu'arada," *al-Ahram*, June 24, 1987.

parliament to counter Western missionary ideas and to reorient society toward God's law, the righteous representatives of the people must uphold the obligation to command the right and counter the forbidden in the forum offered by parliament (Wa'i 2001, 160–64). No popularly elected assembly, he declared elsewhere, had the right to rule on whether or not God's law was correct; *shura* meant holding the ruler accountable for following God's will, and the Islamic Alliance must channel the positive energies of those who believed that elections could produce *islah* (Rady 1990, 26). General Guide Hamid Abul Nasr stated in an interview in state-owned *Oktobar* that the communist party Tagammu' had no place in Egypt, a pious country, because it rejected religion as a mere opiate of the masses.[37] MB deputies continued to publicly affirm the idea that only Islam, and not any secular ideology, could solve the problems of the nation, and that the term "opposition" did not correctly define the Islamic Alliance's mission in parliament because it connoted a division among people where the MB wished to bring them together to work for Islam.[38]

Conclusion

To what extent did the movement's strategic framing of its political activity in the public sphere change its directive discourse? In many internal statements and assessments of their first few years in parliament, movement leaders engaged narratives about the rightful place of Islam in electoral work and about their own goals and identities that made new kinds of action meaningful and justifiable in terms of existing beliefs and commitments, which Schwedler (2006, 121, 126–27) has noted is a critical test of the lasting impact of strategic moderation on Islamist movements. Both internally and externally directed statements assessing the movement's achievements at the end of the first parliamentary session in 1987 framed MB deputies' work in parliament as work for the Islamic cause through

---

37. "Fi awwal hadith li-l-murshid al-'am li-l-Ikhwan al-Muslimin ba'd al-intikhabat: tatbiq al-shari'a al-islamiyya yakun bi-l-tadrij," *Oktobar*, April 19, 1987.

38. "Al-tahaluf: nihayat tariq 'amma bidayat marhala?," *al-Wafd*, April 17, 1987.

work for the public good. The Islamic Alliance's statement of its parliamentary achievements affirmed its commitment to preserving the message of Islam and reminded readers of its slogan, "Islam is the solution," while listing specific parliamentary achievements, including statements about human rights and against torture, efforts to hold the government accountable for economic and health policies, and work to expand political freedoms and consultation.[39] A parallel statement produced by movement leaders for members similarly described the achievements of MB deputies in parliament as focused on standing up for "Islamic" issues and included calls to defend democracy and free expression, national unity and social morals, alongside efforts to champion sharia, culturally authentic education, and imperialistic threats to the Muslim community in Palestine and in Egypt in this category (Wa'i 2001, 153–55).

Mustafa Mashour, writing in the late 1980s about new paths of *da'wa* after the MB's political experience, argued that *da'wa* and *tarbiya* continued to form the basis of the Islamic mission while acknowledging new strategies and forms of work as tools to work for God in different ways. Mashour affirmed the priority of religious over political goals when he argued that focusing on politics and administration at the expense of spiritual growth would be fatal to the movement's mission, because faith was the nutrition and water that the 'tree' of the movement needed to survive, and faith lay at the heart of all capabilities that allowed human beings to act as individuals and in society (1989, 30). While human reason (*'aql*) was essential in determining how best to apply Islam for contemporary justice, he argued, and Islamic teachings were compatible with human reason and freedom, the human mind was limited and needed the light of religious inspiration to show it the way, just as the eye needed light to see—without this guidance, parliaments and human decision-makers could make ethical errors. He also warned that human freedom that was not religiously correct (*salima*) could not achieve the greater good; spiritual cultivation or *tarbiya* continued to be the first and guiding principle of the movement's work (89–90). Debates around the new tools that the movement should

---

39. "Bayan al-tahaluf: madha qaddam nuwab al-tahaluf?," *al-Ahrar*, August 3, 1987.

employ for its mission were acceptable to the extent that they focused on adapting to new circumstances but did not open up space for factionalism or unbounded pluralism: internal debates on the best instruments for *da'wa* and *tarbiya* must be channeled through formal paths of consultation within the movement and stopped when the leadership made its decision, so as to prevent internal debate from producing disputes and factions (32–34). Similarly, he contended that political pluralism was valuable in allowing people to work for God in different ways, but harmful in encouraging the chauvinism (*ta'ssub*) around individual and other identities that Banna had abhorred, which could occur if spiritual education was neglected (29, 35). Divided Muslims needed guidance, correction, and cures for their social diseases, not politics to divide them further (101–2).

In internal writings, Mashour continued to frame the movement's *da'wa* or mission as an individual religious duty (*fard 'ayn*) that included community outreach, preaching, and teaching, and the righteous individual as one who modeled himself on the Prophet to embody his piety and willingness to work for God in his everyday life (Malik 2018, 221–22). However, he and other movement leaders increasingly accepted that the growing scope (*da'ira*) of the *da'wa* required a broader strategy for adaptation and distribution of work according to specialized capabilities. The movement must consider how to bring in different kinds of people (men, women, youth, students, workers or scholars) and to make use of different kinds of power (the power of unity, of knowledge, of character, of arms, of money, of the media) while recognizing that these were all rooted in the power of faith (Mashour 1989, 48–49, 83–84). In the right hands, the tools of the public sphere were useful in achieving the movement's mission. Cultivating the committed (*multazim*) Muslim, he insisted, must remain the movement's work, and those carrying out its mission also needed ongoing *tarbiya*, because building men and reaching hearts and souls was different from—and more difficult than—building institutions (62–63, 84–85).

While this chapter has shown that the MB leadership did reimagine the strategies that were justifiable and imaginable in "working for Islam," and that the movement's decision to consider new strategies allowed once-controversial ideas, such as participation in pluralist party politics, to become more normalized in its mission, an expansion in the boundaries of justifiable action did not, in the short term, extend to justifying political work unguided by God's will, whether on the part of the MB or on the part of potential allies and other parties. By conceiving the movement's political mission as one of working to uphold God's will in contexts of potential immorality, to resist efforts to restrict the voice of the pious, and to push back against corrupt rivals, pro-politics leaders presented elections as a way to defend and expand an Islamic constituency more than to embrace pluralism and democracy for their own sake. Enshrining public work and deliberation as processes through which God's will could be worked out gradually normalized electoral and parliamentary work within movement ranks as moral, Islamic practices, even if they could not be relied upon to produce Islamic outcomes.

Participation in politics did not change the primacy of the relationship between God and individual believers, but gave it new sites in which to be expressed. Making participation a more accepted part of the movement's mission, however, opened up the space to consider a more comprehensive engagement with politics, including aiming for state influence and using institutions and power to apply God's will in addition to cultivating more upright Muslims—which is the focus of the next chapter.

3

God and Rule

Political Empowerment and Applying Sharia

How did the Muslim Brothers' leadership reconcile power-seeking with ethical practice and accept the state-centered pursuit of social and political empowerment (*tamkin*) as a form of godly work accompanying *da'wa*, rather than its final achievement? The Islamic *minhaj* had always included exhortations and moral suasion directed at rulers in its repertoire of tools aimed at establishing God's will on earth. However, aiming for state power and using the tools of state were strongly discouraged both by the movement's long-standing aversion to partisanship, and by regime restrictions on religious power-seeking. Despite the insistence of the MB leadership on the priority of *da'wa* and *tarbiya* in the mission of electoral politics, in addition to their emphasis on processes of consultation and cultivation, with the individual believer as the key agent in achieving change, Brothers in parliament and in electoral politics became increasingly comfortable with a more statist and institution-driven approach to applying God's will (*tanfidh al-shari'a*) in the public sphere in the period from 1985 to 1990. Although parliamentary and public debates on sharia-compliant legislation, triggered by court rulings, offered the MB an opportunity to promote a religious vision of good governance, they also risked confirming negative stereotypes of Islamists as bent on using the coercive resources of the state to monopolize the interpretation and application of sharia. Additionally, using state power and legislation for sharia application presented a problem for the movement's own understanding of its mission: leaders had generally presented the Islamic state as an end point of social

Islamization, and cooperation with an un-Islamic state as a hindrance rather than a resource for this mission.

In this chapter, I will show how MB leaders in parliament and in the public sphere framed state institutions and influence as opportunities to fulfill collective religious obligations (*fard kifaya*) in new spheres, while keeping their ambitions for political power consciously limited to reassure both internal and external skeptics. While MB leaders had historically been wary of state power as a tool for the Islamic mission, a new generation of MB parliamentary leaders lobbied for a more pragmatic approach to levers of state power as capable of being guided by—and used to apply—the principles of sharia. Parliamentary and public debate, and arguments seeking to persuade sympathizers and movement members that legislative work, however limited, was part of the "Islamic solution," reveal how MB deputies emphasized the practical contributions of "Islamic" political principles for the public good, countering regime efforts to paint Islamist legislative goals as superficially religious. I then consider how the political leadership's arguments for using state resources to command the right and to cultivate a more Islamic citizenry changed internal movement interpretations of how state power could be used for the Islamic mission. MB leaders countered state attempts to depoliticize sharia by asserting the religious establishment's authority over it, and addressed opposition concerns about partisan instrumentalization of sharia, by framing its application as a popular demand that required public accountability, but could not be left to any one authority or party.

Finally, I will explore how the movement changed its own interpretation of its mission while grappling with the strategic utility of political work. As movement authorities accepted state institutions and tools as resources for *da'wa*, and ways to command the right (*al-amr bi-l-ma'ruf*) that supplemented the more traditional consultation (*shura*) and advice (*nasiha*) for rulers, they persuaded activists that powerful state institutions could and should be Islamized, however partially, through political pressure, and that the movement must build power (*tamkin*). The idea that Islamizing the state and implementing or applying God's law (*tanfidh/ tatbiq al-shari'a*) could be done piecemeal and in the short term, rather than deferred to a distant future following complete social Islamization, was established in directive discourse, too: movement training materials increasingly embraced participation in state and political institutions as an a form of social *tarbiya* for individual and collective spiritual advancement, allowing activists to cultivate themselves spiritually by doing more, and more effective, work for God (*'amal salih*).

State Power in the MB *Minhaj*

The MB's reputation as "statist Islamists" who wished to pursue their goals through state institutions has more recent and ambiguous antecedents than political scientists have generally assumed (Volpi and Stein 2015). While the MB had historically decentered the state and courts as targets of their activism, state elites had invested in top-down Islamization, bringing religious jurisprudence under state control (Ranko 2015, 91–94; Rock-Singer 2016, 294). In this section, I will show how the MB's goal of "applying sharia" through state and legal institutions was a relatively late innovation, developed as the movement sought to repoliticize and contest the authoritarian state's right to govern religion and to position itself as a better representative of "national Islam" in Egypt than state authorities.

The state and its power posed a paradox for Hasan al-Banna and the early generations of Muslim Brothers. Banna wrote in *Mushkilat fi dhaw al-nizam al-islami* that politics and rule (*al-siyasa wa-l-hukm*) were among the basics of God's sharia, because they defined the righteous social order that was prescribed by God for his followers (Wa'i 2001, 21). The idea that Islam was a matter of rule and worldly life (*dawla*) and not just religious doctrine (*din*), and that believers must ultimately seek to be governed by their highest beliefs, was, for the Brotherhood, a major driver of Islamic activism, and its leaders often cited Banna's statement in the movement's Fifth Conference that Muslims could not perfect their faith without taking an interest in the wider issues of the nation and working for political reform.

Yet state power was always suspect when not yoked to a spiritual mission. In Banna's writing, the comprehensive and perfect order of Islam (*nizam kamil wa shamil*) required reforming the state and politics and infusing them with morality, but it did not depend on a specific set of state institutions. The Islamic state, Banna argued, was no mere administrative formation, but was defined by its ethics: it must be built on the basis of the *da'wa* until it became a state of the message of Islam (*risala*) (Wa'i 2001, 21). Similarly, the Islamic *da'wa* relied on watchful protection and organization to do its outreach (*tabligh*) in order to succeed, but Islamic activism had to focus on individual spiritual cultivation as an operational priority, because the kind of society that could embrace godly rule depended on social Islamization first. The Islamic state or caliphate was traditionally fixed in the distant future, the end point rather than a part of the process of social Islamization. Only after recovering their spirituality could Muslims strengthen their nation sufficiently to resist external cultural and political threats (Mitchell 1969, 6–8, 22–23, 233–34; Wendell 1978, 48–49).

The judgment or rule (*hukm*) of Islam was, for Banna, embodied in the rules that Islam had established for life and that individual Muslims were obliged to follow. Banna's writings, along with movement texts—notably the *Risalat al-Ta'lim*—regularly cited the Quranic verse *Al-Maida* 49, which urged the Prophet to judge between Muslims on the basis of God's revelation in order to remind activists that the only legitimate basis for judging human actions was revelation (Rosen 2008).

Sharia was a set of rules to live by and a moral code rising above human manipulation, to guide, censure, and correct individual Muslims and authorities alike (Kramer 2010, 114–15). Yet it could only be implemented by righteous individuals: forming a sound Muslim who could be capable of commanding the good in his own life and social circles was therefore a priority for the movement (Kramer 2015, 202). Godly individuals and principles, not godly institutions, were necessary for godly rule, and sharia could not be applied by state law.

Banna's suspicion of state power specifically and coercive power more broadly was shared by his successors. He accepted that a state was necessary for upholding the unity of the *umma* and protecting and spreading the message of Islam, but he did not lay out a vision for Islamic political institutions, focusing instead on a ruler who could apply and obey God's law (Jadaane 1990, 256). Abdel Qader 'Awda, the MB's foremost political writer in its first generation, argued that a caliph who was spiritually competent and accountable to his nation and to God's law would uphold God's will in consultation with knowledgeable community leaders (Jadaane

1990, 258–62). All of this depended on proper religious education, as well as moral persuasion, which Banna practiced by cultivating good relations with and offering moral advice to political and religious authorities, notably exhorting Egyptian kings to support Islamic behavior over Western norms (Lia 1998, 97–98; Wendell 1978, 103–4). He asserted that a preacher must always employ *muwazana hasana* or "good admonition" and noted that only a ruler could carry out the requirement of a famous hadith urging Muslims to forbid the wrong (*nahy 'an al-munkar*) by hand first, and then by the tongue and the heart (Cook 2003, 119).

Banna's successor, Hasan al-Hudaybi, emphasized the goal of Islamic governance and rule more prominently—that there was no rule other than through God (*la hukm illa bi-llah*), that divine law had priority over state law, and that the state's principles must be derived from the goals (*maqasid*) of sharia (Zollner 2009, 108–9). But he just as strenuously argued that God's sovereignty did not require a state to uphold it, and that Islamic rule was defined by the principles of God's will and morality in contrast to reason and self-interest, rather than on the state (Zollner 2009, 118). Hudaybi also argued for a nonstatist understanding of sharia application, rejecting the idea that sharia could serve as the *qanun* or legal code of a state, and wrote that an Islamic state must rather be one that defended the faith and ensured that God's will was respected (Zollner 2009, 119). For Hudaybi, the implementation (*tanfidh*) of sharia was the ruler's job, but applying the judgments (*tahkim*) of God's law was an individual obligation for Muslims (Rosen 2008). Hudaybi's best-known tract, "Preachers, Not Judges," which disavowed the idea that preachers could seek to rule or judge all Muslims, was aimed at distancing the MB from its controversial thinker Sayyid Qutb, who had associated un-Islamic rule with apostasy, but the book's vision of Islamic rule was not at odds with the movement's internal vision.

The State as Vehicle for Sharia Application: Law and Righteous Activism

When the MB leadership decided to participate in electoral politics in the early 1980s, the question of how to ensure that power-seeking remained bound to the pursuit of God's will rather than escaping it and competing with the *da'wa* was an important one for leaders justifying the choice to participate in elections to skeptical movement members. They also grappled with public taboos against challenging the Azhari monopoly on sharia interpretation and against theocratic ambition. Yet, in contesting elections on the promise of an Islamic "solution" that could be more effective than existing state policies, the movement's leadership was under pressure to define the "Islamic solution" concretely, to voters as well as to skeptical regime and secular opposition deputies who argued that Islamist political goals were impractical and spiritual when the nation needed practical solutions for economic development.

Two major debates in parliament in the mid-1980s made sharia application a focus of legislative discussion and pushed MB leaders to rethink the purpose of their parliamentary participation within the wider Islamic mission. In 1985, the Supreme Constitutional Court ruled that it would no longer hear lawsuits concerning the sharia compliance of laws, ordering parliament to take up article 2–related questions in the future. For its part, parliament debated the question of whether elected representatives, or state-appointed religious professionals under the aegis of al-Azhar, should be responsible for determining what counted as sharia compliance.

In 1986, the Egyptian government presented parliament with a package of substantially more free market–oriented budget proposals to respond to a foreign exchange crisis that had required loans and, subsequently, economic restructuring agreements, with the International Monetary Fund. This triggered public and parliamentary debates on how economic reform might hurt national autonomy and social justice in which government representatives framed economic policy as a greater priority for public welfare than the sharia-compliant legislation for which the MB-led Islamic opposition in parliament had pushed. In both debates, MB leaders made a case for why sharia application required using the laws and institutions of the state for the public good and embraced pragmatic policymaking as a path to achieving it. They also framed their own role as elected representatives as enabling popular consultation and restoring the state's accountability to God and nation, to produce the kind of public good that sharia envisioned, rather than as challengers to official religious authority.

Before his assassination in 1981, Anwar al-Sadat aimed his amendment of article 2 of the Egyptian constitution, to define sharia as the—not just a—primary source of Egyptian legislation, at demonstrating the state's commitment to Islam and preventing Islamists from gaining popularity. What it meant for legislation to be based in and in conformity with sharia, however, was unclear, and the newly formed Supreme Constitutional Court (SCC) was regularly charged with adjudicating this question in the early 1980s, because article 2 compliance was a matter of constitutional law. Yet the question of who had the right to interpret and define the provisions of sharia for legislative and legal purposes, whether elected or unelected government officials or religious scholars, was far from settled by this arrangement, as various social and political actors jostled to use the new constitutional provision to promote their own vision of the public good.

In the first several years of the MB's electoral participation, the sensitive question of how to change existing laws to conform more closely to Islam was debated largely in the expert realm of the judiciary. Judges and, secondarily, scholars of the Azhari religious establishment, following regime preferences, framed sharia application narrowly as a matter of harmony between existing legislation and the tradition of Islamic jurisprudence and the principles of sharia. They resisted taking positions on the process through which this harmony should be assured, other than to warn against divisive efforts to politicize sharia. Establishment support for sharia as a legal and governing framework focused on the letter of the law, with symbolic state commitments to sharia in the law and constitution interpreted and upheld by qualified experts. MB advocacy for sharia application was shaped in part by these authoritative competitors: formal and textual commitments to sharia offered little scope for political contestation, and the areas in which there was further scope for legal reform, such as in the application of bans on alcohol and usury, were controversial because they risked disrupting economic growth. Yet the government's formal constitutional commitments allowed the MB to frame their own advocacy as a call for more accountability and for putting existing commitments into action, rather than challenging the entire legal order.

For many religious conservatives (generally not members of the MB), using the courts to pressure the regime and make public opinion heard was a productive strategy, learned from liberals, at a time when electoral influence was more limited (Lombardi and Cannon 2016, 141). They brought a flurry of lawsuits to the SCC based on the principle of *hisba* or an individual Muslim's right to sue for violations of God's law, challenging the legality of alcohol production and gambling in Egypt, among other matters (Agrama 2010). The court initially responded to these lawsuits with narrow, scriptural interpretations, resisting calls to amend legislation by arguing that article 2 could not be applied retrospectively to already-passed laws, while affirming that sharia compliance must apply to new legislation (Lombardi 2001, 155; Brown 1997, 372). But these rulings revived, rather than ended, debates around whose job it was to make legislation sharia compliant, whether individuals, their representatives, or religious authorities. A key court decision in 1985 on the legality of interest payments on loans taken out by al-Azhar, affirming that individuals could sue on matters of sharia affecting them personally, but that only parliament was responsible for the sharia compliance of legislation, repoliticized the question of sharia application (Dupret 2000, 74; Moustafa 2010). This decision set off public contestation and outbidding over who was best positioned to speak for the kind of religious law that could serve the public good, in a process some scholars have dubbed "sharia inflation" (Brown and Sherif 2004).

While the MB leadership had stopped short of supporting *hisba* lawsuits, the idea that Muslims were obliged to work to command the good and forbid the evil was central to their vision of *da'wa*, and, as such, parliament's new charge to interpret what it meant to apply sharia through legislation presented a challenge to the movement's mission. In columns in *al-Da'wa* directed at movement members, Tilmissany wrote that the duty of *al-amr bi-l-ma'ruf* (commanding the right) was a collective one that God required of the *umma* and an obligation that the state and its legislation had an important role in discharging. If Muslims were sinning collectively, whether by straying into usury, alcohol use, corruption, and anti-religious media consumption, he argued, Muslims were obliged to work collectively to put a stop to these sins (Kenany 1993, 19, 118–20). If a sound Muslim state that could apply God's will, praise justice, and censure injustice was lacking, and if existing religious authorities had neglected their responsibilities, it was up to pious activists to keep rulers on the straight path (73, 112, 118–20). The movement's political leadership similarly made the case for working through the state, and for the importance of Islamic morals and practices in state institutions, in two draft manifestoes for potential political parties attached to the MB, that were submitted to regime authorities for approval in the mid-1980s. The manifesto of a proposed "Shura" party included a call to "establish the Islamic Egyptian state that aimed to combine between being a state of guidance, guided by the light of Islam and committed to its rules, and being a welfare state that provides services to its citizens and works to ensure freedom and security," while the manifesto of the alternative "Islah" party vowed to "reform the affairs of the Egyptian state so it becomes able to provide its citizens with services and ... freedom and security" (Awadi 2004, 83–84).

In writings and speeches aimed at both internal and external audiences during the 1987–88 parliamentary cycle, such as parliamentary speeches and election manifestoes, MB leaders emphasized that state institutions and tools were important in cultivating ethical citizens, and that their power must be used for the cause of Islam. In an open letter to President Mubarak, the MB's new general guide, Hamid Abul Nasr, urged the government to draw on sharia and the Islamic legal tradition to use the power of the state to cultivate good social morals by banning the religiously forbidden, sponsoring better preaching and religious education, and developing sound economic practices and policies, which would lead to national renewal.[1] In a speech in the People's Assembly in June 1987, another MB parliamentary deputy, Lashin Ali Abdallah Shanab, echoed the idea that state power mattered for the proper moral upbringing or *tarbiya* of the nation's children and called on the government to do its duty in applying God's will by replacing vulgarity and materialism in televisual media with popular religious values (Rady 1990, 51). In the same session, Mahdi Akef, another MB leader in parliament, asked the government to use both the culture ministry and the education ministry to deliver morally correct education in the cultural environment that could support it (55).

---

1. Hamid Abul Nasr, "Risala min al-ikhwan al-muslimin li-l-rai's Hosni Mubarak," *al-Shaʿb*, February 17, 1987.

In addition to recommending that government officials use their authority over the tools of mass cultural uplift to uphold Islamic values, MB deputies, such as Ahmed Seif al-Islam Banna, also made the case in parliament that the state could apply Islam better by encouraging its own employees to be better Muslims (e.g., by offering them prayer breaks) so that they might be exemplars to others and by implementing the obligation of *zakat* or charitable contribution to build solidarity and piety among government officials (89). Hodeiby went further in arguing in parliament that applying sharia was both an individual duty and a public matter (*amr*), and that the state must apply sharia both for religious reasons—faith (*din*) required worldly application (*dunya*)—and as an obligation to the pious Egyptian people, who wanted to be ruled according to their faith (71). Hodeiby and other MB intellectuals and leaders argued that Islam, beyond being a faith, was a national moral code, and a system of government that even non-Muslims could accept and participate in without accepting Islam as belief. They contended that the state was obliged to uphold this moral code more forcefully and signaled both internally and externally that existing "secular" governance structures were compatible with, and could be used to implement the laws and goals of Islam (Wa'i 2001, 47–53).

MB leaders championing parliamentary activity as a tool for the Islamic project, increasingly defined the application and implementation (*tanfidh*) of sharia in terms of state policies that could help citizens live better, more Muslim lives, and a sharia-governed society as one where a constitutionalist vision of rule by law and accountability to God's will could prevail. Islamist deputies responded to the government's legislative proposals on economic and security reform with what they considered more Islamic alternatives that would be more effective in achieving the public good and in using state power ethically. In making the case that Islamic sharia contained practical prescriptions for economic and public welfare, requiring interpretation and application by the people's representatives, MB deputies challenged government elites who contended that religion belonged in the private, spiritual sphere and should be governed by religious experts alone, and they also countered non-Islamist critiques of Islamism as a distraction from real-life public welfare priorities by proposing a practical, if somewhat partial, Islamic policy agenda.

In their first major policy debate after expanding their seat share in the 1987 parliamentary election—in which they responded to the government's proposals for substantial neoliberal economic reform to address the national debt crisis—the MB-led Islamic alliance presented Islamic solidarity as a solution to economic problems and a source of moral and cultural autonomy from the West, and sharia as a tool for social justice and economic growth. In June 1987, MB deputy Ahmed Seif-al-Islam Banna argued in a speech in parliament that state implementation and enforcement of *zakat*, the charitable contribution required of pious Muslims as one of the pillars of faith, could promote economic and social solidarity (Rady 1990, 89). In a statement responding to the government's economic proposals, the Islamic Alliance asserted that economic policy must be part of a broader vision of moral society, and that the best path for social and economic reform was by the "divine door."[2] Deputies in parliament argued that changing regulations on unlawful financial gains, allowing mosques to work freely, closing down alcohol production, and generally increasing the state's stewardship of religious values were necessary steps for moral-economic reform. MB deputies also contended that citizens who were committed to their faith would help the nation grow, and that religious cultivation built more productive as well as more righteous individuals. Lashin Ali Abdallah Shanab declared in parliament that as religion (any Abrahamic religion) was the most powerful motivator of individuals, and faith-based discipline the most powerful kind of discipline: a call to the bodily jihad of hard work was also a call to faith (Rady 1990, 51).

MB deputies also urged the government to apply God's will and expand Egypt's economic growth and self-sufficiency by implementing Islamic financial rules and increasing cooperation with other Muslim countries. When Ahmed Seif al-Islam Banna made a speech in parliament maintaining that Islamic finance, of the kind prevalent in Turkey,

---

2. "Al-qissa al-haqiqiya li ma dar fi-l-jalsa . . . wa asbab insihab al-mu'arada; bayan al-tahaluf al-islami raddan 'ala bayan al-hukuma bi Maglis al-Sha'b," *al-Sha'b*, June 22, 1987; "Al-aghlabiya wa-l-mu'arada tatanafisun amam Maglis al-Sha'b fi-l-radd 'ala bayan al-hukuma," *al-Ahram*, June 22, 1987.

could help resolve Egypt's economic problems, he appealed to both religious and nationalist frames, arguing that it was more ethical, because of nonreliance on religiously prohibited usury, and better for the nation than Western financing, citing the early twentieth-century nationalist economist Talaat Harb's arguments for "self financing" in support (Rady 1990, 89). MB deputies challenged the argument of the speaker of the assembly, ruling party member Rif'at al-Mahgoub, that Islam's ban on usury (*riba*) could be overriden by concern for the public welfare (*al-masalih al-mursalah*) by asserting that banning usury would be good for the public interest. Abdel Hamid al-Ghazali, an MB deputy and professor of Islamic economics argued that if it was possible to participate in the global economy and reap its benefits through Islamic alternatives to usurious finance, the government should seek this alternative, and that Muslims must save more in order to avoid usurious borrowing. Hodeiby made a similar case in parliament that sharia could solve contemporary economic problems and advocated for expanding Islamic banking domestically and using *zakat* to fulfill the nation's social responsibility and religious obligation to provide for the poor.[3] MB deputies framed an Islamic economic policy as part of a wider reinstatement of Egyptian national strength and leadership in the Muslim world, calling on parliament to protect Egypt from "missionary" and "American" institutions that had influenced and weakened Muslim values in the 1980s, cooperate with countries like Pakistan in their battle against Soviet communism instead, and help Egypt reprise its traditional leadership role in the Arab world (Wa'i 2001, 157; Rady 1990, 107).

Partisanship, Religious Authority, and Popular Accountability in a More Islamic State

In making a case for why the state mattered for the Islamic mission, MB leaders had to counter public skepticism about their claims to religious

---

3. Magdy Mustafa, "Al-'ulama' yusahahun khata' ra'is Majlis al-Sha'b: al-qurud al-rabawiyah la tadakhal dimn al-masalih al-mursalah wa-l-badil mawjud," *al-Nur* May 6, 1987; "Munaqasha hawl tatbiq al-shari'a al-islamiyya, tashtarik fiha al-aghlabiyya wa-l-mu'arada," *al-Ahram*, June 24, 1987.

authority, and their commissive discourse on sharia application reflected strategic considerations about positioning themselves as moderates.

Arguing for the application of sharia via state policy, MB deputies consciously distinguished their pragmatic approach to religious restrictions on economic activity from that of more conservative, literalist Salafi scholars and deputies, who believed that banning alcohol and adultery should be priorities for a more moral society (Rady 1990, 45). The managing editor of *al-Sha'b* publicly debated the hardline leader of the Gama'a Islamiyya, 'Ala'a Mohieddin, in the newspaper's pages, countering his claim that an Islamic state must focus first and foremost on forbidding evil (*nahy 'an al-munkar*) by suggesting that vigilante justice against drunks and abusive police authorities was not the mark of an Islamic state, but that an Islamic state must be achieved through legal reform and social reform to produce a more just society.[4]

MB leaders and deputies faced accusations that efforts to apply sharia risked strengthening intolerant, unelected Islamist power. State supporters such as the influential liberal judge and columnist Said al-'Ashmawy had warned against the MB's mission to apply sharia by equating it with an effort to move from a state that basically upheld the core of the Islamic creed (which, he argued, the Egyptian state did) to one that sought to introduce a heretical sixth pillar of *wilaya* or government into a faith that did neither contained this nor rules for religious *hukm* or rule.[5] The Islamist project in parliament was also publicly critiqued in newspapers by leading secularist intellectuals like Fouad Zakariyya, who accused the MB and its allies of wishing to install human rule with a claim to divine rule and of treating others as apostates.[6] MB public discourse countered these accusations with the claim that their project would strengthen, rather than challenge, the existing religious establishment by making it

---

4. Adil Hussein, "Ahbatna al-fitna . . . wa lina arba' mulahizat," *al-Sha'b*, January 24, 1989.

5. Muhammad Said al-'Ashmawy, "Haqiqat sha'r al-Islam huwa al-hal," *al-Akhbar*, July 13, 1985.

6. Fouad Zakariyya, "Takfir al-tafkir: Radd 'ala al-duktur Yusuf al-Qaradawy," *al-Sha'b*, June 2, 1987.

truly representative of the believing public, and uphold the voice and the rights of believing citizens.

Mamoun al-Hodeiby and other MB deputies thought that al-Azhar, as the institutional guardian of "national" Islam, needed to be headed by a popularly elected council of senior clerics in order to be responsive to a (presumably pious) majority who wished to see sharia implemented in Egypt, and they insisted that non-Muslim minorities would be treated equally in such an order (Wa'i 2001, 178–89). Echoing Tilmissany's argument that the state must be founded "on an Islamic basis," and that it should participate in the collective religious responsibility of raising the word of God but must not coerce or seek to control the conscience of individuals of minority faiths, Muhammad Abdel-Quddus contended that an Islamic state based in God's sharia was not a theocratic project, because the MB rejected the monopolization of power or any claim that they were uniquely qualified to represent Muslims.[7]

As the MB increased its parliamentary presence in 1987, deputies claimed that more individual freedoms and more religious accountability for the regime were essential for applying Islam through the state. In a speech in parliament urging the government to apply God's will in deference to the popular religious awakening and attachment to Islam in Egypt, Muhammad Habib, an MB deputy and rising leader, argued that pious citizens should be allowed to exercise their conscience in the public sphere, and that free elections for al-Azhar would allow clergy to work more effectively for Islam; in the same parliamentary debate, another MB deputy, Hasan al-Gamal, asserted that a more autonomous clergy, closer to the people's sentiments rather than to the corrupting forces of state power, could help the state fulfil its obligation to provide for young people spiritually as well as materially (Rady 1990, 85, 97). In emphasizing public pressure and accountability as reasons for rulers to live up to their religious commitments, MB leaders also positioned themselves as a necessary moral conscience and public voice for sharia application. Rather than

---

7. Muhammad Abdel-Quddus, "Al-Ikhwan al-Muslimin wa tatbiq al-shari'a," *al-Wafd*, June 8, 1984; *Al-Ahrar*, "Umar al-Tilmissany yaqul: Al-Ikhwan al-Muslimin laysu intihaziyin," May 7, 1984.

developing a structured alternative Islamic agenda, the MB maintained that the state was falling short in its own responsibilities and must do more. Further, they strengthened their argument that sharia application was a collective religious obligation to be fulfilled through public work as much as an individual one to be achieved in individual lives and interpersonal relations and resisted regime efforts to depoliticize it.

MB leaders responded to accusations of religious partisanship and power-seeking by framing their vision of a more Islamic state as one that respected religion while rejecting theocracy (*hukuma diniyya*) (Ibrahim and Awad 1996, 110). Hodeiby framed Islamic law as compatible with, not contradictory to, popular freedoms: an Islamic state required popular participation and was built on the agency of moral, cultivated individuals rather than their disempowerment. In a speech on sharia in the people's assembly, he argued that the state had a duty to apply God's law because it must "respect what the overwhelming majority desires" in addition to applying it out of religious obligation, because a modern president had the same responsibility to protect the faith as caliphs of old (Rady 1990, 71). Similarly, MB and Islamic Alliance leaders made the case in parliamentary sessions in 1987 that mobilizing the public to act on the basis of their religious principles was the best guard against the corruption of the political process and urged the government to follow "the wishes of the popular masses (*jamahir*)" in reforming Egypt's laws to better conform to God's sharia.[8]

Even as MB leaders framed their mission as one that supported Azhar and the state's religious stewardship, rather than challenging it, Azhari leaders pushed back against what they saw as Islamist attempts to contest a long-standing depoliticization of religious authority. When MB leaders like Mustafa Mashour asserted that legal and legislative action was required to make the state Islamic, and that the MB must use its presence in parliament to oppose laws that opposed sharia (Wa'i 2001, 160–61), regime actors and Azhari leaders suggested that calls for sharia application

---

8. Mustafa Mashour, "Kharij al-majlis," *al-Sha'b*, May 5, 1987; "Ibrahim Shukry, za'im al-mu'arada al-jadid fi Maglis al-Sha'b: Al-dawla al-diniyya la tatafaq ma' al-din," *Oktobar*, April 26, 1987.

outside the aegis of responsible state actors reflected purely cynical political ambitions.[9] In interviews with the state-run *Mayo* magazine, Shaykh al-Azhar Gadd al-Haqq argued in favor of the idea that Islam should be Egypt's guiding philosophy, and a practical religion that could solve social problems, while warning against individual and dissident efforts to determine how the faith ought to be applied in social and political life.[10] The Shaykh and other Azhari leaders averred that scholars of religion must guide rulers in how to advance Islam, and that this must be left to qualified authorities (Abdo 2002, 58–61; Rady 1990, 45). Regime-owned newspapers accused Islamists who called for applying Islam through politics of sloganeering and of giving a religious patina to political opportunism.[11] The minister of endowments rebuked Islamists for sullying the image of a nation that had already made most of its laws sharia-compliant and urged people to focus on applying God's law in their own lives rather than pushing for state action to do so.[12] Yet MB leaders continued to present their calls for more sharia application as a way of holding the state accountable for its incomplete commitments, and representative institutions as better able to do this than existing religious authorities.

MB leaders increasingly advocated parliamentary and representative institutions as an ideal path to applying sharia in modern times, not as barriers to the Islamic state. Tilmissany argued that the ruler was obliged to implement sharia before his subjects could obey him, and that this bond of accountability and obedience between rulers and ruled, based in God's law, would strengthen and be strengthened by parliamentary institutions (Ranko 2014, 101–5). According to another MB scholar, the rule of law and

---

9. Abdel Azim Ramadan, "Ahlam al-haraka al-islamiya al-mu'asira . . . wa ihzanuha," *Oktobar*, October 19, 1989.

10. "Hiwar ma'a al-imam al-kabir Shaykh al-Jama'at al-Azhar: al-dimuqratiyyah fi-l-Islam a'maq athran min dimuqratiyyat al-gharb," *Mayo*, May 16, 1988; "Shaykh al-Azhar yaqul li-Mayo: Al-hall . . . an na'awd ila al-Islam," *Mayo*, May 26, 1988.

11. "Kayf tahawalat al-shari'a al-islamiyya ila sha'r siyasi?," *al-Gumhurriyah*, November 13, 1988.

12. "Dr. Muhammad Ali Mahgoub: 90% min qawaninuna la tata'rid al-shari'a: al-hukuma multazima bi-'adam isdar qanun mukhalif," *al-Gumhuriyya*, July 12, 1987.

equality of all before the law would be strengthened by applying sharia, because sharia would restrict the power of rulers and protect individuals from the excesses of those in power.[13]

In speeches in parliament and in public discourse, MB deputies regularly framed popular and religious freedoms as essential to an Islamic form of government and their political advocacy for more public freedoms as "Islamic work" in internal writings. In both kinds of discourse, they inverted the regime's accusation that Islamists sought an exclusive and coercive right to represent Islam over the wishes of the masses, by presenting their own work as a corrective to the state's repression of religious and political freedom. In a parliamentary debate on the state's extension of emergency law to permit the detention of Islamist radicals, Islamic Alliance deputies criticized the interior minister, Zaki Badr, for declaring these detentions were necessary for national security and grouped them with other violations of religious freedom, such as banning Alliance members from delivering Friday sermons at well-known mosques. More comprehensive social *islah* and more religious freedom would, they contended, produce a more secure society than repression could.[14] Indeed, MB leaders such as Farid Abd al-Khaliq argued that youth radicalization was due to a crisis of trust and proper religious education, and that reviving Islamic values such as freedom, *shura*, equality, and justice was essential to addressing it.[15]

A collection of MB parliamentary speeches published in 1990 assessing the contributions of parliamentary work to the Islamic project similarly depicted political freedoms and religious freedoms as intertwined. It highlighted a June 1987 speech by Mokhtar Noh, an Islamist deputy

13. Tawfiq al-Shawy, "Sayyadat al-shari'a al-islamiyya wa sayyadat al-qanun fi Misr," *al-Sha'b*, October 15, 1985.

14. "Al-qissa al-haqiqiya li ma dar fi-l-jalsa . . . wa asbab insihab al-mu'arada; bayan al-tahaluf al-islami raddan 'ala bayan al-hukuma bi Majlis al-Sha'b," *al-Sha'b*, June 22, 1987; "Al-aghlabiya wa-l-mu'arada tatanafisun amam Majlis al-Shaab fi-l-radd 'ala bayan al-hukuma," *al-Ahram*, June 22, 1987.

15. Abdel Sabour Fadel, "Afwan ya qanun, inta mutaham," *al-Nur*, December 14, 1988.

and a lawyer, in which he criticized the interior minister for understating the number of political detainees in Egypt and berated the government for not upholding its obligations to quickly process detainees and allow them a fair trial, urging the assembly to fulfil its responsibility of *riqaba* (oversight) of government actions to prevent the injustices of extrajudicial detentions and torture (Rady 1990, 113). It touted Essam el-Erian's parliamentary speech exhorting the government to remove laws that restricted student freedoms and democracy on university campuses (59). It also reproduced Ahmed Seif al-Islam Banna's June 1987 parliamentary response to a government statement on emergency law, in which he described public freedoms, a free press, more democracy, and fewer limitations on the formation of political parties as the "Islamic way" and Islam's support for individual freedom as the best guarantor of the rights of Egyptian citizens (89).

Reframing Righteous Action and *Tarbiya* to Incorporate Political Work

Participation in elections and in parliamentary and public debates on the Islamic uses of state power changed the ways that the movement represented its mission internally as well as externally. As they championed state action and the use of state power for social Islamization in politics, MB leaders had to address concerns about whether this new approach replaced the traditional vision of the Islamic state as something that could only exist in an ideal future, after social Islamization was complete. Both internally and externally, they advocated increasingly for public, state-centered policies, however piecemeal, as goals for Islamist activists to work toward and argued that a state guided by Islam not only depended on increased popular piety but could also act to create the social and material conditions under which people could flourish as Muslims. By the late 1980s, MB leaders' internal discourse around what it meant to apply sharia and to work for the empowerment (*tamkin*) of God's will on earth reflected the more pragmatic principles they had generated in political work and acknowledged a range of actions limited to specific social and political spheres as steps toward the application and implementation of God's rule.

The leadership framed lessons gained from electoral experience for the movement for the purposes of the movement's own mission and *tarbiya* in ways that suggested that *tamkin* and power-seeking for the purpose of commanding the good were forms of *'amal salih* (righteous work) and should be part of the movement's short-term mission of *da'wa* and cultivation. In the movement's directive discourse, "implementing" sharia at the individual and the collective or state level came to be viewed as interchangeable processes, requiring similar skills, with the *usra* as a building block and training ground for both. This marked both a boundary shift, in terms of acknowledging state-based power as part of the Islamic mission, and continuity, in terms of locating the pious individual, cultivated through traditional organizational tools, as the main instrument through which the movement would seek to apply and establish God's rule.

In a text on *da'wa* written in 1989, Mustafa Mashour, a senior MB leader associated with the conservative old guard, made a more explicit case than the leadership since its political reemergence for why power, government, and rule were important tools for the Islamic mission, setting aside the taboo against power-seeking that had governed the movement since Hudaybi's "preachers not judges" statement. In this text, Mashour argued that political and social power mattered for Muslims who wished to work for the empowerment (*tamkin*) of God's religion on earth: the power of faith came first, but the power of unity and of arms were both goals for Muslims to work toward (1989, 50, 59). The MB, he insisted, would never give up this goal for any fear of controversy over whether *hukm* (rule or judgment) and jihad (struggle, including armed) were appropriate goals for an Islamic movement (60). Mashour also lauded the MB's success in creating widespread public awareness of the comprehensive and perfect Islamic social order (*nizam kamil wa shamil*) over a decade of political outreach and claimed that it had transformed the call for sharia from an unusual to a popular demand in Egypt (129–30). The long-term goal of establishing a global caliphate, he argued, required patient work from those trying to spread God's word in the present: just as every great building needed a large and solid base, constructed patiently, a strong Islamic state that could unify Muslims, stand in the face of evil, and regain occupied lands would take time to build (10–12).

Mashour was careful, however, to clarify that this did not mean that Muslim activism must be governed by the logic of political power-seeking. Echoing an older MB wariness about autonomous human sovereignty, he warned that, while it was important to make detailed plans for the goal of making God's word reign over earth, it was God, not humans, who ultimately decided the success of any such plans (1989, 77, 84–85). Mashour also argued that investing in local state power must not come at the cost of the goal of a global state that unified all Muslims, and yet reforming existing government (*hukuma*) until it was truly Islamic was a positive step in the *da'wa* ultimately aimed at ensuring that God's word was highest (13, 65).

The MB leadership's more open embrace of political institutions and power as tools for the Islamic mission was also reflected in its directive discourse on how to work for Islam, most notably its educational program for the social and spiritual cultivation of members. In a text titled *Wasa'il al-tarbiya 'aind al-ikhwan al-muslimin* (The Means of Cultivation for the Muslim Brothers) on the goals, and methods of *tarbiya* for the movement, published in 1989, the head of the MB's committee on internal education and cultivation, 'Ali Abdel Halim Mahmoud, explicitly included training for public activism and capacity-building for political work in the list of priorities for a Brother's *tarbiya* and highlighted rule or governance (*hukm*) as a goal that should guide everyday movement activities.

Hasan al-Banna's writings on the cultivation of good Muslim activists defined a sequence of *ta'rif* (acquaintance or knowledge), *takwin* (formation as a movement member), and *tanfidh* (ability to apply Islam) as key to each member's progress within the *gama'a*, both as a pathway for bringing new members on board and as a general approach to ethical organizational practice within the movement. This approach, repeated in subsequent movement writings on *tarbiya*, defined *tanfidh* or applying the message of Islam as something that people would do after reaching a certain level of advancement in their spiritual training and focused more on how to cultivate committed Muslims who were ready to take on *tanfidh* than on a broader vision of what it might look like in the public sphere. Mahmoud argued that because the movement's mission was fundamentally about translating the goals of Islam from ideals to realities, its education and organization should focus on applying Islam, within the movement as well as in activists' relations with the broader social order (1989, 13).

The *Wasa'il al-tarbiya* text contended that these priorities could be pursued in parallel and emphasized the kinds of *tanfidh* that must be pursued in the public realm, not just in movement circles. While this vision for *tarbiya* still focused on moral and spiritual cultivation as the main goal of the Islamic mission, it made a strong case that rule according to God's sharia was both an ultimate goal for the movement and a means for carrying out a broader social *tarbiya*. Like Banna, Mahmoud defined government (*hukuma*) as a sphere that was closely tied to ethics and argued that the "corrupt political systems" that had come to dominate the Arab world were the products of Western influence and "moral occupation" (*ihtilal akhlaqi*), as were the moral and cultural decay of Arab societies (1989, 53–59). Like Banna, he also believed that all social and public institutions were governed by norms that were either Islamic or un-Islamic, that political and moral norms were inextricably related, and that Islam's values and culture required a government committed to maintaining them. Consigning Islam to the spiritual sphere alone and limiting its authority over law and the public good had made Western understandings of culture, trade, education, and industry hegemonic, to the extent that Muslim societies were defined by a predominantly Western tint (*sabgha*) rather than an Islamic one (82–83). He blamed materialistic and atheistic Western philosophies, from Machiavelli to Sartre, that elevated possession and power over human morality, for political ideologies that enabled rulers to justify oppression by promising that it would bring material success (39–44). Islamic *hukuma*, by contrast, "led the people to the mosque" and "protected Islam" by standing up for Muslims, their unity, and their liberation everywhere (27).

Despite bemoaning the importation of laws and legislative systems from Europe, which meant that authority was no longer derived from God, Banna did not elaborate a vision for an Islamic political order, declaring only that a pious ruler must respect God's law and stay accountable to the believing people (see chapter 1). Mahmoud went a step further, arguing that the rules and procedures for selecting rulers, and for all kinds of governance, must also be derived from God's law: ruling officials must be chosen for their piety and Islamic work, deal with people with justice and equity, and not give any preference to the wealthy or to foreigners, for those who were given broad powers without meeting these criteria, and without oversight, would neglect citizens' rights (1989, 84–85). He offered two main lines of justification for why movement members, and anyone who wished to work for Islam, must focus on politics: one, that rule (*hukm*) was a founding principle, and even a pillar, of Islam; and, two, that applying Islam (*tanfidh*) via the state or in one's own life were both ongoing obligations for believers.

The first argument focused on the place of governance or rule in religious scripture and jurisprudence. Mahmoud thought that governance was central to Islam because Islam required application and execution (*tanfidh*) as much as guidance (*irshad*), teaching, and legislation, quoting a saying that God could show people truths through a ruler (*al-sultan*) that He could not through scripture (*al-Qur'an*) (1989, 106). Using theological argumentation, he wrote that rule was among the constants (*'arwa*) and founding principles (*usul*) rather than branches (*furu'*) of Islam—even a pillar of Islam (106). As such, reformers and workers for Islam could not be content to be jurisprudents (*fuqaha*) or guides, reciting religious lessons and delineating categories of religious rules, while leaving executive authorities to legislate and govern as they saw fit: the voice of the reformer could "not merely echo in a valley while implementation occurred elsewhere" (106). A state governed by Islam, he stated, would ensure that educational and media institutions were staffed by upright and properly educated people and use them to instill correct virtues and responsibilities in human souls. As such, it was an extension of *tarbiya* and would promote the cultivation of a Muslim society just like the *gama'a*'s traditional *usra*-based system of bottom up, peer-driven *tarbiya* (113, 146–47). Such a state would also uphold an Islamic economic system, which was, in contrast to Western systems like capitalism and communism, driven by accountability for public welfare, justice among people, sympathy for people in the state's care, and protection of righteously earned wealth (*mal salih*), in order to encourage work while banning wrongful gain, would protect property as long as it did not hurt the public interest, spend for the public good, and encourage *khayr* or charity and cooperation for benevolence or *birr* (90–91).

The Islamic credentials of the state depended on the extent to which it carried out the key functions of ethical governance, such as ensuring security, upholding law, protecting public welfare and health, strengthening morals, and spreading *da'wa*, as well as on a righteous Muslim leadership (Mahmoud 1989, 90–91, 162). Evoking an older Islamist norm, Mahmoud cited examples of the early "rightly guided" caliphs' condemnation of ill-gotten wealth, nepotism, and bribery as an implicit rebuke and idealized alternative to the corruption of contemporary government, while citing these rulers' reminders to the people that they worked for the *umma* as a mark of their exemplarity (90–91). This leadership was not just important at the top: good Muslims willing to support Islamic obligations and apply Islamic rulings (*ahkam*) were needed to staff the government of any Islamic state; non-Muslims could serve as well, but only in positions of secondary authority (162). A government was Islamic to the extent that it upheld a socioreligious contract with Muslim citizens: if it upheld its duties, people were obliged to obey it and contribute their resources to it, and, if it fell short, these citizens, after attempting to correct it with advice and guidance, were religiously obliged to defect from it, for they could not obey a creature of God (here, a human ruler) if this required disobeying their creator (163).

The second argument for political empowerment as a path for applying Islam (*tanfidh*) focused on how an individual Muslim's ethical cultivation and obligation to command the right extended to political and social activism. Dealing (*ta'mul*) with the earth and all living beings ethically was every Muslim's duty, Mahmoud reminded readers, and, while political work required its own skills, working for the *tanfidh* of Islam and its empowerment (*tamkin*) on earth was everybody's job (1989, 21). Because the Islamic *minhaj* called for God's will to prevail over God's devotees, he added, working for God's *khalifa* (vice-regency) and *wilaya* (authority or jurisdiction) were goals for Islamic *tarbiya* (23). Public work also included one's obligation to carry out acts of righteousness (*salihat*), he argued, because a good Muslim was rewarded in the afterlife for all kinds of actions to command the right, and working for God's rule and convincing others of its necessity were important righteous acts. Citing the well-known hadith about changing what was wrong by hand, heart, and mind, he explained that commanding the right included active practices (*mumarisat 'amaliya*), and that working for excellence in everything that one did (*ihsan*) required acting with justice toward others and wanting the best for them, which included working for what was right (*haqq*) and against oppression (*zulm*) (29–30). The text presented political activism as as an extension of the requirement to command the right (*al-amr bi-l-ma'ruf*) in individuals' everyday lives. Just as Brothers were obliged to cultivate their own personalities, homes, and social spheres in an Islamic way and encourage virtue, command the good, and do good works (*khayr*), they were obliged to win over public opinion for Islamic thought, and to color public life with the "tint of Islam," just as the *gama'a* was obliged, as a public organization (*haya' 'amma*) to work for Islam in the public sphere. Both kinds of obligations were aimed at liberating the homeland from any un-Islamic authority, whether political, economic, or religious, reforming the government until it was truly Islamic, and serving the nation and working for its *maslaha* or benefit (161–62).

The text framed the obligation of *tanfidh* as something that must be tackled in movement *tarbiya* because pious Muslims had to be trained for the work of mobilizing people and preparing souls for God's rule and for holding rulers accountable to God. Working for Muslim reform meant working to get righteous (*salih*) people in positions of power and exhorting those with the power of *tanfidh* to listen to and execute God's commands, but, in line with a long-standing MB commitment, not seeking power for oneself (Mahmoud 1989, 87, 107). Working for *tanfidh* through *da'wa*, by instilling a concern with public interest and upright rule in the souls of people to prepare ground for the return of the caliphate, and cooperation between Muslim nations, could, in Mahmoud's view, continue in parallel with work to pursue *tamkin* (108). Following the traditional MB view of *tarbiya* as an ongoing process for individuals as they learned through work and instructed others, Mahmoud construed political activism as requiring prior ethical formation and constituting a kind of practical *tarbiya* that allowed activists to participate in the cultivation of others as well. He argued that individuals with a correct knowledge of Islam would recognize that righteous action was a form of worship, and that the implementation (*tanfidh*) and application (*tatbiq*) of Islam were religious obligations (28–29). The stages of *tarbiya* required the first step of individual formation (embracing Islam in worship, one's way of thinking, and one's behavior), which included following religious social obligations such as paying *zakat* out of obedience to God (28). In addition to cultivating oneself, one was obliged to increase *ta'ruf* between Muslims by promoting brotherhood, cooperation, and solidarity, along with Islamic morals and a general love of God (31).

Muslim activists' own cultivation and their cultivation of others had to include a political component, in Mahmoud's framing: the *takwin salih* (upright formation) that Brothers were taught to give their peers had to include education on issues of society, governance, politics, economics, and judiciary, and everyone's spiritual cultivation required working for the *tamkin* (empowerment) of God's religion on earth, preparing to build *hukm* according to revelation, and developing the strengths, capacities, experience, and specialization that such rule required (1989, 32). The skills required for religious cultivation and for establishing godly rule, he argued, were closely related and could be honed through similar methods and activities in the movement's *tarbiya* system. The *usra* or family unit in the MB could function both as a training ground for skills that would prepare good Muslims to form an Islamic public order and as a building block for the kind of applied Islam and empowerment (*tamkin*) that an Islamic state would be a culmination of, with application as its own practice and form of *tarbiya*. The *usra* system must, Mahmoud asserted, produce upright humans (*bashariyya saliha*) who would participate with all their sincerity and ability in work, under God's supervision, to take people from aberration to guidance, ignorance to truth, and from the tyranny (*jawr*) of existing rulers to the justice (*'adl*) of Islam; they must help society progress in manners, morals, politics, economics and institutions (146). The *usra* system was also required to train people in governance-related skills, such as solving problems in all social sectors, so that they could participate positively in all public activities and work for the public good and implement the goals of Islam in various public sites, like schools, universities, factories, farms, and the institutions of government (147–48).

This kind of training would be a natural extension, Mahmoud stated, of the kind of practical, applied righteousness that Brothers learned and had to practice in *usra*. Activists would learn to command the right in society by learning to command it in their own *usra* and their everyday lives: for instance, helping a fellow *usra* member develop and apply his talents to God's work and revive his faith and commit to Islamic ethics and morals in the face of social barriers, or faith-weakening forces, functioned as a way of applying Islam oneself and preparing for applying Islam in society (Mahmoud 1989, 116). Training individuals in how to serve God, whether by building bodily and social strength to work for Him; cultivating *ihsan* or perfection in their actions, such that one always behaved as though God were watching, and *'adl* or equity in how one treated others; commanding the right; and undertaking jihad in God's path against the enemies of faith also built the capacities and skills that Muslims needed to empower God's will further on earth (117–18, 125).

Mahmoud argued that the *usra*'s training and practices were also useful for building and organizing Muslim social life, even if they were primarily aimed at religious cultivation. Through practical training, application, and mutual monitoring to hold others accountable to high moral standards, the *usra* cultivated social bonds in addition to intellectual skills (1989, 125–26). Through *usra*, one learned to work with and serve people, to meet their needs, to attract and gather people, and to lead them; individuals discovered how to release the power of reform (*islah*) and good (*khayr*) in every Muslim and to put different skills and capabilities in the service (*tawdhif*) of religion (126). *Usra* and movement activism cultivated management and people skills that were good for public outreach and governance, such as time management, listening skills, constructive dialogue, cooperation, and tolerance (129–35).

As the movement leadership had positioned debate, consultation, and political freedoms as essential to applying sharia in governance, so, too, did it emphasize the importance of training members in *shura* internally. Mahmoud presented the practice of *shura* or consultation within the *usra* as a key method for cultivating individuals' capabilities in the service of

Islam, because listening to all members helped reveal their talents and wisdom and allowed them to generate solutions to difficulties in Islamic work, while emphasizing that the kind of *shura* and *nasiha* practiced in Islam was aimed at unifying people rather than dividing the nation and entrenching *ta'ssub* or chauvinism (1989, 134). Outreach-oriented skills such as visiting neighbors, setting up mosques and clinics, speechmaking, and earning a living would allow individuals to serve God in many spheres of life, whether within the Islamic movement sphere, or by achieving worldly success that could serve the cause of Islamic mobilization (135).

Mahmoud's text explicitly highlighted mobilizational (*haraki*) skills as key to applying Islam within the movement and to preparing activists' capacity to apply Islam at a social and institutional level. Such work, Mahmoud argued, included persuading people of the necessity of collective action and social work, and recruiting them for Islamic work (1989, 131). Those trained in the movement's *usur* could transfer skills to new networks and generations, and the collaboration skills that activists learned in *usra* would be useful in building cooperation with other groups that wanted to work for Islam and resisting and confronting tendencies that were hostile to it (154). He considered political knowledge as essential for the training of Muslim activists, arguing that *usra* training could include political and economic analysis; practical knowledge of various topics essential for governance, such as housing, education, energy, traffic, and energy and banking policy; and knowledge about organizations and institutions that could support Islamic work, in addition to training on commanding the right and forbidding the evil, teaching children correctly, and identifying Islamically appropriate media (176–77, 181).

Rather than being pursued in parallel to or as separate from religious cultivation, Mahmoud framed training in social and political skills as rooted in, and essential for, cultivating religious ethics as well: citing Banna and the sayings of the Prophet, his text argued that a good Muslim knew that helping a brother was a pious act just as much as going to a mosque, and that whoever brought joy to the home of Muslims would be rewarded in paradise (1989, 157). Further, the solidarity (*takaful*) that *usra* members developed with each other was a reminder of the principle that every Muslim was the brother of any Muslim (except for those who had betrayed or oppressed him), and that Muslims must feel each other's pain as members of one body and care for each other enough to set people on the right path (158–59). Commanding the right in various spheres of life required a broader, more strategic perspective on outcomes and goals—for instance, it made sense in *usra* and in public work to postpone a decision to forbid a wrong if it might lead to a greater wrong, or not permit a righteous act if it might lead to a forbidden one (148).

Mahmoud's text also exhorted activists to prioritize *tamkin* or empowerment, and capacity-building, as a way for good Muslims to command the good and to extend their obligation of *da'wa*. Movement members were obliged to be activist (*mutaharakan*) in addition to being preachers for God's word, to the extent that their strength and knowledge allowed, as both were forms of work for the cause of religion (1989, 129). *Tamkin* could be pursued through movement institutions and public institutions at the same time, and both kinds of institutions allowed people to apply and expand the power of Islam. Citing Hasan al-Banna and Hasan el-Hodeiby to make his case, Mahmoud argued that Islam could be implemented on a practical level within the *usra* (*tahqiqan 'amaliyan*), by building understanding (*tafahum*) and solidarity (*takaful*) between members and by encouraging them to help one another financially and emotionally to address problems in everyday life (127). A properly run *usra* functioned as a fortress for its members by defending them all and working for their benefit, and every member who did his duty in the *usra* would help it become a building block for an Islamic society (114–15). Broader social Islamization and the *tamkin* of God's religion on earth required expanding the circle of *usur* and of those who were willing to work for Islam in their social spheres, until schools, media, the street, and all social institutions had an "Islamic pulse," and the world would be prepared for rule by what God had revealed (154).

In his text, Mahmoud affirmed the *usra* as the social, individual, and financial sinew (*'asb*) of the *gama'a* and, eventually, of a properly Islamic society, because of its role in building bonds of unity and solidarity among Muslims, but he urged those who wished to work for the good of Islam to use both religious and nonreligious social spaces to build support for their cause (1989, 116). Mosques were obvious starting points, because building them and contributing to their maintenance enabled more people to pray and contribute *zakat*, and allowed activists to do good by offering people a more correct understanding of religion than a public school education might (150–51). Mosques also allowed activists to organize events and seminars that met the material as well as spiritual needs of believers and to demonstrate to believers the benefit (*nafaʿ*) that Islam offered to them (151). Yet, echoing earlier MB arguments for participation in imperfect parliaments, Mahmoud urged activists not to neglect spaces like sports clubs and other youth establishments that permitted immoral activities, because workers for Islam did not benefit from having these spaces occupied by the wrong ideas, and it was part of their *daʿwa* to infuse them with more upright ideas (152). Every social establishment could, and should, have an Islamic "pulse" and form, and it was the job of the MB to send its trained activists out to work for the good of people in this world and the next and to make their group known as one that had worked for Islam. Building power and capacity in public and social institutions was useful for the movement's broader *daʿwa*, Mahmoud explained: Brothers who proved themselves in important social fields and gained social skills could guide people better in Islam, because a person who attained leadership had the means to implement the good that he was calling for and would therefore be more persuasive to people, who were always more liable to hear the truth from someone with power. Attaining excellence in any field allowed people to guide others under their influence in all areas, because people would seek to learn from them, and a Muslim activist who treated others with wisdom and good advice offered *tarbiya* by emulation that was more effective than a hundred sermons (148).

Mahmoud's text did not frame empowerment as something that would happen independently of God's will, and it directed movement members to remember that their moral and spiritual practices and influence remained most important. Those who had commanded the right, established prayer and given *zakat* had the right to expect God to grant them victory, and, while social and political work was part of what good Muslims were required to do for God, they must pursue a godly rather than a partisan, democratic vision of power, using social, material, and political tools of empowerment to serve Islam first (1989, 115, 120–22).

Politics driven by leaders' personal ambitions were harmful for the public good and morals (85–87). Mahmoud reiterated Banna's warnings about the dangers of partisanship and cited cautionary tales from Egypt's interwar experiment with multiparty democracy and attempts by British political officers to barter money and influence for compliance, to remind activists of the corrupting potential of power-seeking (120–22). Similarly, he suggested that while it was incumbent on activists for Islam to pursue godly rule and use opportunities for empowerment where they could find them, this was not meant to legitimate or enshrine the "rule of the people" (*hukumat al-sha'b*) in the Western sense of democracy, because such fallible rule was a poor alternative to the rule of Islam (40). Those who worked for God had to engage in politics so as to achieve moral rule, but the goal of political empowerment was to apply God's sharia, or get others to apply it or demand its application, not to attain offices of state or ministries for their own sake (339). Nor did recognizing the utility of public institutions for the Islamic mission require the movement's *tarbiya* leadership to accept the logic of conventional party politics: Mahmoud insisted that the MB would always focus more on the formation (*takwin*) of youth and on productive work than on self-promotion and would not seek to expand for the sake of numbers, but would continue to educate people to achieve its carefully thought out goals and objectives (101, 109).

Mahmoud presented the uses of power for the Islamic mission pragmatically and conditionally, in outlining how power-seeking would affect the movement's operational practices and *tarbiya*. Citing Banna's argument that *quwa* (power or strength) was important for Islamic organization and legislation, he affirmed the need to seek, and act with, strength; yet, he noted, the strength of faith and belief, and, secondarily, of unity and connectedness, must take priority over the strength of armed force as a means of achieving God's rule (1989, 105–6). While recognizing the urgency of political reform, and the need to act for it, he also warned against revolutionary methods, recalling for activists that revolution and its subsequent upheaval had served Egypt poorly over time, and that direct action or force (*quwa 'amaliyyah*) might be a tool of last resort but could not be understood as a desirable method for doing God's work (105). In his text, Mahmoud cited multiple instances in the movement's history in which its leadership had chosen patience and quiet suffering over revenge on oppressors, to make activists remember that the religious ethics of their actions mattered more than outcomes (338).

Mahmoud emphasized that the movement remained defined by its mission of *tarbiya*, which *tamkin* would support, not replace. Countering those who called for the movement to adapt its methods for new political goals, he argued that traditional *tarbiya* methods had never stood in the way of the movement's expansion before, and that *tarbiya* and governance would continue to rely on each other after the formation of an Islamic state. Implementing Islam (*tanfidh*) required that a state be staffed by properly cultivated Muslims, and *tarbiya* was an ongoing need, rather than a preliminary step for *tanfidh*. Moreover, those who worked for Islam in the public sphere had to do so with the recognition that God's legislation was always aimed at promoting the right morals (*akhlaq*) for Muslims, just as the *naqib* or leader of an *usra* ultimately sought to bring people closer to God by educating them in good values and nurturing their talents (1989, 112–13, 194–95).

Conclusion

By the end of the 1980s, MB leadership's directive internal discourse echoed public-facing discourse on applying God's will through public institutions and empowering Muslims to do good with political and social power, embraced the need for collective action to serve God, and encouraged organizational educators to incorporate political skills in movement *tarbiya*. Tanfidh or the execution of God's will was adopted within this discourse as a goal that could be pursued in the public sphere as well as within the *usra*.

Movement leaders increasingly emphasized leadership skills and power-building as helpful for the *da'wa*, in that they pushed individuals to cultivate their own perfection and to develop the necessary capacities to convince others that Islamic governance was the best kind. Organizational leaders, particularly those in charge of *tarbiya*, advocated for building political capacities and skills in every movement activist, rather than seeing governance as a specialized task that required the rank and file's involvement only once the work of social Islamization through proselytization was complete. In Mashour's view, earning a living, setting up businesses that followed Islamic norms, and financing Islamic work, among other kinds of social action for Islam, were all forms of worship (1989, 109–15). Skills cultivated in the *usra*—especially in terms of people management and mobilization—were transferrable and convertible to political capacity-building (see above). By situating the goals, skills, and tools of Islamic organizational work as effective both within the movement and in the public sphere, *tarbiya* leaders signaled that political work for Islam could build on and reinforce *usra*-based cultivation and expansion, rather than occupying a separate space.

Movement discourse by the late 1980s gradually reframed *tamkin* as something that could be attained through various kinds of institutions, capitalizing on social and political influence of Brothers in different spheres of life, instead of only through a diffusion of *da'wa* to the maximum number of Muslims, who would then call for an Islamic state. Arguments for using positions of social influence to allow workers for Islam to deliver tangible benefits to people and to show them the material and spiritual benefits of Islam also treated political and religious capacity as more convertible than older approaches to *tamkin* had done. Rather than treating a pious political order or an Islamic state as something that relied on a leader willing to uphold God's will, the newer discourse on the political order emphasized the kind of social and political mobilization that might place upright people in a range of positions of power and allow righteous citizens to hold leaders accountable. Movement leaders also framed *tamkin*, through control or influence in a variety of social institutions, as helpful for *da'wa*, by allowing committed Muslims to draw others to the cause by showing them what justice looked like, rather than occurring as the result of *da'wa*.

This helped to justify political and social work (and training for it) as part and parcel of everyday *da'wa* work: pursuing political and social activism that allowed the movement to leverage a wider range of resources to form good Muslims, and cultivating political skills to enable activists to apply God's will in positions of power, ensured that movement work served God first and foremost. In this argument, *hukm* was not a function that individual believers and activists were being asked to transfer to public institutions, because applying Islam and ruling by what God had revealed in one's everyday life, in *usra*, and in the public sphere all counted as forms of *tanfidh*. Similarly, by insisting that success in social and political activism would depend on, and be measured by, the ethical conduct of Muslim activists, and that the function and social obligation of righteous representatives and rulers were the same as those of righteous citizens in Islam (e.g., working for reform, promoting Islamic education), movement leaders incorporated political work into a unified religious mission more effectively than if they had defined the goals of Islamic politics in terms of state policies and structure.

As the MB's organizational leadership normalized the idea of using the state and political influence of various sorts to apply sharia and to carry out collective religious obligations to work for an Islamic society, their directive discourse interpreted the movement's work in parliament and politics in terms that were not very different from those that they used externally. In a text collecting interpretations of political thought from the MB leadership in the 1980s and 1990s, leaders insisted that sharia was applied through practice and comportment (*suluk*), morality (*khalq*), and seriousness of work (*jiddiya*), not merely by law, and called on Islamic deputies in parliament to both use their positions to apply sharia and to apply it in their own conduct and be accountable for it before God just as members of government had to be (Wa'i 2001, 155–56). MB leaders did not designate statecraft as a separate, or higher, form or goal of Islamic work than other kinds of work; they believed that different Muslim workers might build mosques, preach, command the good, do jihad, and so on, but that everyone's goal was to help and unite Muslims, and to find cures for social diseases due to a decline in faith (Mashour 1989, 94–102).

According to leading MB thinkers, the state's power and social position made it a key site for applying sharia in the political realm, but this did not necessitate specific kinds of political institutions or laws. The "Islamic solution" was defined largely by its values and culture: it elevated God's vision of the good, and spiritual growth, over that of secularists, capitalists, and leftists, who prioritized material growth, and defended Islam from the "enemies of Islam." While MB leaders insisted on the comprehensiveness and distinctiveness of the Islamic *nizam* or order, and the superiority of the divine over human *minhaj*, they did not challenge the state and its religious establishment's ultimate authority over sharia compliance through legislation, or the basic structure of the Egyptian state. They viewed the state and its laws as important sites and instruments of social Islamization, and upright representatives, an enlightened electorate, and an autonomous religious establishment as essential in allowing these instruments to be put to the right use, but were careful to note that the requirement to engage with politics and infuse it with morality did not necessitate wholesale institutional change, and that Islam could be applied by reforming existing institutions (Wa'i 2001, 293).

The state was meant to uphold a collective obligation to build individual morality and empower it in social institutions and community life, rather than to simply enforce or sanction religion through a fixed set of institutions. Movement leaders continued to affirm, in both directive and assertive discourse, that *hukm* and *tanfidh* remained matters of primarily individual responsibility and applied to the norms that guided a person's choices and actions: a believer obeyed God's commands through all his or her actions, by having faith in God, by being governed by his or her faith in every form of work, while those who sought to legitimate anything that contradicted God's will were not applying God's commands (Wa'i 2001, 295–97). Movement-affiliated scholars and intellectuals like Yusuf al-Qaradawi argued that the individual and the institutional logics of commanding the good relied on each other. Qaradawi stated that the requirement of commanding the right and forbidding the evil was a collective one, because Muslims could not be a force capable of commanding, prohibiting, monitoring, and warning rulers without building some power; the obligation to correct rulers who disobeyed God was difficult to achieve against the coercive power of contemporary rulers, and, therefore, working to set up a righteous state, which would enable believers to carry out their duties of *nasiha* (advice) and commanding the right, was a religious duty by association (103–4).

In framing sharia as something the state owed to its people, and as a commitment that required everyday public action in various spheres of society and the economy to achieve its goals of social and individual justice, MB leaders kept it active as a mobilizing mission for supporters and sympathizers, and positioned Islamic activists as a necessary moral conscience to ensure that, where relevant, the collective obligations of Islam would be fulfilled through public institutions. By conceiving of individualized political work as religiously meritorious, they destigmatized it, associating it with capacity building for a godly mission instead of personal ambition. Yet they also defined the work of righteous politicians and representatives, not just righteous citizens, as central to the work of building a more Islamic society.

Similarly, leaders asserted in both external and internal discourse that the results of Islamic political activism would depend on God, and on the willingness of Muslims to conduct themselves as God wished, rather than on state or economic rewards, resisting the notion that political work would be driven by its own logic, or take the movement in a different, more state-dependent, direction. The Brothers had run election campaigns on the promise of promoting sharia application, but insisted that a sharia-governed society relied less on attaining executive power and more on building the social, material, and political conditions under which upright citizens could hold rulers accountable to sharia.

The state and its levers were important to sharia application and social Islamization, as MB deputies and political leaders reasserted in parliament and in electoral discourse, and the law was a particularly powerful and symbolically important tool in ensuring that Muslims were governed ethically. But, leaders argued consistently, capturing the state was less important than ensuring that it was directed by and for properly cultivated Muslim citizens. For the Brothers, the state and its power mattered indirectly in ensuring the application of sharia, because they offered resources to those who wished to cultivate Islamic social morality, and tools to build the kind of social solidarity, economic justice, and cultural autonomy from Western-style materialism that defined the sharia-governed society. In internal mobilizational and directive discourse, empowerment (*tamkin*) to apply God's will in broader spheres of life depended on the personal qualities of those with institutional power, but good Muslims could pursue *tamkin* on the way to achieving an Islamic state, not just through it. Rather than generating a vision of what an Islamic state might look like, in contrast to the existing Egyptian state's institutional structure, MB leaders framed policies and proposals in parliament as more "Islamic" moral alternatives that could represent the interests of believers seeking better, more godly lives and argued for ways that existing state institutions could use their power to implement sharia piecemeal.

Why did movement leaders choose this approach, and to what extent were they responding to state incentives? Movement leaders' discourse on politics reflected a pragmatic awareness that electoral opportunities were limited, and that parliament offered, at best, a chance for greater public visibility and reassurance to followers that the movement was committed to promoting Islam in all spheres of life. The fact that movement leaders' directive discourse—including that of leaders responsible for internal discipline and education—advocated for political engagement as a path for religious cultivation and movement building, with or without electoral success, and that *tamkin* was framed as part of *da'wa* and *tarbiya*, suggests that leaders were as pragmatic in their embrace of politics internally as they were externally. Leaders' assurances in directive discourse that politics would always serve the religious mission and not drive the movement in a new direction appeared directed as much at those who resisted politics within the movement as at external audiences.

The movement's embrace of *tamkin* though social and political institutions allowed it to justify individual participation in, and mobilization for, political work alongside *da'wa*, rather than deferring politics to another time, and to motivate those who wished to serve God to see political work as building capacity for *da'wa* rather than distracting from it. Embracing political work that pursued *tamkin* through different nodes of social influence, particularly by placing committed Muslims in public leadership positions, allowed the movement to build a pro-politics position on some older norms of movement activism, such as the norm that centered individual spiritual growth as the ultimate goal of Islamic activism, by asserting that political work helped cultivate and liberate the moral energies of both activists and those to whom they reached out. Presenting political and social skills, such as the ability to draw supporters in different spheres of life, or build economic success, as transferable to *da'wa* work and convertible to religious influence, also allowed the movement to maintain a flexible commitment to political work despite reversals in electoral opportunities. As the next chapter will show, this flexibility mattered in sustaining the movement's commitment to politics through the 1990s and early 2000s.

4

Political Work and the Practical *Tarbiya* of Welfarism

Scholars have extensively studied the Muslim Brothers' political evolution in the 1990s and early 2000s, with a particular focus on how a rivalry between a new generation of politically minded activists and an old-guard leadership seeking to limit challenges to its control shaped this evolution (Wickham 2004; Stacher 2001). Wickham's influential argument points to "middle-generation" Brotherhood activists who developed political skills in university and later parliamentary and syndicate politics, as the key drivers of the movement's shift to greater electoral participation. Both Wickham and Stacher have argued that interactions in public institutional settings and with non-movement activists were critical to this generation's political evolution (Wickham 2004, 216–21; Stacher 2001, 50–70). Scholars like Baker (2003) have emphasized the influence of "new Islamic intellectuals" from outside the Brotherhood, like Tariq al-Bishri, Mohammed Selim al-Awa, and Fahmi Howeidy, in shaping the ideas of the moderate *wasatiyya* faction within the Brotherhood, which produced the breakaway Wasat party initiative in 1995–96. In a similar vein, Wickham and others contend that the more open and outward-looking Wasat faction, headed by many reform-minded middle-generation leaders, was sidelined by the movement's leadership hierarchy in part because the leadership chose a more inward-looking, survival-oriented strategy for the movement in response to regime repression in the early 1990s. Tammam has pointed out how an influx of conservatives into the movement from rural areas and from Saudi Arabia and the Gulf states in the 1990s reinforced the power of leaders aligned with the Qutbist faction who were keen to return the movement to its religious roots and reduce electoral investment (2010a).

The Mubarak regime created new electoral rules designed to limit the influence of Islamist candidates and dissolved parliament in 1990 after ruling the 1987 elections illegal. In the 1990s, it began to use anti-extremism laws to arrest and jail MB leaders alongside Islamist insurgents, dealing a blow to those within the MB leadership who had championed electoral participation and further strengthening the conservative position; the "organization men" used the opportunity to stack the movement's guidance council leadership body with their own loyalists, reducing the influence of more liberal, politically open middle-generation leaders (Wickham 2013, 84–88, 113–14). Despite these clear institutional pressures to downgrade political and electoral work, as well as reduced external opportunities, the movement continued to encourage political skill-building and to embrace a range of public institutions as sites for activism and capacity building. By the early 2000s, even as conservatives cemented their control of the movement leadership, the MB returned to electoral participation, and a new training curriculum for full members centered politics and government as a key goal of Islamic activism.

This poses a puzzle: why, for what purpose, and in what form, did conservative and *tanzimi* leaders embrace political work? Squeezed between a regime seeking to marginalize Islamists as extremists, and an activist faction ready to embrace politics more fully, how did movement leaders use politics without being steered by politics? In this chapter I will show how the *tanzimi* leadership incorporated political work into training and organizational rebuilding efforts after quelling the Wasat rebellion because they understood the benefits of politics for ethical cultivation and capacity building, even while resisting the middle generation's vision of partyism. Politics was incorporated into the *tanzim*'s tools as a form of practical *tarbiya*, and its benefits were framed in terms of the resources it could offer to *daʿwa*; this understanding of the benefits of politics, distinct from that of the *wasatiyya* faction, was embedded in the movement's routine directive discourse. While the Wasat leaders' actions forced the movement to confront the organizational implications of political work, the Wasat faction was not the primary driver of political education and professionalization for the movement, with the *tanzimi* leadership focused more narrowly on organizational discipline. Rather, *tanzimi* leaders' approach to politics evolved as well, and they used political education in part to assert control and discipline over the movement's rank and file. Several *tanzimi* leaders had participated in electoral politics and took different lessons from it than the more middle-generation Wasat faction did, framing social work and constituent service as opportunities to perform and cultivate righteousness, while remaining wary of electoral coalition building that risked diluting the movement's mission and discipline. Their understanding that activists could do good for fellow Muslims both materially and spiritually through social and political empowerment was translated and reinforced within the movement through increasingly standardized training curricula. As such, these conservative "organization men" were important players in the movement's ideational evolution, and, I will argue, their understanding of politics as a form of Islamic work, and their control of *tarbiya* within the movement, mattered as much as generational tensions and factional divisions in driving the movement's politicization in the 1990s–early 2000s.

This chapter first examines the movement's internal framing of political work in professional syndicates in the early 1990s, focusing on how both middle-generation and *tanzimi* leaders interpreted the opportunities of syndicate work in terms of building *da'wa* skills and offering opportunities to command the right, while also cultivating activists' piety through social *tarbiya*. The movement leadership's simultaneous rejection of calls to form a political party and issuance of statements supportive of democracy and pluralism in the mid-1990s framed *shura* and political work similarly, as helpful for Islamic empowerment and cultivation, and politics as valuable only insofar as it served individual and collective piety. While the literature on Islamist social welfare networks has emphasized how the social capital of religious services was convertible to political capital, I will suggest that the reverse was also true: political capital was framed as valuable for *da'wa* purposes in directive discourse.

The chapter then analyzes how political training was included in a new curriculum for full members introduced in 2003, using a format for ethical cultivation that justified and directed political work in terms of religious arguments and goals. The curriculum presented governance as a source of *tamkin* and opportunity to practice *shura*, and political mobilization as a form of jihad, and framed the goals of political action and power in terms of their contribution to the Islamic cause, specifically in building moral capital, enabling Muslims to fulfill collective religious obligations and in furthering activists' own ethical cultivation. After this, the movement leadership framed new political opportunities due to electoral liberalization in 2005 as opportunities for further *tamkin* and *da'wa* and continued to treat political and religious skill-building as interchangeable, whether for electoral candidates or promotion within movement ranks, and activists themselves framed election campaigning and constituent services in terms of ethical practice rather than clientelism.

As I will show, the *tanzim* sought to form a political party because its vision of religiously guided political activism supported mobilization, electoral outreach, and service provision that served *tamkin* and practical, social *tarbiya*. Disagreements on the question of whether the movement should seek broader political change, particularly after a renewed period of state repression, hardened in 2007 as the *tanzim* issued a political party platform that upheld a religious view of the goals of politics, while younger activists sought a political project separate from the religious one. Yet a second generation of activists who participated in electoral politics generally upheld the *tanzim*'s framework of political work as a form of *tamkin* that allowed Muslims to cultivate their piety. I will argue that this commitment was a pragmatic response to changing electoral incentives, and, rather than being a conservative force, was helpful in sustaining movement support for electoral politics through rounds of repression and reopening. Moreover, while different factions within the movement may have disagreed on internal leadership issues and strategy, they did not differ substantially on the utility of politics for the *da'wa*.

Changing Political Opportunities and Political Specialization in the 1990s

As the regime restricted Islamists' opportunities for electoral power after the 1987 election, MB leaders turned to different sites for public outreach and *da'wa*, as Wickham's influential study (2002) of Islamic mobilization first analyzed in detail. The movement leadership embraced professional syndicate elections as resources for building broader support networks, as Wickham has shown, but, whereas she emphasizes the utility of civil society for supporting a "parallel Islamic sector" and cultivating a new kind of upwardly mobile, professional activist, I will demonstrate that the MB leadership's internal and external framing of syndicate work also suggests that this was a site where the religious meanings of activism were elaborated further, similar to the *tanzim*'s framing of parliamentary work. In particular, I will focus on how movement activists framed the value of syndicate work as an opportunity for ethical practice and the kind of capacity building that the movement leadership, in prior political mobilization, had argued could serve God.

Several scholars have noted that institutional resources such as funds, patronage networks, and access to the public offered by syndicates and other civil society organizations were important for the MB's survival as a political and social force under authoritarian repression in the 1990s and early 2000s (Wickham 2002; Ranko 2015; Brooke 2017). In particular, Wickham (2002, 103–5, 109–12) has argued that the independent mosques, savings and mutual aid groups (*gamaʿiyyat*), and service organizations connected to syndicates and other state bodies allowed the MB access to resources that could show people how Islam might serve them and to build institutional power to resist the authoritarian state. Professional syndicates, such as the Doctors Syndicate, the Engineers Syndicate, and the Lawyers Syndicate, were particularly important sites for political contention, as rare institutions in a corporatist, authoritarian order that were allowed relatively free elections, and the right to distribute resources autonomously. Wickham (179, 101–5) argues that an Islamic "counter-elite" that worked its way up the ranks of syndicate representation, as the MB targeted syndicates for political influence building, were able to use syndicate experience to build their own political skills, and that syndicates offered alternative avenues for upward mobility and social influence, just as the growing Islamic publishing and media sector did. Both Wickham (160–61, 190–91, 199) and Ranko (2015) emphasize the economic and political resources offered by syndicate elections, and Wickham contends that the religious habitus of Islamist activists in these professional sites allowed the MB to benefit from an upright image, converting religious into political capital. As Wickham also notes, however, MB activists emphasized the religious value of political work, urging syndicate members to see voting as a religious obligation.

Reports and records of the MB campaign for and debate over syndicate elections also show that Brothers framed syndicate work as a kind of social and practical *tarbiya* for Muslim activists, and that they used syndicate space to build more "Islamic" policies to guide doctors, lawyers, and engineers in using professional life to better serve God. Elections were themselves a way to bear witness for God, MB leaders argued, because they both gave the silent, pious majority a voice and supported a democratic process that was helpful in achieving an Islamic social order. Notably, these arguments were proferred by leaders from different segments of the movement, not just *wasatiyya* leaders: both internally and externally, Brothers emphasized the religious goals of public work. Syndicates were not only a space in which to cultivate a different kind or generation of activist for the movement; they also offered opportunities for religiously meaningful activism for all kinds of activists.

As in parliament, some MB leaders framed their work in syndicates as representation of a pious majority. Countering accusations from regime members and leftist politicians that Islamists were terrorizing a silent majority of Egyptians, Essam el-Erian, a rising middle-generation leader who had been elected to parliament and was active in the Doctors Syndicate, asserted that the success of Islamist candidates in syndicate elections, despite being excluded from parliament and hounded by a regime willing to use its patronage resources to win support, served as evidence that Islamists were able to give a voice to young people who had been denied a voice in the past.[1]

Again, as in parliament, MB activists framed electoral outreach for syndicates as religiously valuable work. Mokhtar Noh, campaigning for the board of the Lawyers Syndicate, argued that elections were an act of worship, bringing people closer to God, while Yusuf Kamal Muhammad

---

1. Essam el-Erian, "Niqabat al-atba' wa hissar al-aghlabiya al-samita," *al-Sha'b*, September 15, 1992.

Yusuf, also on the Islamic Alliance list, said that elections were a kind of jihad that must be waged to achieve *shura*, and an obligation like any other kind of jihad.² MB candidates maintained that syndicate work was a chance to perform and encourage Islamic behavior while addressing the broader moral failings of contemporary society: in campaign materials for Lawyers Syndicate elections in 1992, candidates promised to "straighten out" syndicates and purify them of immoral, irreligious behavior that included corrupt uses of syndicate funds, arguing that such behavior was due to a lack of Islamic ethics and promising that Islamic alliance candidates would protect people's interests and serve "our beloved, renascent Egypt" through upright practices like limiting syndicate-funded trips to religious pilgrimages rather than foreign junkets.³

When Islamists organized seminars in the Engineers Syndicate on challenges for the profession, such as unemployment, they framed "Islamic" solutions to these problems in both policy terms, such as keeping up with the needs of industry and ensuring research on productive fields, and in terms of moral-social reform, insisting that social problems were fundamentally due to a lack of a comprehensive social philosophy and required individual and social reform through religion.⁴ Brothers started to use the slogan "Yes, We Want It Islamic" (*na'm, nuriduha islamiyya*) in syndicate election campaigns, promising to address everyday constituent concerns like financial and medical services, as well as fighting injustice through courts and offering Islamic education through professional summer camps, as they traditionally had in movement summer camps.⁵

---

2. "Al-niqabat al-fara'iyah fi-l-Iskandriya wa Tanta wa Beni Sueif wa Aswan: ta'yid wasi' li-l-murashihin al-islamiyin bi-niqabat al-muhamin," *al-Sha'b*, August 28, 1992; "Al-yawm, 12 murashihan li-l-tayyar al-Islami yukhawwadun mu'araka niqabat al-muhamin, haqana injaz malmusa fi-l-niqabat al-fara'iyah wa nuqaddim barnamijan kamilan li-l-nahud bi-l-niqaba al-'amma," *al-Sha'b*, September 11, 1992.

3. "A'lan al-barnamij al-intikhabi li-murashihi al-Ikhwan fi niqabat al-muhamin," *al-Ahali*, September 2, 1992.

4. "Madha ba'd taza'id al-batala bayn al-muhandisin?," *al-Sha'b*, January 17, 1989.

5. "Al-yawm, 12 murashihun li-l-tayyar al-Islami yukhawwadun mu'araka niqabat al-muhamin, haqana injaz malmusa fi-l-niqabat al-fara'iya wa nuqaddim barnamijan kamilan li-l-nahud bi-l-niqaba al-'amma," *al-Sha'b*, September 11, 1992.

In addition to enabling righteous action by Islamic activists and those who supported them, MB leaders argued that syndicate work must promote Islamic policies in different professions in order to enable them to do social and religious good and to build their capacity to do more social and religious good in the future. They aimed to persuade people that religious commitment was essential to professional success and to guide professionals in what it meant to "apply sharia" in medicine, the law, and other professions. Islamist representatives in the Doctors Syndicate in particular used their position to propagate the idea that following God's law and practicing medicine were inseparable endeavors and should be promoted in tandem.

At one professional conference, delegates recommended grounding medical education in the regulations of Islam and advocated for the teaching of medicine in Arabic. One delegate, a professor of medicine in Saudi Arabia, argued that teaching *fiqh* or Islamic jurisprudence to doctors would allow them to know the religious rules guiding their profession and be better able to guide patients on the ethical norms surrounding assisted reproduction, organ transplants, brain death, and so on. One delegate emphasized that doctors must see their work as religious duty: Muslims were not created in jest but, rather, to do good work, and, as such, were obliged to fight the epidemics of their age, just as those in other spheres, such as the media, were obliged to direct their art toward the good, and toward God. Abdel Moneim Abul Futouh, then secretary-general of the syndicate and prominent middle-generation MB leader, stated at this conference that the guidance of sharia was important in ridding society of injustice and tyranny and in helping Muslims see work as a form of worship, and scientific research as a religious duty. Some conference delegates who were described as American-trained or were employees of the World Health Organization also compared Islamic approaches to health favorably with Western ones, noting that Islamic rules about sexual morality offered protection against diseases and the negative effects of sexual freedoms that plagued the West. Religious norms could therefore be valuable in promoting public health, while professional skills and knowledge allowed Muslims to live up to their religious commitments, by solving people's problems and doing social good.⁶ Similarly, in the Lawyers Syndicate, Islamist representatives helped constituents purchase law books and copy machines, organized summer camps, and arranged medical care, and also started a newsletter titled *Difaʿ Islami* (Islamic Defense) to deepen lawyers' familiarity with sharia and organized a conference to raise awareness about torture in prisons.⁷

Brotherhood representatives used the freedom of expression and resources offered by syndicates to organize conferences and promote ideas about Muslim values and solidarity more broadly and to call for Islamic action for justice understood in terms of what they considered an alternative, indigenous universalism, in contrast to a flawed Western secular scientific framework. For example, the Doctors Syndicate organized a seminar on Islam and secularism with leading New Islamist and secular intellectuals, as well as a conference on medical miracles in the Quran and the role of Islam in regulating medicine, and seminars on terrorism, supporting the Afghan jihad and the Palestinian uprising; they organized a further conference on Islamic unity and attacks on Muslims throughout the *umma* that convened Islamic delegations from the Balkans and from Somalia to discuss challenges faced by Muslims in those areas.⁸ Similarly the Engineers Syndicate cosponsored a conference with the Higher Council for Islamic Thought and a New Islamist research center on "Western biases" in modern scientific thought that brought together former leftists like Adil Hussein of the Hizb al-ʿAmal and "civilizational Islamists" like Christian leader Rafiq Habib to consider culturally appropriate alternatives to Western style economic development and modernization theories in Egypt.⁹

Islamist leaders and representatives writing for Islamic publications touted their work in syndicates as a form of righteous action itself, as

---

6. "Al-mu'tamir al-thani li-l-ʿagaz al-tibbi fi-l-Quran wa-l-sunna yu'akkid: Dharurat tatbiq al-sharia al-islamiyya," *al-Shaʿb*, November 29, 1988.

7. "Al-ittijah al-Islami athbat jadaratuhu fi qiyadat al-niqabat al-mihniyya," *al-Nur*, February 1, 1989.

8. "Al-ʿalam al-Islami yataʿaradh li-l-mu'amirat wa-l-amal maʿqud ʿala wihda al-muslimin," *al-Liwa' al-Islami*, September 17, 1992.

9. "Naqd li-l-fikr al-ʿarabi . . . wa daʿwa li-l-ijtihad tuhayyaz li-l-ʿadl badlan min al-tahayyiz li-l-huwa," *al-Shaʿb*, October 3, 1992.

much as a means to *tamkin*. As examples of "Islamic work," they cited workshops they had organized on how to teach Islamic regulations in faculties of medicine, and aid campaigns for war-riven Sudan, for solidarity building with Muslims worldwide; syndicate work that Islamist leaders and publications touted as "Islamic" was not clearly identifiable as serving religious identity and values: seminars on addiction and its treatment were included in reports on Islamic work.[10] MB representatives in the Doctors Syndicate, for instance, framed their understanding of Islamic work and justice as defending the rights of all members without discrimination and addressing everyday problems like housing and income.[11] Partly in response to concerns from Christian and secular professionals who worried about sectarianism in syndicates, Islamist candidates emphasized their mission of unifying lawyers and serving them regardless of their religious affiliation; they argued, too, that an Islamic understanding of *shura* meant that they would not ignore the interests of minorities, but would guide and mobilize the public (*harakat al-jamahir*) toward an Islamic understanding of justice, welcoming any sincere participation to help solve problems.[12]

MB cadres in syndicate work framed welfare initiatives as another opportunity for good Muslims to do good and to show people that Islam had practical benefits. When the MB-led Doctors Syndicate used its humanitarian relief committee to aid victims of the 1992 Cairo earthquake, and MB leaders in the Engineers Syndicate volunteered their expertise in inspecting building construction and collecting donations for those affected, with banners at emergency relief centers bearing the MB electoral slogan "Islam Is the Solution," the regime framed this work as a partisan

---

10. "Al-ittijah al-Islami athbat jadaratuhu fi qiyadat al-niqabat al-mihniyya," *al-Nur*, February 1, 1989.

11. "Al-tayar al-islami yasa'y li-l-husul 'ala al-aghlabiyya wa ba'd bi-l-tasaddy li-l-fasad," *al-Ahrar*, April 7, 1986.

12. "Al-niqabat al-fara'iya fi-l-Iskandriyya wa Tanta wa Beni Sueif wa Aswan: ta'yid wasi' li-l-murashihin al-islamiyin bi-niqabat al-muhamin," *al-Sha'b*, August 28, 1992; Dr. Fouad Hanna, "Ayn al-aqbat fi-intikhabat al-niqabat al-mihniyya?," *a-Sha'b*, December 8, 1988.

exploitation of religion and issued a decree preventing anyone other than the Ministry of Social Affairs and the Red Crescent society from distributing relief (Stacher 2001, 71–72).[13] Syndicate work was also appealing to Brotherhood professionals who had returned to Egypt from the Persian Gulf and Europe in the 1990s, such as Khairat al-Shater, a businessman and future deputy General Guide, and Essam al-Haddad, who sought to build a stronger economic base for the movement (Willi 2021, 160–64).

While MB leaders viewed syndicate work as offering opportunities and resources to do good, regime leaders touted such work as evidence of a stealth campaign for political revolution. The regime raided Khairat al-Shater's business offices, specifically those of his Salsabil computer company, and argued that documents seized in the raid outlining the MB's Empowerment Project (Mashru' al-Tamkin), which focused primarily on how to rebuild the movement's organization and create new committees for politics and other functions, were evidence of an Islamist plot to seize power from the state (Wickham 2013, 90). A rising Islamist insurgency in upper Egypt and the poorer parts of Cairo, and anti-Christian attacks and political assassinations by the Gama'a Islamiyya in the early 1990s, gave the Mubarak regime the justification it needed to accuse the MB of being a conveyor belt for radicalism and distorting religion in order to encourage political violence (Ranko 2015, 124). After the MB decided to boycott parliamentary elections in 1990 following a regime-pressured court decision declaring the 1987 assembly election invalid, as well as made clear their opposition to Mubarak's cooperation with the United States over the 1991 Persian Gulf War and the Madrid peace process, the Mubarak regime restricted political opportunities for the group, painting it as a sectarian threat to national unity and progress (Ranko 2015, 118–23; Stacher 2001, 52–54). The regime amended the Egyptian penal code in 1992 to define acts of terrorism more broadly and altered syndicate election rules to render Islamist victories invalid. Further legislation that year reasserted state control over the press and funding for civil society organizations,

---

13. "Dr. Muhammad Ali Bishr yatahaddath bi-l-Nur: "1/2 million guineah min niqabat al-muhandisin . . . li-dahaya al-zalzal; 200,000 muhandis yu'ainun al-misakin . . . majanan," *al-Nur*, October 28, 1992.

allowing the regime to justify seizing assets from MB-owned companies and arresting many politically active MB leaders, including prominent middle generation leaders (Ranko 2015, 112, 120–21; Stacher 2001, 65–66).

The expansion and contraction of political opportunities in the 1990s encouraged, rather than discouraged, those who wished to move the MB in a more political direction at this time. Wickham (2002, 91) notes that there was pressure from syndicate activists to separate the work of the *gama'a* from that of electoral politics and to formally apply for a party license; moreover, because pressure to engage more openly and wholeheartedly in politics came largely from middle-generation activists, she suggests that those who had internalized more tolerant, pragmatic political values from electoral experience were the most important drivers of a demand for a party. The *tanzimi* leadership was, however, in favor of party formation as well: former leaders of this group confirmed in later years that they had proposed different formats and names for potential political parties in 1992 (Wickham 2013, 72; Ranko 2014, 137). Just like the middle generation, the more conservative organization men of the *tanzimi* faction benefited from the lessons of a generation of electoral participation in weighing the risks and benefits of party formation and favored a more professionalized and specialized kind of Islamic public activism. They disagreed, however, about the terms and pace of this specialization, and the matter of who would lead a proposed party (Ranko 2015, 152). The *tanzimi* leadership disciplined those who led the breakaway Wasat party initiative, which had called for greater youth representation and transparency in the *gama'a*'s internal elections and organization, both because this initiative threatened the movement's unity and its hierarchical norms, and because accepting state laws governing political parties at that historical moment meant agreeing to a formal organizational separation of *da'wa* from political work—something the movement leaders were not ready to do as yet (Wickham 2013, 71, 87–94). In a statement on the "virtues of hardship" that they issued after the Wasat conflict, the movement leadership argued that the movement must not lose its sense of purpose in changing times, reminding members that *da'wa* remained the ultimate mission (93). Yet many Wasat-supporting activists were brought back into the movement fold, and activists who had been associated with a pro-politics position moved up the organizational hierarchy in subsequent years (Wickham 2002, 221; Ghobashy 2005).

Partly in response to regime efforts to group them in with anti-system radicals, regime leaders put out high-profile public statements in 1994 and 1995 on pluralism, *shura*, and the rights of women and Christians under Islamic political norms in Egypt. While these statements were written with external audiences in mind, they also reflected changing internal norms about how politics could serve a religious mission. The leadership issued a statement on *shura* and pluralism in 1994 that echoed internal, directive discourse on the value of parliamentary debate on consultation, arguing that *shura* was an essential tool for determining how sharia was to be translated into policy and legislation; responsibility for deciding how to command the good in different situations was vested in the people, the statement said, and consultation among people, pluralism, and input from as many people as possible were important tools for commanding the right (*al-amr bi-l-maʿruf*) (Ranko 2015, 130–33; Ghobashy 2005, 384–85). Echoing the movement's internal emphasis on the importance of religiously guided and oriented political work, the statement also asserted that political pluralism must remain bounded by the limits of the "highest constitution" of God's law, in that groups should be free to disseminate ideas and programs as long as they did not violate sharia (Wickham 2013, 69–70). The goals of democracy and pluralism, went the statement, were to "return God's rule to the peoples of Islam," enabling them to choose their representatives freely, according to their religious conscience; this right, and the right to hold rulers accountable, belonged to citizens, under Islam, regardless of their personal faith (Wa'i 2001, 130).

The next year, as militants in upper Egypt were using violence against tourists and the state, and the regime jailed dozens of MB leaders and put them on military trial for allegedly plotting to overthrow the regime, the MB released a statement on democracy. In 1995, MB syndicate leaders organized a conference on freedoms and civil society, together with representatives from opposition parties and with public intellectuals, to attempt to reach an accord on political freedoms and to condemn political violence. However, while affirming a shared commitment to freedoms and democracy, the MB leadership refused to sign an accord that did not adequately refer to sharia (Ghobashy 2005, 384–86).

The movement leadership continued to make space for political specialization within the organization even as it shut down calls for greater internal transparency: when general guides Mustafa Mashour and Mamoun el-Hodeiby died in fairly quick succession in the early 2000s, the leadership replaced them with Mahdi Akef in part because Akef had electoral experience and good relations with the electoral wing of the group (Wickham 2013, 99–101). A parliamentary committee was added to the MB leadership structure in 2000, to be followed by a political committee in 2005, and, while the MB fielded candidates in only half the seats in the 2000 parliamentary election as it had in the 1995 election, the movement leadership sought as much electoral influence as possible without risking a regime crackdown (Vannetzel 2016a, 234–36; Wickham 2013, 101–5).

The fact that the movement's internal reorganization and retrenchment in this period reinforced the power of a conservative *tanzimi* leadership, notably over the *tarbiya* division, did not mean that politics was no longer encouraged internally (Willi 2021, 171–72). Leaders associated with the *tanzimi* leadership incorporated pragmatic commitments to political work into their methods for movement discipline, and their internal directive and public-facing commissive discourse converged, by the end of the 1990s, on similar understandings of the religious meanings of political work. Mamoun el-Hodeiby, who had served as deputy leader of the MB's parliamentary delegation and rose to become the general guide in 2002, affirmed the religious purpose of politics for the movement in a new parliamentary program that he issued for the 2000 election and included in a statement of reform presented to the regime in 2004, under some American pressure. Hodeiby stated that the MB were committed wholeheartedly to political and economic reform, and that service to God and individual religious perfection remained the ultimate mission of human and political life (Wa'i 2001, 166–77). Arguing that Islamic activists were nothing without God, and that calling people to God must be the basis of all their work, Hodeiby noted that the well-being and spiritual growth of individuals remained the goal of all progress as well as the best tool for further development, and that Egyptians must purify the pious essence of their national personality if they wanted reform (166–68). Political reform, the statement continued, required political freedoms, participation, freedom of religion, and an independent judiciary, which would serve as forces for the national good in tandem with reform to bring laws in line with sharia; judicial watchfulness against actions that violated social etiquette (*adab*), and, in turn, economic reform depended on *salih* (religiously pure) capital and Islamic investment. Women were essential to a reformed Egypt, and Coptic Egyptians were brothers in the nation; religious freedom was no less essential and required that Islamic religious endowments (*awqaf*) and preaching must be free of state interference, and that al-Azhar must be able to elect its own leadership (Wa'i 2001, 178–81).

Directive Discourse and *Tarbiya* for Politics in the Early 2000s

The argument that politics, for the committed Muslim, was too tainted to be worth engaging was put to rest in the MB's internal discourse by the end of the 1990s. A book by an MB-affiliated scholar, Tawfiq Yusuf al-Wa'i on the major trends in the movement's political thought (published in 2001 and referred to me by several members) assessed the costs and benefits of political participation concretely and pragmatically, arguing that political engagement was essential for the *da'wa* in contemporary times. While the MB had believed in its early years that education would suffice to Islamize society, he wrote, the greater challenges that *da'wa* faced in the twenty-first century, through technology, globalization, democratization, and Zionism, all required different responses (235). Citing the prophet Joseph's pragmatic decision to work with Pharaoh to salvage what influence he thought he could have, the text declared that Muslims should join governments, even in an era where a return of the caliphate was not in the cards, if this allowed them to prevent wrongdoing; further, religiously forbidden (*haram*) acts could be permissible (*halal*) if they permitted the doer to achieve a greater good (189–92, 200–201). Therefore, Wa'i concluded, if political participation could offer Islamic activists access to knowledge, restore people's faith in Islam and its ability to govern, and serve Islamic interests through government representatives, it was a positive thing for religion (216–17). Yet he cautioned that political participation, while helpful for the *tamkin* that allowed Muslims to live under sharia, never had unconditional religious approval, and that Muslims must weigh the costs and benefits of each act of participation and see politics as a duty that would bring them closer to God, rather than being motivated by personal ambition or greed (221). Legitimate political participation must be defined by the religious intent of the participant as much as by the religious consequences of their participation; participation that simply sought a role in government, without using that role to serve Islam, was wrong, because participation should increase, not reduce, people's ability to speak up for Islam and oppose violations of its norms (239). Muslims were accountable to God for their intentions, and only the best and most honest members of the MB should take up the task of political participation and be closely monitored, so that they didn't participate in anything that would violate Islamic teachings (220, 240).

The idea that political work could be an important part of the *da'wa* mission and required specialized training, with careful religious framing so as to ensure that it reaped religious benefits, was translated into changes in the training curriculum for *tarbiya* in movement *usra* units as well. As part of a broader effort to reinforce discipline and unity in movement ranks in the early 2000s, following the release of many middle-generation leaders from prison, the *tanzimi* leadership began an initiative to bring some uniformity to the educational materials used to cultivate movement recruits and members at different levels. Up until that point, the *naqib* (leader or captain) of an *usra* had generally been entrusted with choosing materials and activities for weekly sessions, and *usra* leaders drew on a variety of texts that generally included Banna's letters and some other writings by MB leaders but were not standardized. In 2003–4, however, the MB's central educational council (*lignat al-tarbiya al-markaziyya*) produced a series of standardized instructional texts for use in *usra*: *Min Mabadi' al-Islam* (From the Principles of Islam) was aimed at the *muhib* or sympathizer level, *Fi Rihab al-Islam* (In the Vastness of Islam) at the *mu'ayyid* or supporter level, and *Fi Nur al-Islam* (In the Light of Islam) at the full member or *muntasib* level.[14] It is not clear that these curricula ever fully replaced other texts, or removed the *naqib*'s discretion in choosing what to focus a lesson on, and both my interlocutors in the movement and Brothers interviewed by other scholars like Kandil (2015) and Willi (2021) noted that other texts, including some by Sayyid Qutb, remained in use as well. However, the initiative for curriculum centralization mattered in laying out and structuring priorities for activist education, and in the boundaries it set for what was included within the *da'wa* mission. It also represented, per one of my interlocutors with historical family ties to the leadership, an effort by the Khairat al-Shater faction to ensure control over the movement rank and file through *tarbiya*.[15]

The instructional texts for the introductory and secondary levels focused primarily on religious knowledge and correct ritual worship practices, with practical guidelines for ethical practice, and it was only at the advanced *muntasib* level that the curriculum dealt with politics and governance and the nature of an Islamic social order, as part of a sequence on faith, worship, and ethical behavior. This multivolume curriculum, made available to me by a movement interlocutor, was designed at all levels in a similar way: emphasizing correct religious knowledge and practice, each section laid out practical goals for behavior (*al-ahdaf al-ijra'iyya al-sulikiyya*), explaining and justifying their importance with relevant extracts from religious texts, mostly the Quran, *sunna*, and hadith, and with historical movement leaders' teachings and writings; in some sections, these were followed by discussions of contemporary circumstances, and choices for working for Islam within them. Each section ended with a quiz, and these curricula may have served as texts to prepare for the examinations used by the movement to allow activists to proceed from one level of membership to another (Vannetzel 2016a, 366). The last text in the series, *Fi Nur al-Islam*, aimed at full members, was the only one to focus on political work, with the last third of the volume devoted to explaining why politics mattered for ethical cultivation, and what the religious justifications and reasons were for seeing political work as *'amal salih* (Abou Rayyah, 2006).

14. Interview, AK, Cairo, May 18, 2013.
15. Interview, AG, Cairo, September 24, 2013.

The fact that political work was discussed only after religious and spiritual knowledge, following the traditional *tarbiya* sequence of reforming the self and the home before reforming society, and appeared only in the final volume, affirmed arguments from Wa'i and others that only those who had reached a certain level of spiritual cultivation could be entrusted with politics. The text was striking in presenting political work as essential for the religious mission and in arguing that political and religious skills must be cultivated together: where *Wasai'l al-Tarbiya* focused on the *usra* as the primary site of cultivation and the arena in which the movement could best build its capacity to do good, *Fi Nur al-Islam* argued that the political arena offered the greatest opportunities for cultivating their spiritual abilities and discharging their religious obligations. By presenting political work as part of religious cultivation for average members, the last third of the curriculum approached politics in four ways: first, by making a case for why politics and the state were important in maintaining the religious community; second, in arguing for political work as a religious obligation for Muslims, both individually (*fard al-'ayn*) and collectively (*fard al-kifaya*); third, in instructing Muslims to cultivate *shura* skills in their movement and political work as a way to build an upright political order; and, fourth, in framing political work as a kind of jihad that could both count as work for Islam, and serve as a form of practical *tarbiya*.

The section began by making the case that nationalism and the state were important concerns for all those who worked for Islam (Abou Rayyah 2006, 621–26). Quoting extracts from Banna's writings, it declared that liberating the nation (*tahrir al-watan*), reforming government, and restoring a global entity for the Islamic *umma* and for the guidance and mastery (*ustadhiya*) of the world were duties for all Brothers, and for the *gama'a*; nationalism (*wataniyya*) was valuable for Islam inasmuch as it strengthened bonds between people for greater strength and guided them to use this strength for the welfare and good (*masalih*) of people, rather than the nationalism that segmented the *umma* into factions based on interest-seeking (Abou Rayyah 2006, 620–21). A Muslim of true faith must devote themselves to and sacrifice for the cause of *wataniyya*, for serving the nation and working for its good were religious duties (623). The "nation" (*watan*), here, was framed as interchangeable with the *umma* or community of believers, but the work of being a good citizen included cultivating feelings of brotherhood for Christian citizens as well: the text cited Quranic verse on why believers must befriend those who were of their kind (*Al 'Imran* 118) and cooperate with those who didn't attack one's faith (*Al-Mumtahina* 8), as well as a hadith of the Prophet saying that the servants of God should be brothers, to support this point (622–23).

The curriculum contended that working for the unity, strength, and liberation of the nation required working to liberate it from the moral, political, economic, and intellectual hegemony of the West—indeed, it was as much of a legitimate obligation (*wajiban shar'iyyan*) as the obligation to fight colonial rule had been. Non-Islamic rule or government (*sultan*) was key to the breakdown of Islamic morals, and the replacement of sharia with foreign ideas, and this rule had been enabled by various forms of cultural imperialism: secular education, propaganda about Islam being radical, and materialistic and atheistic culture had allowed the West to exercise political *sultan* through rulers in the region (Abou Rayyah 2006, 624–26). Citing Banna's principle that Islam was *din wa dawla*, and that the *dawla* (state) was necessary to protect religion and its *da'wa* and applying the laws and upholding the conditions that made it possible to practice the faith, the text argued that the traditional sequence of Islamic cultivation, building the good Muslim individual, home, community, and global government, required a fifth intermediary stage as well: reforming the government until it was Islamic (*al-'amal 'ala islah al-hukuma hatta takun islamiyya bi-haq*) (629, 653).

The text was careful to anchor its arguments about governance and the state in traditional movement literature, particularly quotations from Banna, citing as references for further reading only texts by *tarbiya* division leaders like Abdel Halim Mahmoud, with the "new Islamic intellectual" Muhammad Imara as the only external reference (Abou Rayyah 2006, 628). Quoting Banna from the movement's Fifth Conference that the Islam that the Brothers believed in made governance one of its pillars and relied on execution as much as on guidance (*hadha al-Islam alladi yu'min bihu al-ikhwan . . . yaja'l al-hukuma ruknan min arkanuhu, wa yu'tamid 'ala al-tanfidh*), and arguing that the Prophet had made governance a knot in the bond of Islam, the text defended governance as a central concern for religious faith rather than a secondary matter (630–31).

To make its case, the text used traditionally religious arguments and a range of religious references. It also quoted Banna's epistle "Between Yesterday and Today" and various hadith, including by Bukhari, to support its contention that it was necessary to establish a free Islamic state in a free nation, and that if governance were to be left to those who were not qualified for this, Muslims were collectively responsible for this before God (Abou Rayyah 2006, 633). Quoting a well-known saying from the third *khalifa*, the text argued that God could sometimes draw people closer to Him through the *sultan* than through the Quran, and cited a Quranic verse (*Al-Baqara* 251) to argue that if it were not for God checking some people by means of others, the world would be corrupted. It quoted another Quranic verse instructing believers to obey God, the Prophet, and those in authority among them (*Al-Nisa'* 59), and drew on jurist Ibn Taymiyya to reinforce the principle that governance was one of the greatest duties in religion, and one could not have religion without it. Governance, it affirmed, was grouped in with matters of belief, and not *fiqh* or jurisprudence, in books of religious learning (631–32). The text described an Islamic government in terms of its functions and duties to God and to a believing public. These included ensuring that laws conformed to sharia and supporting a leader (either a president or imam) responsible before both God and the *umma*, who would staff government with believers charged with carrying out the laws of Islam (with non-Muslims acceptable in some administrative positions. The *umma* was responsible for ensuring that the leader followed the righteous path (Abou Rayyah 2006, 634–35). It cited Quranic verses to remind activists that they were religiously obliged to judge between people justly (*Al-Nisa'* 58; *Al-'Anfal* 27), but also cited Banna and scholar Yusuf al-Qaradawi to assert that Islamic government did not mean a theocratic state: rulers could not be God's delegates, but must be chosen, monitored, and removed, if necessary, by the *umma*, and it was the right and duty of individuals in this civil state to advise the ruler, consult with them, and command the right and forbid the evil (635–36). Muhammad Imara was referenced again to support the claim that a sharia-governed state would protect the lives and safety of Coptic Christians in Egypt better than "imported" laws (637). Continuing to quote Quranic verses and Banna's sayings, the text defined an "Islamic government" as one that spread Islam, maintained the unity of the *umma* and respected its opinion, established justice, handled public funds with integrity, and respected citizens, treating them with parental compassion and equity (645–48). It discussed modern systems of government that could be compatible with Islamic rule and concluded that constitutional, republican government, with a parliament to hold the head of state accountable, rather than monarchy or autocracy, were more likely to respect Islamic law (640–41).

The text argued that an Islamic government (*hukuma*) depended on certain kinds of religious and political work by believers, as much as on what those in power did: Muslims were obliged to consult among themselves, scrutinize their leaders, and understand the end results of politics. The definition of positions equivalent to those of the *ahl al-hal wa-l-akd* (people who loose and bind)—a group that included scholars, public leaders, and heads of large families and tribes—needed to expand to accommodate changing realities, and members of this group had particular obligations to participate in political work (Abou Rayyah 2006, 643–44). But all believers must be driven by religious duty and a desire for unity that surpassed partisanship, so as to participate effectively in politics (642). The curriculum instructed Brothers to consider political work a religious obligation (*wajib*), as it was part of the process of liberating the Islamic nation (629). Arguing that God had made Muslims a just community so as to serve as witnesses over people, and that they would be as good as *jahil* (people in pre-Islamic ignorance) if they did not, the curriculum laid out a series of obligations for Muslims to achieve Islamic governance (673). These were both individual and collective obligations: working to reform government so that it could apply the rules and follow the principles of Islam was a collective obligation (*fard kifaya*), and Muslims were collectively sinners if they did not work for it. But even though this obligation belonged to the *umma* as a whole, it imposed religious obligations on individuals (*fard 'ayn*) according to their position in society, and fulfilling a collective duty was not possible without fulfilling individual duties—one could not perform one's obligations of charity, prayer, and so forth, without governance that protected and implemented God's will (633, 647–49. 654). Individual Muslims were urged to act like the early companions of the Prophet (*al-salaf al-salih*) and work to free and dignify their countries and to prepare what they could of power (674).

The curriculum also made a case for *shura* as a religious obligation and a way of cultivating and achieving religious merit, in addition to being a practice that allowed people to build a more Islamic polity and to work for the reform of *hukuma*. Where in the past the movement leadership's public-facing, commissive discourse and writings on political goals had focused on defending electoral politics' compatibility with, and utility for achieving, an Islamic order, the *Fi Nur al-Islam* text emphasized the utility of consultative and representative norms for individual religious perfection. The curriculum cited Quranic verses on religious obligation (*Al 'Imran* 104 and 159; *Al-Nisa'* 59; *Al-Tawba* 111; *Al-Shura* 38) and quotations from caliph Abu Bakr, as well as contemporary Muslim scholar Qaradawi, to exhort believers to invest their time, money, and effort to help any government that was serious about *islah* and to advise, guide, and set right any ruler who deviated from the path of Islam, so as to command in him the right and forbid the evil and to counter oppression (*zulm*) wherever they saw it (Abou Rayyah 2006, 643, 654–55). The ruler, it continued, was the delegate of the community (*wakil al-umma*), not the delegate of God, and must be held accountable to the law as well (659). The curriculum argued that a state as financially and militarily powerful as the modern one required political organizing to hold it accountable, because rulers might kill a few individuals, but could not silence large groups of people in civil society, professional associations, and political parties (658). Therefore, the good Muslim must organize and connect people, educate the young, carry out *tarbiya*, personally refuse to do anything the government asked them to that contradicted sharia, and struggle constitutionally until the state was won over for the *da'wa*, because this was their moral obligation, whether or not the state was doing its job (659–60). The quiz that followed this section tested students on the role of the individual in political consciousness raising and on differences between religion and state in Europe and in Islam, asked them to provide religious justifications for why the government must be accountable to the *umma*, and assigned them to read Mustafa Mashour's writings on the importance of *shura* and on the question of why there was no Islamic state as yet (661–66).

The curriculum then argued that *shura* was a uniquely Islamic concept, important as an educational practice, and valuable for the spiritual cultivation of Muslims, tethered closely to religious meaning and obligation, rather than sectioned off as one that applied mainly to the political sphere and political activism. As an ethical practice, *shura* must imbue all of Muslim social life, including family life and everyday decision-making in *usra*, and activists were encouraged to see *shura* as not merely or even primarily a political practice (Abou Rayyah 2006, 729–30). In this section of the curriculum, *shura* was figured both as a religious obligation and a faith-driven practice (*mumarisa 'imaniyya*): it was established in sharia not only as a principle to be implemented according to circumstances but also as one that must be learned through practical education (*'amal tarbawi*) rather than through bodies of scientific knowledge (*'ilm*) (726, 728, 730). A substantial section on "understanding and practicing *shura*" asserted that it was a "form of worship (*'ibada*) and a means to reach the correct solution to any problem," as it harnessed the reason, strengths, and knowledge of human beings for the good (718–19). The text quoted Quranic verses such as *Al-Shura* 38 and *Al 'Imran* 159 to describe believers as "those who obey their Lord, establish prayer, and conduct their affairs by mutual consultation" (724). It cited Sayyid Qutb's text *Fi Zilal al-Qur'an* to emphasize that *shura* was important in the lives of Muslims, with a deeper and broader meaning than that ascribed to it in the affairs of state: it framed *shura* as an early characteristic of the *gama'a* itself, listed by God as an important rule for Muslims alongside the profession of faith and prayer, preceding even *zakat*, and an important quality for a group chosen to manage humanity (720).

The text framed individual spiritual cultivation as something that both allowed *shura* to proceed and that benefited from the practice of *shura*. It offered examples from stories of the life of the Prophet and of his successor caliphs to illustrate that *shura* was essential for training (*tadrib*) and building (*bina'*) young Muslims in the best way to respond to God's commands: the Prophet, it maintained, accepted consultation from others during the Battle of Uhud, despite his misgivings, because he prioritized the *ta'lim* (education) of the group and the *tarbiya* of the *umma* above temporary losses and recognized that *shura* was necessary in allowing the *umma* to learn how to be prepared to manage its affairs, just as trial and error were important in allowing toddlers to learn to walk (Abou Rayyah 2006, 721, 724). Because the Prophet intended for Muslims to be ready, wise, and well guided in leading and to learn to bear the outcomes of their opinions and behavior, everyday practices of *shura* were a form of real-life, practical *tarbiya* to this end; *shura* also allowed people to avoid mistakes and learn what was the right thing to do, and to reduce chances of *fitna* (social dissension) or decisions that were sinful, by encouraging good decision-making and by allowing the *umma* to benefit from—and unify—a range of talents (724–25). The text emphasized the pedagogical utility of *shura* for individual *tarbiya* (*tarbiyya shuriyya*) by noting that the exchange of views in a loving, trusting atmosphere of *shura*, where people both offered and sought guidance, helped people grow in all kinds of social contexts, including the family environment (730).

According to the text, the kind of *shura* that allowed positive social outcomes relied on properly Islamic personal characteristics, bringing the emphasis of the chapter back to individual spiritual growth: the Islamic *nizam* didn't have a fixed form (*laysat ashkalan jamida*) but relied, above all, on a spirit that acted with steadfast and true faith in the heart (*ruh yinsha' 'an istiqrar haqiqat al-iman fi-l-qalb*), conditioning feelings (*shu'ur*) and behavior (*suluk*), because *shura* could not be practiced correctly without faith (*'aqida*) (Abou Rayyah 2006, 728). To reach a majority decision, people must practice *shura* in a spirit of brotherhood (*ikhwa*); give advice in a sincere, not a confrontational manner; and disagree in a climate of faith and brotherliness, following Islamic etiquette (*adab*), such as focusing on the collective good, not withholding information or belittling others, and respecting the decision of the majority as one's own, once it had been taken (726–27, 730–32). While *shura* was instrumental for producing positive social outcomes, it could only do so when guided by religious considerations: people participating in *shura* must be concerned with increasing their piety (*taqwa*), following the truth (*haqq*), and implementing and realizing God's blessings (*tahqiq al-baraka*), rather than making decisions for their own sake (728).

Strikingly, the curriculum also framed everyday electoral and political outreach work as a kind of jihad that both defended and upheld Islam against threats and cultivated the good Muslim individual. While it depicted jihad as the duty of those who had already achieved a certain level of religious advancement, it folded various forms of social, *da'wa*, capacity building, and outreach work into its definition, all of which it defined as important for individuals seeking salvation. It also framed the goals of jihad in terms of individual spiritual advancement and work for God, rather than political outcomes, and laid out a vision of preparing for jihad that did not distinguish between political and spiritual training. The curriculum argued that a student must cultivate the right qualities in himself in order to be a jihadi, and that jihad was, like *shura*, both a kind of righteous action and means of practical education (*tarbiya 'amaliyya*) in being a good Muslim (Abou Rayyah 2006, 678). First, jihad constituted a religious duty: as long as good and bad existed in the world, all Muslims were required to do jihad, through prayer and charity, as well as obeying the *ma'ruf* as established by God, calling people to the good, fighting injustice, and advising rulers (678). Citing Pakistani Islamist thinker Abul Ala Mawdudi, the text asserted that "our lives are, from start to finish, jihad" and then described which forms of jihad applied to different stages of life, presenting a hierarchy of its different forms. It explained that they were all related, assuring students that all kinds of jihad were valuable in attaining salvation because they were rooted in, and aimed at regenerating, religious commitment, for the jihadi was one who exerted all his energies, in world and deed, for God, without fear or regret (681). Every Muslim was required to first engage in the jihad *al-nafs* or jihad of the self, to understand truth, and then jihad to act on, and make sacrifices for it (681). The text cited Quranic verses (*Al Baqara* 216; *Al-Tawba* 41, 82) to remind students that they must commit their lives to jihad for God, who had purchased their lives, and warned them that those who were cowards would suffer in other ways (682).

Quoting Banna, the text laid out a continuum of self-cultivation and commitment based on different kinds of jihad, beginning with the jihad of the tongue, consisting of denouncing the wrong and advocating what was right and speaking truth to rulers; living one's life as a believer, and denouncing the enemies of God and of his path; and finally, fighting, the highest form of jihad (Abou Rayyah 2006, 682–85). Yet it also framed political work and quotidian acts of citizenship as obligations and forms of jihad that the common Muslim, not just those of a righteous vanguard, must undertake. Muslims were dominated politically and humiliated by others, lacking autonomy to decide their own fate, with their religion crippled in their own homes, and *daʿwa* restricted in their communities; therefore jihad was a duty for all (684). Every Muslim must be a jihadi in whatever way possible, because everyone had something to offer, the text argued, citing Quranic verses and examples of a range of MB activities over time—whether bodily, emotional, or intellectual efforts—to encourage people to see a range of work that involved giving money, time, and personal effort, as jihad. For instance, supporting and paying for *daʿwa* was a legitimate form of jihad, as was advising people and working with them, while refusing to work with those who offended religion (686–89).

The text reminded people that activism for God would be judged by its spiritual, not political, merit. All kinds of jihad ultimately had the same goal, which was to advance Islam and establish a properly Islamic state and society (Abou Rayyah 2006, 688–89). The prophecy had established Muslims as a striving community (*umma mujahida*), the text argued, so that it could lead humanity to the truth and out of oppression, by commanding the right and forbidding the evil (677). Quoting Banna, the text stated that *daʿwa* was the individual obligation (*fard ʿayn*) of jihad, while fighting Islam's enemies was a collective obligation (*fard kifaya*), and they were mutually dependent, because *daʿwa* called on people to act for the good, while jihad enabled *daʿwa* by working to form a state that would rule according to revelation and allow faith to flourish (690, 683). While the text urged the student to focus on what he could do for the salvation of the community and to combat the enemies of Islam and Muslim government, it directed him to see his individual spiritual growth as the measure of successful Islamic mobilization, rather than any public or political outcome (695–97). Those who sought to please people above all could not please God, the text warned, clearly referring to political initiatives (710–11). The goal of jihad was to serve God, and jihad did not count if a person was motivated by ambition or worldly desires such as a love of money, for only working for the glory of God made activism halal—indeed, the text warned, one must not confuse work to exalt God's word with other issues and goals (685).

The bulk of the curriculum's discussion of jihad focused on both the individual qualities that a student must cultivate in himself to do jihad for God, and jihad's spiritual rewards. More than thinking about the outcomes of his work, the student was urged to cultivate himself ethically and emotionally in order to do it well. A good jihadi was urged to be jealous of his religion, as he was of his spouse, and to fill his mind and emotions with thoughts for fellow Muslims and to feel the pain of the Muslim nation (Abou Rayyah 2006, 696–97). The student was also encouraged to focus the work of the movement on feeding and renewing people's faith, and the instinct (*fitra*) of piety in their hearts, so that they had the moral strength for jihad, comparing faith to the oil that a lamp needed to stay lit and maintaining that no jihad could succeed without producing and sustaining the right kind of individual to carry it out (692). Just as it had cited Quranic verses and hadith and stories from the life of the Prophet and his companions to define some kinds of behavior and social practices as desirable for the good Muslim's ethical cultivation all round, it also cited similar sources to define good Muslim behavior for those who did jihad, citing scriptural arguments for what made jihad just that emphasized the spiritual discipline of the jihadi—for instance, Abu Hurayrah on fasting and praying as important qualities, and *Al-Anfal* 45–47 on the proper etiquette of fighting (682–83). It emphasized all kinds of jihad, including work for an Islamic sociopolitical order, as resources for individual spiritual advancement: God did not need human beings as much as human beings needed God in order to attain salvation (697). The text urged every striving jihadi to keep an eye on the spiritual rewards promised to those who carried out their obligation, in the form of merits (*thawab*) toward salvation, which would accrue to those who made sacrifices for God, regardless of the outcome of their sacrifice: money spent for jihad would be returned seven-hundred-fold in *thawab* as well, making jihad a spiritually lucrative deal (*safqa rabiha*) for believers who wished to go to paradise (693, 697). Students were also exhorted to think of time as a resource that was available for them to use for jihad, and that they would be accountable for before God, along with many other kinds of resources that God had blessed them with, whether knowledge, efforts, or money, that they might profitably use as their "capital" to apply to *daʻwa*, jihad in God's path, and the *tamkin* of God's *daʻwa* (710, 714). By contrast, worldly concerns such as self-preservation were pointless, because earthly life was temporary, while heaven was eternal (713).

Electoral and Service Work as Religious Performance, 2005–2010

The influence of arguments and interpretations of political work set out in the *Fi Nur al-Islam* text on activists' practices and understanding of the meaning of their political work was evident in MB internal and external discourse during their renewed engagement with elections and welfare outreach in the mid-2000s. The idea that political outreach was a kind of ethical practice that served as social *tarbiya* was echoed by political activists in neighborhood welfare work and electoral campaigning. At the same time, activists doing social and electoral work used the argument that religiously cultivated individuals could build the movement's support networks and social capital through their moral influence on others in social and political outreach. This section will look at how *tanzim*-directed electoral efforts treated social and electoral outreach not as separate activities guided by separate logics, but as guided by the shared logic of religious motivation, and how political specialization did not necessarily produce a clear separation between political and preaching cadres within the movement.

When the Mubarak regime agreed, under pressure from its American ally, to allow less restrictive electoral rules for the 2005 parliamentary elections and to permit multiple—if carefully screened—candidates to contest the presidential election that year, the new general guide Mahdi Akef, in a statement explaining the movement's electoral platform, reaffirmed that the movement's goal in participating in parliamentary institutions, "just as in entering elected bodies, syndicates, and civil society institutions, was to establish a Muslim society, which would lead to the establishment of a Muslim state, in which the good can be achieved for everyone."[16] Even after issuing statements in 2003 and 2004 supporting political pluralism and equal rights for women and Christians under an Islamic political order, Akef and movement leaders continued to frame the movement's political mission as a continuation of the Islamic *minhaj*, arguing that its focus on ethical formation and religious values made it a good basis for a political project aimed at national development, because only capable, cultivated human beings could make the nation strong and renaissant, while moral failures and weak belonging produced problems for the nation. The platform argued that the state's job, and one that the MB would advocate for in parliament, was to revive morals as well as undertake administrative reform; the Brothers considered themselves preachers (*du'a*) in advocating for sharia in government as in society and would use opportunities for advice and teaching in the political sphere, as they had in other spheres, while supporting individual freedoms and *shura* for people to choose their representatives and hold them accountable. The platform also presented the elected representative's duty to and relationship with constituents through a religious understanding of charity or "doing good" (*khayriyya*), citing a hadith saying that "the best of people benefited other people" (*khayr al-nas anfa'hum li-l-nas*).

The 2005 parliamentary election offered MB candidates more opportunities to build new social networks and develop more specialized policy skills, and this period in the movement's political evolution is broadly analyzed as one of political professionalization. Scholars have shown how candidates who represented the movement in an unprecedentedly large opposition cohort in the people's assembly that year used parliamentary debate and interpellation to demonstrate that the Islamic political project was capable of addressing the pressing problems of the Egyptian people and to display their political and technical expertise on a range of policies (Shehata and Stacher 2006; Wickham 2013, 136; Shehata 2012, 132). MB activists also used the legal protections, visibility, and resources of

---

[16]. "Al-barnamij al-intikhabi li-l-ikhwan al-muslimin," IkhwanWiki, 2005, https://www.ikhwanwiki.com/index.php?title=2005_البرنامج_الانتخابي_للإخوان_المسلمين (accessed April 27, 2023).

parliamentary offices for Islamic activism and social *tarbiya*: there were new opportunities for contact with the public that MB activists found valuable in changing people's "mores, their impressions, visions, their political rearing" (Shehata 2012, 128). MB activists used the opportunities provided by electoral liberalization to not only raise their political profile but also their neighborhood and community profile and to expand the constituency-level services and neighborhood charitable work that they had encouraged activists to see as a kind of "righteous action" important for their own spiritual growth as well as that of their constituents (Shehata 2012, 130–31; Vannetzel 2016a).

At the neighborhood level, MB activists who had kept a low public profile while doing charitable and religious outreach through local mosques and institutions like the Gami'yya Shar'iyya were able to finally "come out" to their communities, using their own insignia and slogans as Muslim Brothers, rather than doing social outreach indirectly (Vannetzel 2016a, 133, 377). MB electoral candidates pointed to their work in community charitable networks in promoting their candidacy for parliamentary office, framing Islamic charitable work as evidence that they could do good for people and parliamentary office as something that, in similar ways, would allow them to do even more good. Two separate analyses of MB campaign literature in 2005 note that MB candidates' promotional materials regularly advertised their positions in the Gami'yya Shar'iyya and their participation in a range of community-based religious welfare work, such as charity for orphans, food and medical "caravan" services, and their experience with neighborhood reconciliation councils (*majalis 'urfiyya*) as qualifications for parliamentary office and as proof that they would continue to serve people if elected (Vannetzel 2016a, 133–40; Masoud 2014, 31–34, 88–91).

Vannetzel's (2016a, 138, 145–46) sociological and ethnographic study of MB candidates and social networks from 2005 to 2010 shows that the *tarbiya*-driven argument for emphasizing religious qualifications in candidates for political work was influential in how candidates were actually promoted in elections: those who had some experience in religiously based charitable fundraising and outreach, whether in communities or in workplaces, were generally chosen as most likely to use the new resources offered by elected office for righteous action and to serve the movement. Echoing the directive discourse of the *Fi Nur al-Islam* curriculum, political activists in Vannetzel's study saw their work as an effort to capitalize on existing social networks and build skills that helped both electoral and religious outreach: candidates were encouraged to build competence in communication and connect with local service networks in their electoral constituencies and to draw more people into networks of righteous action and service through constituent service in a way that increased the ethical cultivation of both service providers and recipients (134, 289–90). Brothers who became members of parliament often tapped the older *zakat*-based networks they had been part of, via the Gami'yya Shar'iyya charity and other *zakat* associations, to offer their electoral constituents services such as medical care, while the funds and office space they were able to access as elected representatives helped them to further their resources and reputations as people who did good in their communities (238–55, 286–89).

MB activists represented this kind of welfare-driven social outreach as something that allowed them to enact Islamic ethics by engaging in the ethical treatment of others and to build more networks of righteous action. In everyday discourse and campaign rhetoric, they argued that both their social welfare and electoral service work were kinds of *khidma 'amma* (public service), motivated by sincerity (*ikhlas*) and an attachment (*widd*) to those they were serving (Vannetzel 2016a, 164). MB members of parliament emphasized their moral obligation to people as their representatives, arguing that they were serving God through their service to people, and presented themselves, in interviews and in electoral tracts, as working for the satisfaction of their Lord, driven less by a desire for political credit or public gratitude than by the desire to obey God and do good for others (Vannetzel 2016a, 193–94, 197, 204–5). As with the practical *tarbiya* that solidarity work in *usra* was meant to promote, activists argued that political work that allowed Brothers to build solidarity and fraternity with all Muslims was also a kind of practical education (*al-tarbiya al-'amaliyya*) and social education (*al-tarbiya al-ijtima'iyya*). This work that taught activists to do good for others and learn to enjoy altruism was, they argued, the final stage of education in faith and ethics (368–69, 373–75). Public-facing welfare work was important for a Muslim individual's own spiritual progress, with popular support as a by-product that also helped the *da'wa*.

MB candidates and elected representatives perceived moral capital and virtuous behavior (*tasarruf*) as central to their credibility and appeal as candidates for election, as well as to their ability to build more social capital. MB political activists and participants in popular councils sought to present themselves as "virtuous citizens" (*muwatinin salihin*) who modeled Islamic behavior in the public sphere as a kind of *da'wa*, in a way that would inspire others to follow them (Vannetzel 2016a, 333–34, 340). Offering examples of ethical dealings (*ta'mul*) that they said were key to Islam, they argued that social interaction could allow community members to earn religious merit themselves by participating in work that enabled *takaful* or solidarity (326, 335). Opportunities to participate in virtuous and "positive" action, such as conciliation councils or neighborhood support networks, would, they argued, help people cultivate their own virtue (340–41). For MB activists, expanding support for the movement and its mission in society through such interactions was a religious rather than a transactional process. Expanding support for the movement and its mission in society through such interactions was a religious rather than a transactional process, for MB activists. They argued that people trusted and supported MB activists because they recognized that their motivation to do public work was religious, rather than being a political quid pro quo, and that activists' ethical behavior in face-to-face interactions and community service was more of a calling card than any political program (200–204, 207, 287).

In line with internal, directive discourse on what it meant to empower and apply Islam and its sharia (*tamkin wa tanfidh al-shari'a*), MB activists framed their efforts to build social services for constituents as a way to perform Islamic ethics and put the message of Islam into practice. In studies of MB-run Islamic hospitals and clinics, activists claimed that those who worked at the hospitals did so to "live the social message of the MB, not for speeches, but for the manner in which they mobilized in society;

they act with compassion and carry out service well. . . . The hospital is itself a message . . . we establish the idea and then people can see that it is a good idea, and they implement it themselves (Vannetzel 2016a, 296; see also Brooke 2017). While studies on the MB's social service institutions have tended to emphasize how these institutions allowed the movement to build trust with voters, converting socioreligious credit into political capital, activists in Vannetzel's study considered their work to build service capacity as helpful for both *da'wa* and electoral outreach and were as likely to see electoral institutions as helpful for the religious movement's *tamkin* as the reverse. For instance, those who developed positive reputations through services provided in Islamic hospitals were often able to recruit more people to contribute to MB-run religious service networks: in some districts with MB deputies, *tanzimi* networks organized medical caravans publicized by the local MB deputy, which then allowed the deputy to become a respected neighborhood figure who drew others to participate in and contribute to further services that he organized as acts of religious obligation (Vannetzel 2016a, 296–307). In an interview, Muhammad Habib, a future deputy general guide and parliamentary leader for the MB, stated that local service brokers were community ambassadors for the MB, and that, if the Brothers could show what they were able to do for the community via parliamentary work, they would build more trust and support in community networks (Vannetzel 2016a, 212). MB activists involved in public work argued that social Islamization could happen through community work or parliamentary work. For these activists, social work was not subsumed under or secondary to electoral work, but rather worked in parallel toward the same goals (349–50).

New social and political arenas offered new fields in which to pursue social Islamization. The MB leadership contended that while the movement was ready for the stage of *tamkin* or empowerment, this could be achieved by extending the movement's established, pragmatic, bottom-up approach to a wider social sphere instead of through a control of political institutions, but for the same ends. Political tools and institutions mattered because they allowed the movement to spread its ideas more effectively, and these ideas and their influence on people were more responsible for electoral success than any political work.[17] The leadership, therefore, reconciled its increasing comfort with politics and state institutions with its commitment to the *da'wa* mission as a priority by remaining committed to the idea that political and *da'wa* work required, and promoted, the same kinds of *tarbiya*. However, by 2007, the argument that politics did not require a distinct kind of training and strategy began to face increasing criticism from younger MB activists. These activists supported the decision to contest new elections in 2007–8 as a way of working for the public good, but asserted that ethical performance could not be the only criterion for nominating candidates, and that failing to reward and develop political skill while granting tickets only to those members who performed a "disinterested" kind of piety was ultimately self defeating for the movement's ability to attain and use state power (Vannetzel 2016a, 383, 405–11). They were frustrated by the mid-level leadership's lack of political savvy and promotion norms within the movement that depended more on organizational preservation than political experience and became more open in their criticisms of the *tanzimi* leadership and its inflexibility, notably through online media and blogs (324–85). When some activists argued that pragmatically cooperating with other political factions and doing more to empower people to transform society, beyond just building their religious cultivation, was necessary for the movement to be able to build a more just society, they were disciplined by the *tanzimi* leadership for disobedience (Vannetzel 2016a, 324–85; Wickham 2013, 106–13, 131–37).

The Mubarak regime changed electoral rules, jailed MB leaders, and introduced constitutional amendments in 2006 that aimed to clip the MB's wings once more, most notably requiring legal party membership for representation in parliament and banning parties formed "on a religious basis" (Wickham 2013, 120–23). This pushed the MB leadership to present a party platform in public for the first time ever and to show its

---

17. Rafiq Habib, "Al-ikhwan wa marhalat al-tamkin," IkhwanOnline, March 28, 2006, https://www.ikhwanonline.com/article/19081.

commitment to the democratic process, with strong incentives to separate religious and political work (International Crisis Group 2008, 12–16). Yet the platform that the MB leadership presented continued to center religious motivations and values in democratic politics, while accepting the institutional structures of electoral democracy. In an interview, deputy general guide Mohammed Habib stated that while the *gama'a*'s ideology and the party program emphasized different tools, they both shared a moral and religious ideology, because politics that was not grounded in faith would not succeed, as it would be purely Machiavellian. He also described politics as work that could be a form of worship and increase the effectiveness of the movement's ideological mission, rather than something separate from it.[18]

Despite substantial pressure and political incentives to the contrary, the draft party platform that the movement leadership issued and circulated to the press and to intellectuals in 2007 reflected the movement's directive discourse that grounded politics in religious norms, while acknowledging the compatibility of modern electoral and state institutions with these norms. One draft, published in an independent newspaper under the title of the program of the Party of the Muslim Brothers, upheld the ideal of "the people" as bearers of a collective burden for reform (*'aba' yujib an ahmaluhu al-jami' li-l-islah*) and emphasized that Islamic values accepted the equality of all citizens and nondiscrimination between them on the basis of religion, gender, or color, declaring freedom a "gift from God" and the natural right of all citizens.[19] The platform affirmed a number of principles for a democratic, constitutional state, including majority rule, separation of powers, judicial independence, and the right to free association, by citing their religious foundations, rather than their roots in a positivist, liberal tradition. For instance, a constitutional state was effective for protecting the God-given gift of human freedom, and "God's pronouncement that consultation (*shura*) between them is imperative" meant that

---

18. Ethar Shalaby, "Freedom Ends When It Violates the Freedom of Others, Says MB Deputy Head," *Daily News Egypt*, August 27, 2007.

19. "Barnamij hizb 'Al-Ikhwan al-Muslimin': mabadi'," *al-Masry al-Youm*, August 10–11, 2007.

the *umma* was required to consult to achieve the general welfare, and that it was the source of authority, with the right to dismiss whoever breached the contract between it and those in authority (part 1, points 9 and 11). Accountability and *shura* were, in this framing, religious obligations that could be discharged through democratic institutions, which were not valuable in and of themselves, but only if they operated within the boundaries and for the goals of Islam. The section on principles similarly made the case that the goal of an Islamic political party was to solve the nation's problems (particularly tyranny and corruption), in accordance with the principles of Islamic sharia, the human being was the primary goal of development, charged with executing God's requirements, and that, therefore, the program's goal was to build the individual Egyptian to constitute the means for change (part 1, points 6–7).

In subsequent sections on the goals and policies proposed by a new MB political party, the platform also argued that the state was obliged to implement article 2, which held that the principles of sharia were the main source of legislation in Egypt, in addition to undertaking political and constitutional reform that affirmed the principle of rotation of power; to establish a state of institutions and a rule of law; and to diffuse and deepen the true concepts of Islam as a comprehensive system for all aspects of life (part 2, points 1–4). Echoing the *Fi Nur al-Islam* curriculum's framing of the empowerment (*tamkin*) and implementation (*tanfidh*) of sharia as important reasons to embrace the state, the platform also laid out the goals of a party or any elected authority in terms that were defined by Islamic ideals of justice and welfare. For instance, the platform said that the state was obliged to apply Islam to productive work by making solidarity (*takaful*) and religious tithing for charity (*zakat*) key pillars of its economic policy and prohibiting exploitation, corruption, coercion, and usury so that Muslims could worship God through righteous behavior and serve as the drivers (*muharrak*) of a just, Islamic economy (part 3, point 4). The state's job was to strengthen national security and revive the Egyptian economy; to provide a dignified life for the citizen, while developing a sound educational system for the formation (*takwin*) and upbringing (*tanshi'*) of upright citizens; and to protect belief and worship (part 3, point 10; part 4, points 3–4).

By emphasizing the state's duty to cultivate and empower righteous citizens and free them to push for institutional reform, while presenting the function of its main representative and executive institutions as enacting Islamic norms of *shura* and justice, the platform hewed closely to internal, directive discourse on the implementation of an Islamic state as something that relied on religiously guided activism by individuals more than on specific kinds of institutions. An MB parliamentary leader affirmed this principle when he argued that people must have freedom before the movement was able to call for the application of sharia (Wickham 2013, 137). However, one draft of the platform controversially proposed a religious review mechanism for ensuring that the state's legislation and policies conformed to sharia: reviving an older proposal from the MB's history, it called for an advisory council of senior religious scholars (*haya' kubar al-'ulama*), elected freely by religious scholars (*'ulama*) from among licensed religious scholars and preachers, to offer its recommendations to the legislature on the sharia compliance of proposed laws. The MB framed this proposed council as an effort to make already existing religious authority in Egypt more democratic and accountable to the nation and to religious expertise, rather than to an authoritarian regime, and emphasized that this council would be independent of the executive in all ways and part of a broader initiative to allow more autonomy to religious institutions like *awqaf* (endowments) and al-Azhar.[20] This proposal was strongly condemned by both external political actors and younger MB activists, for the former because it potentially instituted religious control over elected government, and for the latter because it represented a barrier to alliances with other opposition actors, which were necessary, in their view, to win elections. Yet all agreed on the importance of pursuing state and electoral empowerment as a means of instituting more godly governance.

Middle-generation activists who were growing more influential in the *tanzimi* leadership sought to reassure those both within the movement and

---

20. "Ikhwan Misr yu'atarafun bi-khata' fi barnamijuhum li-l-hizb al-siyasi hawl 'haya' al-'ulama' al-muqtaraha," *al-Sharq al-Awsat*, October 16, 2007.

on the outside of it who worried about the potential shift that the platform signaled, from a bottom-up to a top-down approach to social Islamization, that the state would remain subsidiary to the religious goals and obligations of individual Muslims in the MB's vision. Essam el-Erian, a middle-generation activist via student and syndicate politics who had become the head of the MB's political committee, formed in 2005, wrote a tract in 2007–8 titled "The Muslim Brothers and the Concept of the State" that laid out the Brothers' vision of the Islamic state as one very much in line with both internal, directive discourse on accountability and individual moral agency, and external democratic norms.[21] The tract argued that the state could serve its intended goals in Islam through the institutions of democratic politics: applying the principles of sharia, defined as justice, and just rule that brought everyone closer to God, using the freedoms and *shura* allowed by parliaments and constitutions to ensure that rulers and ruled alike were accountable to God's law. Moreover, the state could undertake jihad by building strength to defend the nation from its enemies. Erian reaffirmed that the movement's ideal for an Islamic state was a civil state, with the *umma* as its source of authority and accountability, and no class of people above any other in terms of religious authority—anyone could acquire and apply religious knowledge, and the ruler was only owed obedience through his contract with the people. Erian listed some specifically collective religious obligations that the state must undertake, that individuals could not themselves perform, such as the duty to think of citizens' afterlives (*ma'aduhum*) as well as their livelihoods (*ma'ashuhum*); it was also obliged to spread the *da'wa* of Islam and to care for and protect citizens and motivate society to uphold and fulfil its duties under religion. The state's duty to uphold belief, he contended, could be translated in practical terms (*al-tarjuma al-'amaliyya li-l-wadhifa al-'aqidiyya*) by its ability to build a sound Islamic society (*bina' al-mujtama'*), one of the stages in Banna's project of social Islamization), which would depend on its ability to achieve the good for the people and establish equity and

---

21. Essam el-Erian, "Al-Ikhwan al-Muslimin wa mafhum al-dawla," Fikercenter, November 8, 2007.

justice between them, while learning from all kinds of political experiences and schools of thought (*madhahib*). When the state fulfilled its obligations under Islam, it could serve as what Banna had termed "a state of the message" (*dawlat al-risala*), an exemplar to the rest of the world for its justice, freedom, equality, and preservation of human rights and dignity, and an exemplar of Islam.

Both this document and the 2007 electoral platform drafts presented the state and its institutions as places where a political leadership committed to upholding Islam could do good, and as resources to expand *tarbiya* and to allow righteous citizens opportunities for empowerment. Directive discourse in this period urged Islamic activists to target their work at representative institutions and norms that allowed pious citizens to hold rulers accountable, rather than executive power, which had its ideal function and duties but would not carry them out without popular mobilization. Getting the state to command the right (*al-amr bi-l-ma'ruf*) through its laws and executive authority were eventual goals, but not the purpose of Islamic activism in the short term. Activists were encouraged to use public institutions and gain political and economic skills to be able to deliver justice and do good for people on a larger scale than previously, both to fulfill their own religious obligations and to show people what Islam could achieve.

Conclusion

Institutional incentives and intramovement politics in the 1990s and early 2000s shaped the movement leadership's framing of its mission in electoral politics, without fundamentally changing its goal of putting religious cultivation at the center of all political work. Both the reformist middle-generation leadership and the *tanzimi* faction believed that forming political parties and expanding electoral participation would allow the Brothers to work for a godly society in new, and more effective, ways. Reformist activists and bloggers who were disciplined for their criticism of the leadership and, in some instances, left the movement in 2008 because of their frustration with the leadership's resistance to internal democratization, tended to disagree on methods and priorities for the movement's political strategy, more than on the meaning of political work. They believed that pragmatic alliances and organizational separation between political and religious leaderships would be more effective for the political success that the MB needed in order to do good and to offer a successful model of just, Islamic rule to people, and they argued that the *tanzim*'s refusal to see political skill as something distinct from religious cultivation was self defeating (Wickham 2013, 132–35). While those who were more open to pragmatic, alliance-based political strategies than those focused on preserving the organization frequently broke away from the movement leadership, they did not necessarily come to view politics outside a moral, Islamic frame of reference as a result.

Most significantly, the political leadership that emerged out of the MB in this period was very likely to have its roots in the *tanzimi* wing of the movement. As Vannetzel (2016a, chapters 2 and 4) points out, more elected representatives through the 2005–10 period were likely to be rooted in the *tanzimi* wing and to see their work as a kind of *da'wa* than to identify with the reformist wing of the MB. Movement leaders keen on preserving the organizational hierarchy subsumed political work, and training for political outreach, under the aegis of regular movement *tarbiya* and *da'wa* and incorporated the more practical, piecemeal ideals of how to apply or implement sharia that MB deputies had developed in parliament into regular movement work. The fact that *tanzimi* leaders found politics important enough to restructure *tarbiya* around it, and yet potentially divisive enough to want to control what young members learned about it, suggests that they were willing to adapt their vision of religious work for politics, as long as it did not challenge the primacy of *da'wa* or of their own leadership. If anything, embracing political and social outreach and *tamkin* as an operational priority to enable *da'wa* and social *tarbiya*, rather than an eventual, natural consequence of these processes, made political work more credible and welcome among a broader internal base. It also ensured that welfarist outreach, via charitable work or electoral networks, remained a key part of the education of movement members, and that political skills were seen as enhancing rather than distracting from an activist's spiritual development. A more "pragmatic conservative" leadership in the MB even became open to arguments for separating the organizational and financial wings of *da'wa* and electoral initiatives, while rejecting arguments that the MB should take a more assertively oppositional stand against the Mubarak regime (Wickham 2013, 144–47; Crisis Group 2008, 19).

This evolution is important in understanding the MB's choices in 2011, when an uprising that overthrew Mubarak created new incentives for fuller electoral engagement and offered opportunities for substantial control of executive power. The *tanzim*'s insistence on keeping any MB-run political party under its control, staffed by those who reflected the priorities of the organizational hierarchy, arguably had its roots in this period. The leadership's framing of political work as a kind of spiritual and social *tarbiya* and focus on recognizing and rewarding pious action also explained why the project of Islamic revival that the Brothers and their new Freedom and Justice Party proposed in the following years focused more on individual spirituality than on generating substantive new policy proposals. Highlighting individual religious achievements and interpersonal skills as the movement's main mode of signaling its political capacity to wider publics also kept the movement and its new party tethered to a grassroots strategy that depended on being able to deliver welfare goods and be recognized for it. Rooting political work in the language and logic of religious virtue also reduced opportunities for pragmatic compromise, and a reduced policy agenda further reduced alliance-building possibilities with other opposition parties after 2011. The project of the Islamic revival, once given an opportunity on the national stage, reflected some of these adaptive weaknesses, as the next chapter will discuss.

5

Shura, Sharia, Shar'iyya

Applying Islam in Government

The Egyptian uprising of January and February 2011 that resulted in the removal of president Hosni Mubarak dramatically changed the strategic and political context in which the MB had operated. While for decades electoral majorities and control of executive power had remained a distant possibility, and a cautious, survivalist strategy was justified as necessary for upholding the *da'wa* mission, the MB transitioned, in quick succession, from a semilegal movement to a legal party, then to part of a majority coalition in parliament, then to controlling the presidency in the 2011–12 period and leading the assembly that drafted a new constitution late in 2012. While the Supreme Council of the Armed Forces (SCAF) took over a guardianship of government from Mubarak and manipulated the transition process to limit challenges to its power, access to governing power nevertheless allowed the MB to show, for the first time, what its project for Islamic governance might look like. With *tamkin* finally a real possibility, how did new political incentives and choices affect the way the MB framed its goals of applying sharia and governing according to Islam, and how did the leadership frame older concepts of righteous action for an era of power-seeking?

In this chapter, I will show how the MB leadership used older frames of righteous action to justify large-scale political work and power-seeking, upheld religious cultivation as a key tool for electoral skill building in a new training curriculum, and mobilized pious outreach work and social credit-building as effective electoral strategies. Despite some internal pressure to separate and professionalize party work from movement work, the *tanzimi* leadership maintained control of both and ensured that the newly formed

Freedom and Justice Party's selection and promotion norms and its priorities were continuous with those of the *gamaʻa*. The Brothers and their party continued to develop political strategy with religious ideals in mind and to assign religious value to political work, even responding to electoral competition—notably from newer Islamic parties—by positioning themselves more publicly as the best defenders of Islam for a pious nation, and promoting themselves electorally through their reputation for religiously creditable social work more than policy-oriented electoral programs. Leaders prioritized upholding their position as a premier voice of Islam above forming the kinds of pragmatic election coalitions that could have allowed for more durable political victories, but at the cost of some religious commitments. Under pressure to define concrete Islamic policies with competition from other parties and as the winners of parliamentary and presidential elections, they continued to champion sharia, both externally and internally, as something that could be applied by upright people committed to economic justice and good governance and capitalized on opportunities to influence executive power by following older visions of *tamkin* that emphasized installing upright Muslims in positions of authority. They also upheld older commitments to using the power of the state, where possible, to ensure that the state protected and promoted Islam. When given the opportunity to steer the writing of a new constitution, MB leaders defended democratic norms and *shura* as essential to a state governed by Islam, while introducing rules and institutions meant to prevent the violation of sharia following the norms of popular Islamic constitutionalism they had asserted in the 1990s. As I will show, the MB and its government's response to popular opposition, and its eventual overthrow in a military coup, framed *sharʻiyya* or the legitimacy of rule in terms of defenders and enemies of both the people and Islam, and the movement's short-lived experience in political power influenced its understanding of the Islamic project and of individual religious obligations in the political arena.

The 2011 Uprising and the Promise and Perils of Legalization

When public opposition to Hosni Mubarak snowballed into mass street protests that eventually forced his resignation early in 2011, the MB leadership remained cautious in participating despite pressure from younger members and only endorsed protests when it became clear that Mubarak would not remain in power. Movement leaders initially continued private negotiations with political authorities to figure out how best to protect themselves, quickly agreeing to negotiate with Mubarak's deputy as he was about to resign, and later with the military council that replaced him, rather than associating themselves with revolutionaries (Wickham 2013, 154–66). There was a great deal of uncertainty in the transitional process: political parties were legalized, but the transitional military leadership retained some ongoing control of legislation and cobbled together an interim constitution with important gaps in defining the role of elected and unelected executive authority (Brown 2012b, 8–9). Yet the electoral system chosen by the transitional regime rewarded organized political parties more than the prior model, which had emphasized individual candidates and rewarded independents (4). Legalization offered some clear benefits to the movement, notably in reducing the threat of arbitrary arrests and detention and making the Brothers' message formally available to the mass public, but it also potentially exposed the movement's membership structure and finances to the public eye. Thus, even as it chose to form a party, the MB refused to register itself as a legal social organization in 2011 (Vannetzel 2017, 219–21). In choosing to establish a political party, the MB leadership capitalized on an opportunity for legal protection and empowerment while protecting the primacy of *da'wa* and the organizational hierarchy and practices of the *gama'a*.

In the weeks following Mubarak's overthrow, the leadership decided to form the Freedom and Justice Party, repeating the wary promise of "participation, not domination" that it had used in prior years to reassure the regime that it would not seek to use electoral success to shake up the political order. While acknowledging a need to rethink its political strategy and listen to younger members as part of the transition to formal party status, the leadership also affirmed the *tanzim*'s control over the party hierarchy. Younger members who saw the uprising against Mubarak as a chance to push for more transparency and participation within the movement held a public conference in April to propose changes in the MB's internal organization and by-laws; some lobbied for a political party that would be independent of the *gama'a*.¹ While it recognized the need to get members on board with a new political party and its specific norms, even going so far as to organize a "listening campaign" and online survey of movement youth under the aegis of deputy general guide Khairat al-Shater, the leadership was committed to keeping the party's and movement's mission unified (Martini, Kaye, and York 2012, 45–46). Younger leaders who wanted a separate political party, or multiple Islamic parties for the Brothers to choose between, including former parliamentary leaders like Ibrahim al-Zaafarani and Abdel Moneim Abou el-Fotouh, were expelled from the MB, and youth leaders who proposed broader initiatives under the umbrella of the MB umbrella were either disciplined or removed as well (Wickham 2013, 182–83; Mellor 2017, 194–202; Ardovini 2021, 145). The FJP party leadership was formally separate from that of the MB, but consisted mainly of MB leaders who resigned their leadership positions in the *gama'a* in order to serve the party, like Mohammed el-Beltagy (Martini, Kaye, and York 2012, 47; Wickham 2013, 174–75). Even as the party was carefully nonexclusionary, issuing statements that invited "all forces concerned with this homeland" to work with it, its leaders affirmed that its mission was a continuation of the *gama'a*'s: leader Mahmoud Ghozlan declared in an interview that the party had been formed "to serve our ideas and our wider mission (*risala*)," which was a "matter of belief (*'aqida*)" (Wickham 2013, 175).

External as well as internal messaging reiterated the idea that the party was meant to serve faith. In a pamphlet distributed at mosques in April 2011, produced under the aegis of the general guide, with the slogan "Listen to Us, Not about Us," and the title "Who Are We and What Do We Want?," the MB repeated its traditional description of its mission for new audiences: as bearers of a Salafi call, a Sunni method, and a Sufi truth, as well as advocates of "Islamic" values in government, such as justice, kindness, the general interest, and stronger morals, and supporters of entrepreneurship and "clean profits."² It reaffirmed older MB commit-

---

1. Noha el-Hennawy, "Political Freedom, Competition Drives Rifts between Muslim Brotherhood Factions," *Egypt Independent*, March 24, 2011.

2. "Al-ikhwan al-muslimin . . . Man nahnu? Wa madha nurid?," Ikhwanonline, April 2011, https://www.ikhwanonline.com/article/237677 (accessed April 28, 2023).

ments to *da'wa* and "constitutional struggle" and asserted that "working for Islam, according to the Ikhwan," meant reforming oneself, guiding society, and reforming government until it was just. The pamphlet also repeated the idea that the Brothers' project, rather than being a partisan cause, extended to all Muslims, who must all make sacrifices for the Islamic cause and guide people to the good.

The new Freedom and Justice Party's platform similarly echoed traditional MB understandings of moral reform as the key to social Islamization, stating that its mission in politics was focused on faith, spirituality, and moral politics as essential (*jawhari*) concerns. It declared that the FJP believed that politics was not a necessarily amoral pursuit, but could and should be moral, driven by the goals of achieving justice, progress, and virtue for all people. Reform must be internal (*batini*) as well as external (*dhahir*), and the party's program must begin with purifying souls, ennobling morals, inculcating good values, and encouraging self-monitoring so that people could achieve these goals.[3] The platform also echoed older movement arguments for social and political institutions offering new resources to serve the cause of moral reform and education: mosques, churches, homes, schools, and media could carry out many of these responsibilities, the party suggested, also noting that the *minhaj* it proposed was supported by Christianity as well as Islam. The state and its legislative capacity and oversight institutions would carry out the remaining ethical formation that was needed for social reform, but still with a religious end: the platform cited the hadith used in the *Fi Nur al-Islam* curriculum saying that God revealed through a sultan what He could not through the Quran.

Internally Reframing Movement Training and Political Work

Internally, the movement leadership framed political work to members as an opportunity to achieve long-sought goals, but only if they remained

---

3. "Al-bab al-awwal min barnamij Hizb al-Hurriya wa-l-'Adala," *al-Masry al-Youm*, April 5, 2011.

committed to the *gama'a* as the primary pathway through which this could be done. After the leadership's decision to form the political party and to discipline those who sought to work outside the ambit of the *gama'a*'s hierarchy, deputy general guide Khairat al-Shater addressed young members in a speech in Alexandria in April 2011 titled "The Features of Nahda (Renaissance): Gains of the Revolution and Horizons for Developing," in which he insisted that the much-sought-after Islamic renaissance required the movement to rely on the same organizational methods and goals that it always had.[4] The "constants" of the movement's mission remained: making all of life subject to God's will, while "variables" in the form of modified methods and strategies were needed to achieve goals in new circumstances. The stages of *da'wa* remained unchanged, he declared: the group's main goal continued to be to build Muslim society and promote the *nahda* (renaissance) through individual cultivation. The post-uprising era meant that the movement was also now committed to maintaining the gains of the January 25 revolution. While noting that the Brothers now had the opportunity to build a Muslim society at the same time that they sought a Muslim state, and while affirming that politics was important in undoing a great failure in Muslim history, which was the replacement of "Islamic" with non-Islamic states, Shater nevertheless argued that the *gama'a*, not a political party, remained the organizational tool of choice to achieve this goal. A political party, as an instrument of competition for the sake of power, borne of Western experience, could never replace the *gama'a* as an instrument of integration, borne of the Islamic experience, he stated, but rather must remain subordinated to the *gama'a*'s mission and serve as one of its instruments.

A strong individual formation, both psychological and spiritual, accompanied by strong organizational discipline and commitment, were necessary to build the kind of person who could work for the *nahda*, Shater

---

4. Khairat al-Shater, "Mashru' al-nahda al-islami," YouTube video, 1:32:03, April 24, 2011, https://www.youtube.com/watch?v=JnSshs2qzrM; translation available at Hudson Institute, Current Trends in Islamist Ideology, vol. 13, https://www.hudson.org/national-security-defense/khairat-al-shater-on-the-nahda-project-complete-translation- (accessed April 28, 2023).

declared: a pious person outside of the Brotherhood was not equivalent to a Brother. Similarly, while new political freedoms permitted the *gamaʿa* to work for the *nahda*, free of the state repression it had suffered for decades, the movement's lessons from survival under repression remained valuable for its current strategies. Implicitly rebuking members who sought to separate political organization from the main *gamaʿa*, Shater reminded the young audience that the movement structure had required tremendous sacrifice to preserve itself in the face of repression and should not be taken for granted. The *gamaʿa* and its organizational strength were needed to rally the *umma* as a whole to work for revival and to empower God's law, rather than only working for Brothers. As such, expanding the MB's public influence required reinforcing, not reducing the role of the organization.

In arguing that public outreach was the work of all Muslims, not specialized leaders, Shater used the language of *fard kifaya* or collective religious obligation to fold political work into the broader mission of the *gamaʿa*. While emphasizing that the *gamaʿa* must reexamine its interactions with Muslim society more widely and was at a stage of transformation, Shater explicitly rejected political specialization as a path forward. Promising that different visions for the movement's future would be discussed via *shura* and calling on all members to offer their suggestions for improvement, he nevertheless warned members to be patient about achieving change and painted dissidents as people who refused to accept a majority decision. Another deputy guide, Mahmoud Ezzat, in a speech at the opening of an MB office, reiterated the argument that the *nahda* project was grounded in Islam and did not have a separate political logic, confirming that the *gamaʿa* and the party would work together for political goals: Brothers would be models to the nation in carrying out the *nahda* project, while the FJP would provide a positive model of party practice and ethics.[5]

The *gamaʿa* was, in Vannetzel's (2017, 219–21, 233) words, "transposed" on to the party in its personnel, ideas, and organizational norms,

---

5. "Na'ib al-murshid: al-mashruʿ al-islami alladi tahmiluhu al-jamaʿa 'taklif allah,'" *al-Masry al-Youm*, June 20, 2011.

despite outward signs of separation. The FJP had a separate slogan ("We Bring Good to Egypt") that nonetheless reflected the MB religious ideal that charity had both spiritual and social merit, and while leaders formally resigned their positions in the *gama'a*'s guidance bureau before taking up party leadership positions, they were generally selected for party positions by *tanzim* leaders (223). According to a senior MB leader who took on a founding role in the FJP leadership, the party consciously set out to recruit nonmovement members and set the target of 30 percent of members who would be from outside the movement.[6] Yet FJP cadres were primarily selected from within local MB sections, with those who had distinguished themselves in religious ethics favored over those with political experience and skills, as politically savvy and ambitious members were seen as risky choices (220, 224). Most members acknowledged that the *tanzim* remained in charge of the party, and that the *gama'a*'s approval was important for promotion within the FJP. Those who were loyal to the organization (*sahib al-thiqqa*) were valued more than those who were distinguished for being capable (*sahib al-kafa'*) (Martini, Kaye, and York 2012, 44).

Cultivating Muslim Workers for the Political Sphere

The movement recognized and encouraged political specialization as a necessity for a well-functioning party and offered training that allowed members to choose a party track in 2011, without removing political work completely from the ambit of spiritual guidance. According to MB activists I interviewed, in the months following the formation of the FJP the MB held camps similar to their regular summer camps (*mu'askar*) in which members would set their goals for the coming period and consider how to achieve them, and at the end of every session, they were asked to choose whether they wished to be in the party or not; if they did, they would specialize in political work only and not participate in *da'wa*, but if they wished to work for the poor, be in charge of charitable fairs (*ma'arid*), or carry out educational programs for youngsters, they were put

---

6. Interview, AD, Cairo, September 25, 2013.

into separate divisions.⁷ There was separate training tailored to those with different skills, capabilities, and interests in social work, whether in the contexts of party work, *da'wa*, or syndicate activism.⁸ Training and organizational assignments continued to be divided between party and movement structures. The FJP mirrored the MB organizationally in requiring a pledge of allegiance (*baya'*) from new members and setting up a cultivation office (*lagnat al-tathqif*) similar to the MB's *tarbiya* bureau (Vannetzel 2017, 225). The FJP offered its own separate training for full-time party members, focusing on effective communication, electoral and administrative skills, and "marketing" candidates, often provided by external professionals such as university experts.⁹

But political training was also incorporated into regular movement *usra* sessions, and, in embracing electoral politics wholesale, the *tanzim* changed how the average member was taught about their collective and practical religious obligations as well. Younger MB activists reported that where, previously, *usra* sessions were divided fairly equally between time spent on religious training and on discussion of social and charitable work, after 2011 politics took up more time, in part because of the quick succession of elections following the uprising.¹⁰ One argued that the greater participation of Brothers in political work was a natural adaptation to the social and political opening that the 2011 uprisings made possible, and that the formation of the FJP had allowed members to work with currents and people that they had not previously been able to, while renewing its tools (*uslub*) for a new context.¹¹ Youth activists noted that the movement's educational wing introduced two new kinds of training materials for activists that updated the kind of pious activism that they believed would be needed for a new era. Some training curricula were aimed at younger student activists who would be cultivated as leaders, and one general curriculum, titled *Fann al-ta'mul ma' al-mujtama'* (The Art of

---

7. Interview, AS, Cairo September 29, 2013.
8. Interview, AK, Cairo, May 8, 2013.
9. Interview, AD, Cairo, September 25, 2013; interview, AK, Cairo, May 8, 2013.
10. Interview, AB, Cairo, September 24, 2013; interview, AS, Cairo, September 29, 2013.
11. Interview, AB, Cairo, September 24, 2013.

Dealing with Society) was aimed at all members, replacing the previous series of *Fi Mabadi' al-Islam*, *Fi Rihab al-Islam*, and *Fi Nur al-Islam* texts, and offering a general overview of positive and productive religiously guided social outreach. These texts were assigned for the "variable" current affairs element of *usra* education sessions that were determined by the *tarbiya* committee and accompanied the "constants" of religious education that all members continued to receive: for example, studying the Quran, the life of the Prophet.[12] Movement activists whom I interviewed largely perceived the updated texts as compatible with the *gama'a*'s traditional commitment to working for Islam in whatever sphere one could, maintaining a commitment to the comprehensiveness of Islam—a characteristic of the movement that distinguished it from more purely pietistic and more fully political Islamic movements.[13]

Updated training aimed at college students to prepare them for leadership roles after graduation in 2011 drew on religious traditions and continued to be framed as the "same education" as always, "develop[ed] . . . to be compatible with the atmosphere we are in."[14] An activist who participated in leadership training described these new curricula as directed toward qualifying Brothers educationally, psychologically, culturally, and politically to be leaders, framing the skills they could gain for and through newer social outreach in familiar terms of building stock or credit (*rasid*) with people by doing good for them, and their new role in society in older, missionizing terms of "opening society up" (*fath 'alayhu*) to preachers; whereas they had studied and prepared themselves theoretically in the past, the field was now open for practical application and for a new stage, without any change in the vision that guided the movement's mission.[15] Two new leadership training programs were aimed at students at different levels of education: the Usama Ibn Zayid curriculum, named after a teenaged companion of the Prophet, offered high school graduates examples

---

12. Interview, AK, Cairo, May 8, 2013.
13. Interview, AK, Cairo, May 8, 2013.
14. Interview, AB, Cairo, September 24, 2013.
15. Interview, AB, Cairo, September 24, 2013.

and models of leadership that they could learn from and emulate, as young people; and the Pillars program (*barnamij al-raka'iz*), which offered university students both theoretical and practical training in social leadership and administrative work.[16]

MB activists' experience of religious and social cultivation in this period was different from that of prior years. One activist who had been responsible for *usra* leadership noted that, whereas older curricula like *Fi Rihab al-Islam* had been more narrowly focused on piety and how to be a better person, after 2011 newer training focused on mobilization (*taharruk*) within society, for all members and not just those identified for party roles, even while reminding members that they were acting not so much for people as for God.[17] Another recalled that there was a greater emphasis in *usra* sessions on dealing with disagreement with others (*fikrat al-ikhtilaf ma' al-akhar*), and on how to manage differences through mechanisms (*'aliyat*) of cooperation and comprehension.[18] As with leadership training programs, *usra* programs ran workshops and lectures that drew lessons from the lives of historical figures in Islam, such as early followers of the prophet and caliphs like 'Umar ibn al-Khattab and 'Umar ibn 'Abdel Aziz, coupled with Quranic verses such as those in the *Surat al-Ma'ida*, as guides for proper behavior—for instance, on the protection of public property (*hurmat al-mal al-'am*); self-sacrifice (e.g., serving in syndicate leadership roles while not accepting compensation); and trustworthiness (*amana*), to show members what it meant to be exemplars of good Muslim behavior in serving the nation.[19]

The twenty-page online *Fann al-Ta'mul* curriculum,[20] which was cited by several activists as the main one used to guide movement members on working for Islam through social outreach in the post-2011 period,

---

16. Interview, AB, Cairo, September 24, 2013.
17. Interview, YS, Cairo, September 29, 2013.
18. Interview, AK, Cairo, May 8, 2013.
19. Interview, AK, Cairo, May 8, 2013.
20. "Fann al-ta'mul ma' al-mujtama," 2011, https://www.ikhwanwiki.com/index.php?title=العمل_الجماعي (accessed April 28, 2023).

described its lessons as showing people "how to employ *da'wa* in political work."²¹ Echoing older guidelines for *da'wa*, it noted that good and just dealings (*mu'amala*), equitable treatment, and coexistence with others (*al-mu'ashara al-tayyiba*) should be the movement's message and were more influential than words in reaching people and drawing them closer to God. Where earlier training had emphasized cultivating individual piety in supportive circles and enacting Islamic values in small social groups, the new curriculum urged activists to take the initiative to do good for those outside the movement, even in the face of public hostility. Citing a hadith that said it was better to "mix with people and endure their harm" in order to do good than to stay home and act righteously all by oneself, and another arguing that it was a godly value to do good to one's own people as well as to those who were not one's people so as to transform a previous enemy into one who did good to others, the curriculum emphasized winning people over to righteous causes as key to individual and collective salvation. Individuals could perform and demonstrate their piety (*taqwa*) and sound Muslim ethics (*akhlaq*) by using kindness to draw others to them: the "believing person" was described in this curriculum as "characterized by tact, decency, and gentleness" and was expected to have an optimistic, not a pessimistic, view of others.²²

The curriculum focused on cultivating an "attractive Islamic social personality" that would appeal to others through care, love, and sociability, encouraging Islamic activists to learn to wish for others what they wished for themselves and enjoy caring for others' well-being and spiritual advancement as a way of spreading the movement's message. It reiterated the hadith cited in older curricula and in prior movement messaging that "good people are those who benefit other people" (*khayr al-nas ma' nafa' al-nas*), to make the case that an ability to win people's affections would allow activists new resources that could enable them to do further good.²³ The text laid out a variety of everyday scenarios in which a Muslim activist could spread goodwill and do *da'wa* by following the *adab*

---

21. Interview, AS, Cairo, September 29, 2013.
22. "Fann al-ta'mul ma' al-mujtama'."
23. "Fann al-ta'mul ma' al-mujtama'."

(etiquette) of good Islamic behavior and dealings with others—directives such as smiling, greeting, listening, shaking hands, thanking people, and being thoughtful to friends and neighbors. These kinds of behaviors were religiously valuable, the text argued, both in building individual religious virtue and in creating a more Islamic society. Greetings and handshakes constituted acts of Islamic virtue (*sadqa*) due to the fact that thanking those who had done good (*mohsin*) was incumbent on believers; because the Creator had expressed the good through His creation, and must be thanked, in turn, through people.

The new curriculum framed actions needed to promote a more Islamic society in the new era as broadly similar to those that the movement had always encouraged. It reminded activists that while it was tempting to focus on larger questions and issues—clearly a reference to the movement's turn to power-seeking—small, everyday actions continued to matter in achieving the movement's goal of instituting the highest ethics and morals (*akhlaq*) in the world. These were up to individual Muslims to pursue, including actions like exhorting people (*al-muwa'adh*), establishing properly Islamic rules (*hukm*), spiritual tutelage (*wasaya*), and offering advice. As before, Brothers were urged to serve as positive role models for others, showing them how to do good (*qadwa ghayrak fi-l-khayr*). To build a more Islamic society, one had to make the effort to confront the bad with acts of goodness and charity (*ihsan*), best of all by eliminating want and hardship for others. A society's humanity and level of civilization could be gauged by the quality of its social dealings: advanced and good societies were those that cared for rules and order (including traffic rules). Echoing similar directive discourse in the prior *Fi Nur al-Islam* curriculum, the text argued that good acts accrued merits to the individual believer because the Prophet had said that helping a needy person was equivalent to a tour of the Kaaba in Mecca.

However, the new curriculum was more focused on the outside world than older ones. It more openly discussed and prioritized methods for persuading outsiders, including those who might be hostile to the movement, than prior teachings had done, and drew on examples from a wider range of sources, including Western philosophy, history, and psychology, to support its claims that the methods of Islam could apply universally and were compatible with and defensible against a range of belief systems. While framing the targets of public outreach as people who might be broadly unsympathetic to Islamists, the text contended that good interaction (*hasn al-ta'mul*) was a universal value for all of humanity and encouraged activists to see winning others over as both reasonably possible and religiously desirable. Citing the prophet Mustafa alongside former US president Abraham Lincoln and the American self-help writer Dale Carnegie, the text encouraged activists to remember that they could best fight their enemies by turning them into friends. It also countered Jean-Paul Sartre's aphorism "Hell is other people," framing this kind of thinking as typical of nonbelieving societies, arguing that those who worked for Islam must cultivate the warm and caring social relations that allowed people to build more heaven-like societies. It told readers that the *gama'a* would not have expanded as it had if its members had only interacted with those who were already good Muslims, citing multiple hadith and stories of the prophets stating that mixing with people, even enduring their harm, was more meritorious for Muslims than staying away from them.

More openness to the corrupt world and society was not a sign that the movement had given up on its religious mission, however—kindness and encouragement were meant to draw others to the level of good Muslims. The curriculum noted that affection and care for others could not be unconditional or promote immorality, but must be guided by a concern for their salvation. Popularity for its own sake, as well as sycophancy, were to be avoided, so that young people did not squander their character for peer approval. Social interactions and sincere appreciation (*taqdir*) of the good that boosted everyone's goodness and character were valuable, while fawning (*tamalluq*) was not, because the former led people to God and the latter did not. Once again, righteous practice and intent were emphasized as important ways of working for God, for, even in politics, the outcome was not in human hands. One activist who had worked in political outreach stated that the curriculum taught him that "in political work, we must have honesty, we must have trust . . . [I must learn] now to put up with people's harm and be patient, how to make it so that my goal is not power or a position but more. Why do I work in politics? For God. To communicate the idea of the Islamic project, and because at the end of the day we worship God through this project. The main point is not power or position, it is to implement God's laws in Egypt . . . [and] how we build an Islamic society based on Islamic qualities, so there is honesty and trust . . . I don't care about the result of my work, or that all people join the MB. I care about communicating the message in the best way. The result is from God."[24]

Religious and Popular Credit: *Da'wa* and Capacity Building in Election Campaigns

Parliamentary elections in 2011 and presidential elections in 2012 required a much larger number of Brothers to participate in electoral outreach than prior elections had, because of the larger scale of the MB's participation. The MB leadership decided to pursue the presidency, not just a parliamentary majority, despite having initially promised not to nominate a candidate, both in response to perceived efforts by the ruling military council to downgrade Islamist parliamentary powers, and after justifying power seeking less as "succumbing to temptation [and more as] . . . accepting responsibility" (Brown 2012, 7–9). MB activists who participated saw continuities between this kind of outreach and earlier charitable work and echoed arguments present in older training documents about the convertibility of moral and social capital for different purposes in interpreting the purpose of their electoral work.

Activists recalled that while they had started to discuss political work and what could be done to build Egypt more openly in their outreach to people, whether in student politics or electoral campaigning, tapping their older repertoire of Quranic verses and hadith to support their exhortations, what gave them credibility in talking about politics was still the "stock" (*rasid*) that the movement had with people, due to prior social services and solidarity (*takaful*) work.[25] This social "credit" and the support base (*'ardiya sha'biya*) that it allowed activists to build on gave them

---

24. Interview, YS, Cairo, September 29, 2013.
25. Interview, YS and AS, Cairo, September 29, 2013.

credibility, making it possible to discuss with potential voters how the MB's strength and experience would allow them to govern well.[26] They expected, similarly, that their political outreach would be judged socially (*al-hukm li-l-mugtama'*) by the same standards as their religious and charitable outreach, and by their ability to show that they applied Islamic principles (e.g., honesty, willingness to sacrifice) that made them good Islamic role models. The kind of person who could serve as a good Islamic role model might now vary according to the arena in which he worked—for instance, in economic life, or political life.[27]

Activists continued to do social work, such as organizing charity fairs and medical service caravans, and while in previous years they might have hidden their affiliation with the MB to avoid legal sanction, in 2011–12 they were more open about this. When MB leaders organized medical caravans in 2011, before the first open parliamentary election, they reportedly distributed merchandise and goods with the FJP logo on them, leading those who had been seen previously as local do-gooders to be openly identified with the MB's political party (Vannetzel 2016b, 50–51). The movement's charitable work also adapted to the imperatives of greater public visibility: when a neighborhood MB branch proposed a public cleanliness campaign, the FJP took this over to support its electoral campaign slogan of "doing good for the people" (51–52).

Initially, this strategy worked to build support and political capacity for the movement. In the early weeks after the start of the uprising against Mubarak, MB activists had been well represented in the "popular committees" that offered social services amid disruption, working with "honest people" in neighborhoods to provide policing when policemen left the streets and using their knowledge of districts and ability to identify risks to build public goodwill. Even as they formed a political party, they had continued to be active on these committees (Acconcia and Pilati 2021, 99). Many of them were influential in persuading people to support the March 2011 referendum on a new constitution-writing process proposed by the

---

26. Interview, AS, September 29, 2013; interview, AB, September 24, 2013.

27. Interview, AK, Cairo, May 8, 2013.

SCAF, which the MB supported as more likely to entrench its influence, and popular committees generally helped people become more engaged in the political process (Meehy 2012). Some of these committees were merged into preexisting MB-run local charities (Acconcia and Pilati 2021, 100). Several voters said that they had decided to support the FJP in elections after witnessing the work that the MB had done for them, with some explicitly noting that they did so due to "the relationships of trust built up especially during the previous months of mobilization," even as some members of the popular committees decided to boycott elections (100). Reputational credit appeared to help the MB win parliamentary elections in 2011, with almost half of those who reported having received Islamic health services in the prior year responding favorably to the idea of voting for the FJP in a poll conducted in 2011 (Masoud 2014, 156). A survey of those who had received Islamist medical services the following year also found that providers took pride in offering care as an expression of justice (*'adl*), while recipients' experience of "compassionate" care helped them see the MB as more likable, again confirming the effectiveness of the *da'wa* of public works (Brooke 2017, 48–52).

While the MB's "social credit" permitted the kind of *tamkin* that movement leaders had long hoped would help build support for a more expansive Islamic political project, its partisan work hurt its social credit and image as a movement of morally upright people. A senior FJP leader noted that people who had viewed the MB's social services in transactional terms had to be gradually persuaded to support a policy-driven vision of Islam, which the movement struggled to do in its early party experience.[28] Youth activists who campaigned for the MB's presidential candidate, Mohammed Morsi, in 2012, presented his educational qualifications and experience in parliament alongside his membership in the MB as arguments for why voters should trust him to tackle their problems and do good for them.[29] Yet when notables who had helped run the MB's social service projects in 2007–10 formally joined the FJP in 2011,

---

28. Interview, AD, Cairo, September 25, 2013.
29. Interview, AS, Cairo, September 29, 2013.

community members, as reflected in Vannetzel's (2016b, 50–51) ethnographic research, started to see them as more motivated by political gain than by a general desire to do good. Further, some voters who had participated in and benefited from social services and charitable organizations in which MB personnel were major actors (including the Gam'iyya Shar'iyya) voiced skepticism of the relations of indebtedness that the MB appeared to want to build with residents, which they saw as aimed at partisan gains, and a barrier to effective governance rather than a path to it. In one study, villagers in Fayoum stated: "We need a government that recognizes our rights as citizens, not as recipients of aid! We need people that would help us get our stolen rights. If the Muslim Brotherhood come to power, they will be both the mediators and the government" (Ahmed 2012). Some rural citizens saw MB leaders as beholden to a rigid movement hierarchy more than to local people in making decisions about candidates to field, and ways to resolve local problems; Salafi charitable and *da'wa* work was seen, by contrast, as more willing to help farmers in particular secure their land rights and to forward their concerns to state authorities instead of resolving them through charitable networks (2012).

Electoral Outbidding and New Competition to Represent Islam in the Public Sphere

The MB and FJP leadership's efforts to define an Islamic policy agenda and position themselves as the most credible champions of Islamic ethics and Muslim welfare in Egyptian politics were challenged in 2011–12 by competition from the newly formed Nour Party and other Salafi parties, and by the growing politicization of conservative Islamic televangelists. As fellow Islamists, these new political actors shaped the image of Islamist politics in the public eye and competed for audiences that the MB had considered their natural constituents. Where the MB's *da'wa* had traditionally focused on persuading people through interpersonal influence and conduct to support the Islamic project, elections required larger scale, mediatized outreach, further changing the incentives of Islamic persuasion for the MB and its competitors.

Historically, the Dawa Salafiyya group, which founded the Nour Party, had avoided electoral politics as an impure undertaking, focusing instead on matters of doctrine and faith. But Salafi groups tended to use mosques run by the Gamʻiyya Sharʻiyya to provide charitable social services, just as the MB had long done (Masoud 2014, 168). Salafi preachers also became increasingly influential in the media sphere, thanks to the Islamic satellite television industry, which became popular in Egypt from 2006 onward, bolstered by Gulf Arab investment, and guided audiences not only on matters of worship but also on everyday conduct, and occasionally on how to deal with economic and social problems (Field and Hamam 2009, 7–8). Some star preachers, like Muhammad Hasan and Muhammad Yacoub, even set up charitable medical and education service networks, as the MB had, appealing to less well-off Egyptians (Anani and Malik 2013, 61). After Mubarak's overthrow and the liberalization of party licensing, several newer Salafi parties formed, including the Nour Party, the Asala Party, and the Fadhila Party, with political programs that framed their mission in terms of allowing pious Egyptians to live their faith without compromise (Hamming 2013).[30]

In their messaging on how to "work for Islam" in this new context, the MB had to persuade new audiences not only that the Islamic project was worth voting for but also that they were the best advocates and workers for its goals in politics. MB leaders recognized that they were shaping their messaging for different audiences than they had expected to in electoral politics, and that a *tarbiya*-driven approach did not suffice. A senior FJP leader explained the party's strategy to retain the pious vote thus: in order to be "realistic, you choose the narrative that resonates with people that are listening. . . . As a candidate, you'd like to attract those who really believe in the Islamic reference," even while trying to educate those who were not strict Muslims about "Islamic values, [which] were fundamentally about freedom, justice, and equality." He recognized, however, that

---

30. "With Nour Party, Salafis Attempt to Tap into Party Politics," *al-Masry al-Youm*, May 19, 2011.

there was a tension between educating people on what constituted, in the MB's view, a more "Islamic society" and reaching them, as "simple people" who loved Islam and would elect whoever they thought best represented Islamic values.[31] Newly influential Salafi preachers also challenged the MB's primacy in popular influence and competed for the affections of its own activist base, in addition to shaping public perceptions of Islamism that reflected on the MB, whether they liked it or not. Some MB activists noted that Salafi televangelist *shaykhs* like Ragheb el-Serghali, Safwat Hegazy, Muhammad Husein, and Salah Sultan were influential within the MB and inspired many young Brothers to work, and despite having no formal position in the movement, were frequently seen as its spokespersons and drove its image in the public sphere.[32] One MB youth leader also observed that the emotional connection that television preachers formed with viewers allowed them to shape political opinions, based purely on religious respect rather than political knowledge, with the implication that this influence interfered with the kind of disciplined and gradual cultivation that the MB preferred.[33]

Advocating for and Applying Sharia

While the presence of Salafi parties boosted Islamic influence in Egypt's electoral politics after 2011, particularly as the Nour Party, following elections in November 2011, unexpectedly became the second largest party in parliament after the FJP, it also pushed the MB to defend concrete policies as the most "Islamic" ones in response to external pressures. They offered justifications for why these were good ways to work for Islam post facto, often departing from the movement leadership's preferred messaging. Notably, on the question of how to apply sharia, the Salafi movement pushed for a more state-led enforcement of conservative Islamic social norms, which the MB had moved away from in its years of reframing sharia application as a matter of achieving social justice guided by divine

---

31. Interview, AD, Cairo, September 25, 2013.
32. Interview, AS and YS, Cairo, September 29, 2013.
33. Interview, AB, Cairo, September 24, 2013.

principles (Anani and Malik 2013, 63). The MB had to respond to Salafi claims to represent a popular majority that demanded state enforcement while holding on to the older idea that patient outreach and good works were more important for enacting God's will and drawing support for His cause. At a rally for sharia in the summer of 2011, Salafi protesters evoked the anti-Mubarak slogan "The people want the fall of the regime" to chant "the people want the application of God's sharia," and positioned themselves as the voice of the people against secular elites, arguing that in order to apply sharia, to build a wall around the country for its protection, the state must enact an Islamic penal code and put "one of us who fears God and governs accordingly" in charge.[34] Salafi parties also nominated a popular, sharia-focused presidential candidate, Hazem Salah Abu Ismail, who, while ultimately disqualified, pushed the MB leadership to affirm its own commitment to applying sharia more forcefully.[35]

In framing what it meant to enact and apply sharia as representatives of a pious majority, MB leaders in electoral campaigns positioned themselves as more credible and persistent defenders of sharia application than their rivals, while also trying to persuade voters to see economic and social policies as a pathway to applying sharia. The FJP's party platform presented the goals (*maqasid*) of sharia as a reference (*marja'iyya*) for the elected representatives of the Egyptian people, as well as the cornerstone of Egyptian "civilizational values," and said relatively little about legal reform, rather framing sharia-driven politics as moral politics, with good moral individuals key to a good Muslim state. The platform echoed internal directive discourse and training documents in emphasizing social and political institutions staffed by moral individuals as key to applying sharia, without much detail on policies. Repeating older arguments for using state and social power to reinforce social Islamization, it argued that mosques, schools, homes, and media, as well as churches (given the

---

34. Rime Wassim, "Islamiyya, Islamiyya," Vimeo video, 17:15, July 29, 2011, https://vimeo.com/27130745?fbclid=IwAR00gLp_OuVXuQSD4pKehiulhM9Vmcd3OoJXrH6rDCa2xnS-OA32OrHODns. .

35. Noha el-Hennawy, "Morsy Campaign Discovers Religion's Potency in Politics," *al-Masry al-Youm*, May 3, 2012.

universal applicability of the Islamic *minhaj*) must take charge of purifying souls, inculcating the right values, and ennobling people's morals. At the same time, the state and its oversight and legislative institutions would be responsible for some remaining ethical formation, following the hadith that God could reveal through a sultan what He could not through the Quran.[36] The goal for both socioreligious and state authorities was the same: to build moral individuals, whether by developing their conscience so that they would not accept bribes or commit electoral fraud and protect public funds, or by undertaking constitutional and political reform that would allow the state to build spiritually, culturally, and materially complete citizens.

MB activists who joined the party or did electoral campaign work also continued to see sharia application as a long-term project that required building economic and social justice. They contended that it was not sufficient or honest to promise to apply it at once, because this was not possible: sharia was not something that could be applied from one day to the next.[37] Their job, activists said, was to demonstrate that the Islamic project could benefit people in concrete, material ways, because, even in a naturally religious society, like Egypt's, people needed to be fed and comforted to feel safe before they could really think about and understand what sharia might look like in practice.[38] The sequence for applying sharia remained to build public support, show people what kinds of good governance upright Muslims were capable of, and demonstrate that their effectiveness was based in their ideational and religious commitments. Then, the application of sharia would happen by the "will of the street" (*tatbiq al-shari'a bi raghbat al-shari'*).[39] Thus, while those who worked for Islam must be guided by sharia and aim for its application, the path they had to follow to achieve its application had not changed. This was reflected

36. "Al-bab al-awwal min barnamij Hizb al-Hurriya wa-l-'Adala," *al-Masry al-Youm*, April 5, 2011.
37. Interview, AB, Cairo, September 24, 2013.
38. Interview, AS, Cairo, September 29, 2013; interview, AB, Cairo, September 24, 2013.
39. Interview, AS, Cairo, September 29, 2013.

in election discourse, too: publicity materials for the 2011 parliamentary campaign focused on job opportunities, inequality, education, health, and improved public services, not sharia (Masoud 2014, 138–41).

However, while MB activists sought to use work and *da'wa* to prove their integrity to people, the Nour Party's message, which Brothers described as "just sharia, sharia, sharia," threatened to outflank the pragmatic approach that the MB preferred.[40] To respond, FJP activists in the presidential campaign of 2012 also began to use the slogan "The people want the application of God's sharia" in rallies and debated televangelists on questions of sharia. For their part, MB leaders publicized meetings held with the Salafi Jurisprudence Commission for Rights and Reform over the "shape of the state and the implementation of sharia."[41] The MB invited some popular television preachers like Safwat Hegazy to speak at campaign rallies and to promise that presidential candidate Morsi would realize the dream of restoring the caliphate, while the general guide at similar rallies compared the allegiance that the nation would swear to Morsi to that which the early caliph Abu Bakr had received from the Muslim *umma*.[42] Campaign banners in many parts of Cairo also featured the names and headshots of clerics who endorsed Morsi's candidacy, leaving out the official slogan "The renaissance is the will of the people."[43]

At a campaign rally for Mohammed Morsi at Cairo University, MB leaders positioned themselves as those most capable of applying sharia in its spirit and its form. In his speech, Morsi declared that the MB's constitution had always been the Quran, and that they believed in applying sharia gradually yet comprehensively, and he asked for votes so that the movement could fulfil its pact with both God and people.[44] Leaders emphasized

---

40. Interview, Cairo, YS and AS, September 2013.

41. Maggie Michael, "Egypt Brotherhood Hopeful Promises Clerics a Role," Associated Press, April 4, 2012.

42. Noha el-Hennawy, "Morsy Campaign Discovers Religion's Potency in Politics," *al-Masry al-Youm*, May 3, 2012.

43. Field notes, May 22-24, 2012.

44. Ahmed Owais, "Al-Ikhwan yaftahun al-nar 'ala al-'ilamiyin wa yasfunuhum bi kadhbat faraon," *al-Shorouk* May 14, 2012.

the suffering and sacrifices that the MB had made to work for sharia and for God: Morsi reminded the gathered crowd that many Brothers had been jailed for the cause, while Essam el-Erian emphasized that the MB had never wavered from the path of Islam, but rather had presented an unchanged agenda year after year, in spite of state repression. Speakers at the rally also urged unity in the Islamic vote and presented the MB as the party best positioned to work for Islam and to build the nation: televangelist Ragheb el-Sirghaly called on Salafis, in particular, to support the MB candidate, reminding voters that the enemies of Islam feared the strength of a unified Islamic vote.[45] Erian, too, argued that achieving the Islamic project required unity, but he appealed to national as well as Islamic unity, promising that an FJP-led government would change the situation of the "great Egyptian people," both Muslim and Christian. Evoking older MB arguments for good governance and public welfare as applications of sharia, Erian, along with other speakers at the rally, also made the case that the Islamic project and its sharia-compliant framework for using wealth would make the country better off and could help young people become prosperous and entrepreneurs.[46]

While making efforts to position themselves as better advocates of Islam than Salafis, senior MB and FJP leadership continued to assert, in external and internal discourse, that the state's first task in working to establish sharia was to work for the public good. To build "the nation of the true Islam," MB leaders argued, they had to demonstrate the justice and value of Islamic governance.[47] A senior FJP leader similarly said that the MB's goal in politics was to "pave the environment for the real principles and basic pillars of Islamic sharia" (namely, freedom and justice) to flourish.[48] According to MB leaders in this period, moral reform and economic development both contributed to Islamic justice. Before his candidacy was disqualified for a past conviction, deputy guide Khairat al-Shater

45. Field notes, Cairo University rally, May 12, 2012.
46. Field notes, Cairo University rally, May 12, 2012.
47. Lee Keath, "Islamic Group Seeks Place in a Democratic Egypt," *Associated Press*, June 19, 2011.
48. Interview, AD, Cairo, September 25, 2013.

campaigned on the idea of a "renaissance" (*nahda*) that would allow Egypt to achieve its destiny as a leading Islamic nation, in terms that emphasized economic development as a sign of religious achievement. Launching his campaign with a rally at al-Azhar, Shater positioned the FJP as an inheritor of a prosperity-oriented Islamist tradition and himself as "New Egypt's Erdogan," promising that the FJP's economic development plans would help Egypt quadruple its national income in ten years, just as Turkey's Islamic party had done.[49] Similarly, the Nahda Project, which Shater's successor candidate Mohammed Morsi espoused as his electoral program, touted its plans for person-centered growth as the basis of national rebuilding in terms that were familiar from the MB's traditional "trickle up" approach of religious cultivation. Morsi's platform, however, focused on building the Egyptian citizen and reviving national honor by giving people access to health care, education, and the tools of comprehensive human—particularly economic—development.[50]

The project platform was full of proposals for unleashing what it argued were the creative energies of Egyptians that had been stifled by corruption, cronyism, and bureaucracy under the old regime, including public-private partnerships, and Islamic entrepreneurship associations.[51] The MB's businessmen leaders Khairat al-Shater and Hasan Malek founded an Islamic business and trade association called EBDA, in cooperation with their Turkish counterparts in 2012 and touted entrepreneurial and trade activity as Islamic action as well as a contribution to the national good. The Prophet had himself been a trader, and working for the economic development of the *umma* was a good religious act, while contributing one's *zakat* dues to EBDA was an investment in Egypt's economic growth and employment, which also contributed to the public good (Vannetzel and Yankaya 2019; Adly 2016, 74–75).

---

49. Mohamed Elmeshad, "Shater Faces Early Hiccups on Campaign Trail," *al-Masry al-Youm*, April 11, 2012.

50. Freedom and Justice Party, "Dr. Morsi's Electoral Program—General Features of the Nahda Project," April 28, 2012, https://ikhwanweb.com/dr-morsis-electoral-program/.

51. Nadine Marroushi, "Renaissance Man: Gehad El Haddad Works as the Islamist Project's Pragmatist," *Egypt Independent*, July 31, 2012.

Tamkin and the Tools of State

When the MB/FJP candidate Mohammed Morsi won the presidential election in a run-off vote in June 2012, the movement reiterated its vision of "Islamic governance" as rooted in ethically upright leadership accountable to both God and believers. Morsi's victory speech invoked the ideal of an Islamic social contract, addressing voters with statements such as "I am not the best of you, but I have been put in authority over you" and "Help me as long as I obey God in you."[52] When the SCAF reduced the powers of the president through constitutional declarations after Morsi's election, the FJP's control of policy making and cabinet appointments was limited. However, the MB argued that they would use such tools of state as were available to them alongside the grassroots services and public welfare work and religious education that they would continue to carry out in order to uphold and apply God's sharia. Echoing traditional movement commitments to appointing upright people to positions of power, the FJP-led government prioritized installing loyal Islamists in positions where they might be able to make a difference, yet these opportunities were limited. Where the government was able to set policy on morality in media and education, it did so, but on matters affecting the economy, it framed growth and public welfare as part and parcel of the end goals of Islamic policy. The constituent assembly was the one sphere where Islamists could use their parliamentary majority to set the parameters of future policy and legislation, and they took this opportunity to define the institutional and legal framework they envisioned for an Islamic state.

On policy matters, MB leaders perceived the job of government as similar to that of the movement on the ground, using different means to work for popular welfare and justice and to allow people to live a life that brought them closer to Islam. For instance, despite the fact that the

---

52. Field notes, Cairo, June 24, 2012. For a recording and translated transcript, see "Egyptian President-Elect Mohamed Morsi in Victory Speech: I Will Be the President of All Egyptians," al-Tahrir TV, June 24, 2012, https://www.memri.org/tv/egyptian-president-elect-mohamed-morsi-victory-speech-i-will-be-president-all-egyptians.

minister of trade and supply, who was responsible for distributing subsidized bread, was an MB appointee, MB and FJP activists continued to work through their grassroots service networks to distribute subsidized food to the poor, on the grounds that their work was a form of jihad that also allowed them to build trust and to transform society at the grassroots and yet was ultimately a religious act for God to judge in the hereafter (Naguib 2015, 65). FJP party activists appointed themselves "vigilantes" to monitor subsidized bread outlets to ensure that bread reached the poor and was not sold to mafias, stating that they did so because God cared about fair distribution.[53] Similarly, they set up soccer tournaments for working-class youth to demonstrate what "clean" alternatives to old, corrupt state institutions, of which the national soccer system was famously one, could look like (Rommel 2018).

Even after winning control of a hamstrung government, the FJP continued to carry out grassroots service campaigns aimed at showing people what Islamic governance could deliver and increasing support for the cause, such as the campaign Together We Build Egypt, in which MB activists carried out school refurbishment, medical caravans, and street cleaning campaigns (Brooke 2018, chapter 7).[54] All of this, activists declared, was work for sharia: one student Brother said that he considered the MB-appointed minister of trade and supply, Bassem Ouda, to be "a living example of the application of sharia" because he had worked to get the people "bread and social justice," and that the "ministry of supply is sharia."[55] Activists and FJP leaders similarly argued that government initiatives, such as redeveloping the Suez Canal corridor, improving education and health care, and pursuing self-sufficiency as necessary for a dignified life, were part of a model of Islamic justice and good governance and could win people over to

---

53. Tom Perry and Abdel Rahman Youssef, "Egypt's Brotherhood Turns to Flour Power," Reuters, June 13, 2013.

54. Freedom and Justice Party, "Ready for Parliamentary Elections, Condemning Violence," Ikhwanweb, February 17, 2013, https://ikhwanweb.com/freedom-and-justice-party-conf/.

55. Interview, AS, Cairo, September 29, 2013.

the Islamic cause, folding governance into older understandings of *tamkin* that grew the ranks of committed Muslims.[56]

MB/FJP leaders were under pressure from Salafis and some of their own movement members to use their control of state institutions to uphold religious and social morality, which they did on matters of gender norms and media standards. On issues like tourism, interest-bearing loans, and alcohol, however, they argued that mixed effects on public welfare warranted a more nuanced approach. MB leaders on both political and preaching fronts assured the public that the priorities of sharia were to end corruption and police abuse and to work for the public welfare before banning specific expressions of immorality, because "wherever you find benefit for society, then that is God's law."[57] They promised to protect the tourism industry and to not impose dress codes for women, insisting that they would only consider limits on alcohol consumption if there were eventual popular support for it, in order to not hurt the economy while seeking to bring good to Egypt.[58] The Morsi government, on the other hand, promoted "halal tourism" with alcohol-free resorts that could attract pious tourists even from Shiʿa-majority Iran, as an example of economic development that was based on Islamic values and could therefore enact many forms of the good (Gamblin 2015, 143, 150–51). Similarly, on issues related to media and culture, FJP leaders assured the public that the MB would not oppose the freedom of artistic expression, but instead use their new institutional resources to promote a more Islamically focused kind of art that represented the "true" national heritage, producing, for example, music videos that emphasized the comfort that prayer could bring (Cornet 2021, 8–12).

---

56. Interview, AD, Cairo, September 25, 2013; interview, AS and YS, Cairo, September 29, 2013.

57. Tom Perry and Tamim Elyan, "In Power, Egypt's Brotherhood Seeks Balance on Islamic Law," Reuters, July 25, 2012.

58. Ahmed Feteha, "Egypt Tourism Officials Expect Little Change under Morsi—for Now," Ahram Online, June 27, 2012, https://english.ahram.org.eg/NewsContent/3/12/46334/Business/Economy/Egypt-tourism-officials-expect-little-change-under.aspx

FJP leaders and deputies were willing to use the power of state more directly and coercively to uphold religious norms governing sexual and gender ethics and expressions of support for blasphemous insults to Islam. The public prosecutor appointed by the Morsi government used an existing—albeit weakly enforced—blasphemy law to jail those who profaned Islam on social media, while attempting to appear evenhanded with some punishment of Muslims who tore pages out of the Bible during a rally, but resisted a full ban on insults to the Prophet.[59] In parliamentary debates, FJP deputies joined with Salafis to pass laws that limited women's right to initiate divorce, claiming that laws allowing them to do so had been "un-Islamic" to begin with and contributed to the breakdown of the Egyptian family.[60]

When the MB's legislative agenda was dashed by the SCAF's decision to dissolve parliament following Morsi's victory in the presidential election, the FJP used its access to executive and constitution-framing power to pursue its agenda of social Islamization. An MB leader echoed the older notion that the movement could work for more effective and Islamic rule by placing upright people in positions where they could "command the right" when he told a researcher that the MB aimed to counter the corruption and hostility of a state bureaucracy bent on undermining Morsi's ability to govern by appointing members of the Brotherhood to second-in-command positions in key ministries (Shimy 2015, 88). FJP officials appointed movement members and Islamist sympathizers to important posts in education, religion, and media and also gave them economic portfolios: for example, a senior Gam'iyya Shar'iyya official was appointed minister of religious endowments (Haenni 2016, 29–30). MB supporters were given various positions in the state religious establishment,[61] and

---

59. Kristen Chick, "Egypt Pursues Blasphemy Cases as Morsi Defends Ban at UN," *Christian Science Monitor*, September 27, 2012; "Egypt Salafists Propose Constitutional Ban on Prophet insults," *al-Masry al-Youm*, July 19, 2012.

60. "Islamist MPs Attack Family Laws and National Council for Women," *Egypt Independent*, March 13, 2012.

61. Dalia Rabie, "Egypt's Imams Fight for Their Mosques' Independence," *Egypt Independent*, April 7, 2013.

Islamists jailed under Mubarak for belonging to once-radical movements, now MB allies in government, were freed.[62] Echoing older MB arguments about *tamkin*, one official also noted that Brothers in positions of authority, particularly in schools, would permit the spread of good ethics and the principles of Islam, which would enable the movement to reform and build the nation as it had always wanted to.[63] The MB prioritized control of the ministries of education, media, and religious endowments and worked to hire more preachers sympathetic to the Islamist viewpoint in state-approved mosques and to promote Islamist officials in educational institutions.[64]

MB leaders argued that the representation of Islamists and particularly Brothers in important government posts was a natural consequence of the reversal of the MB's exclusion from politics after Mubarak's overthrow, and of the readiness of competent cadres to serve the nation. They were quick to point out that the Morsi-appointed cabinet still did not have an Islamist majority, in part due to the need to accommodate the military, and because old regime figures often had to be appointed to key ministries to ensure the cooperation of bureaucratic institutions.[65] Despite differences with Salafis on the question of how exactly sharia was to be upheld in a new constitution, MB/FJP cadres solidified an "Islamic alliance" in the constituent assembly and installed more Islamist cabinet ministers as non-Islamist opposition to the Morsi government grew.[66] Invoking the "pious majority," the FJP also appointed Salafis and Islamist sympathizers to its presidential advisory team, to fend off what it saw as secular

62. Tom Perry, "Egypt's Mursi Frees Islamists Jailed by Mubarak," *Reuters*, July 31, 2012.
63. Chaimaa Abdel-Hamid, "Hamdi Hassan: La confrérie a des cadres capables d'occuper des postes importants," *Ahram Hebdo*, no. 963, 2013.
64. "Independent Teachers' Syndicate: Ministry Is Brotherhoodizing Education," *Egypt Independent*, January 7, 2013; Rabie, "Egypt's Imams."
65. Interview, AS and YS, Cairo, September 29, 2013.
66. Mustafa Hashim, "Burhamy li-l-Shorouk: Itafaqna ma' al-ikhwan 'ala hadhaf kalimat 'mabadi' min nass al-shari'a fi-l-dustur," *al-Shorouk*, June 30, 2012; Omayma Abdel-Latif, "Unholy Alliance," *al-Ahram Weekly*, December 27, 2012.

intransigence in respecting the popular will by passing legislation that supported the Islamic character of Egypt.[67]

"Implementing Sharia" through Constitutional Regulations and Policymaking

When the SCAF-led transition assigned the parliamentary leadership to distribute constitutional assembly seats, the MB/FJP had an opportunity to define the constitutional and institutional parameters of a state that applied sharia, which it had not expected in its years of framing sharia as something that required careful cultivation of grassroots support. This opportunity was a partial and risky one, given the military-run transitional council's ultimate veto power over all decisions made by a constituent assembly, as well as the increasing hostility of the non-Islamist political opposition to growing Islamist power. Yet MB/FJP cadres were under pressure to use this opportunity to stake their own claim as champions of sharia, having competed with and sought to delegitimize Salafi parties as impatient newcomers in the field of Islamic politics on the grounds that their legislative proposals to codify the letter of Islamic criminal law were rash and premature, and that a focus on veiling and banning alcohol was a distraction from the main mission of sharia application, which was justice (Topol 2012).

As the political field became polarized, the MB/FJP and Salafis increasingly worked together to shore up what they perceived as the essential Islamic features of the new constitution. The MB leadership saw the opportunity to shape the constitutional framework of a new political order as a significant one and prioritized ensuring a place for Islamic influence in this constitution over more short-term benefits of electoral victory, such as cabinet positions (Brown 2012b, 10). The FJP had used its electoral success to claim a popular mandate to "defend" Islam in the constitution, and the party leadership justified Morsi's majoritarian approach

---

67. Rana Khazbak, "New Presidential Team Hints at Brotherhood-Salafi Rapprochement," *Egypt Independent*, August 30, 2012.

to appointments in the constituent assembly as necessary in the face of an "unfair, unreasonable and relentless campaign targeting the Islamic identity of Egypt today" that sought to halt the work of the assembly in rebuilding national institutions.[68] Salafi pressure to assert Islamic boundaries in the new constitution as legitimate expressions of a majority identity and religious obligation—particularly in the form of street protests and slogans warning the Morsi government not to turn Egypt into a secular, liberal, or American province and to listen to the "85 million Muslims" who "called for the application of sharia"[69]—also reportedly pushed the MB to affirm its visible commitment to Islam in government.[70]

When the constituent assembly debated whether article 2 of the old constitution, which had defined the principles of sharia as the main source of legislation in Egypt, required more institutional and constitutional scaffolding, MB representatives were caught off guard by a Salafi insistence that the constitution should enshrine the judgments or rulings (*ahkam*) and not just the principles (*mabadi'*) of sharia as the main source of legislation.[71] The Brothers, for all their insistence during campaigning that no other group had defended God's law more steadfastly in modern Egypt, defended the existing constitutional language and Sadat-era initiatives to bring law in line with sharia as well suited to Egyptian popular sentiment and sufficient to ensure that Egypt stayed within the path of sharia. Salafis, however, voiced their skepticism that the Supreme Constitutional Court would, as it long had, interpret article 2 to apply weakly to actual political authority. They proposed a new article 219 that defined sharia in terms of concrete, historical Sunni jurisprudence, worrying non-Islamists

---

68. Freedom and Justice Party, "Muslim Brotherhood Statement on Islamic Law and National Identity," *Ikhanweb*, November 4, 2012, https://ikhwanweb.com/muslim-brotherhood-statement-0-27/.

69. Field notes, Tahrir rally, Cairo, November 9, 2012.

70. Interview, AD, Cairo, September 25, 2013.

71. "Constituent Assembly to Vote on Sharia in Egyptian Constitution," *Ahram Online*, August 28, 2012; Gamal Heshmat, "The 2nd Article in Egypt's Constitution Is Supported by Most Egyptians," *Ikhwanweb*, August 4, 2012, https://ikhwanweb.com/gamal-heshmat%3a-the-2nd-article.

and liberals who sought to remove the task of defining the principles of sharia from the control of Islamists.[72] As al-Azhar had reasserted some autonomy and revived its historical Council of Senior Scholars in 2012, the MB proposed to give this newly reconstituted—and somewhat more politically independent—council an advisory role in interpreting what limits sharia should place on legislation, under a new constitutional article 4, echoing their 2007 platform proposal to use the power of the state and the judiciary to guard against violations of God's will, as long as they represented the independent voice of a pious people (Lombardi and Brown 2012; Dunne and Brown 2021). Where Salafis wished to see al-Azhar play a more assertive role in judicial review to ensure that no law violated sharia, both Azhari leaders and MB leaders argued that al-Azhar must retain a unifying, advisory role on matters of sharia compliance, rather than triggering partisan discord around such laws.[73]

The MB leadership did not see this as contradicting its commitment to democracy and political pluralism, despite an outcry from non-Islamists who accused the movement of seeking to establish a theocracy by giving Azhar the right to review legislation, because the latter commitment had always been predicated on the idea that it would allow pious citizens to work together for the good as defined by God's will, and not outside its limits. Indeed, on questions of economic policy where Azhari opinion contradicted the FJP leadership's goals, the party found ways to prioritize its own interpretation of what it meant to apply sharia. The Morsi government in 2012 decided to seek investment from wealthy Gulf Arab economies through Islamic bonds, or *sukuk*, as an alternative to an International Monetary Fund loan, and as a way of demonstrating that Islamic solidarity could be both more ethical and more effective than Western alliances (Henry 2015, 196, 201). Echoing its older framing of just economic policies as those that accounted for both God's will and the public good, the FJP's

---

72. Interview, AD, Giza, September 25, 2013.

73. Ahmad al-Buhayri, "Al-Azhar Insists on Keeping Sharia Law in the Constitution," *al-Masry al-Youm*, July 11, 2012, trans. Naria Tanoukhi, *al-Monitor*, July 12, 2012; "Al-Azhar yanjah fi naza' fatil azma al-mada al-thaniya bayn al-ikhwan wa-l-salafiyun," *al-Mesreyoon*, July 6, 2012.

finance ministry drafted guidelines in early 2012 for a new law to establish *sukuk* at the state level in consultation with legal experts and representatives of the Dar al-Ifta', the official state organization that ruled on matters of religious law. The Nour Party opposed this legislation in parliament and demanded that all kinds of loans be referred to al-Azhar's council of senior scholars for approval, as they risked violating usury prohibitions.[74]

After al-Azhar's council of senior scholars refused to sign off on the law as sharia compliant, due to a provision that allowed for state assets to be used as collateral, which, al-Azhar argued, was tantamount to mortgaging them to foreigners, the Morsi government simply removed the term "Islamic" so that Azhari approval was no longer necessary.[75] This was also intended as a way of refusing the precedent of allowing al-Azhar a veto over laws passed by the upper house of parliament.[76] The government passed the law, arguing that it had taken advice from al-Azhar, the central bank, and from financial experts into account, and that its *sukuk* policy reflected the goals of Islam, and they promised to set up an autonomous sharia board to supervise and offer legal advice on all *sukuk* transactions.[77] In a conference on the issue of *sukuk* in theory and practice, the FJP brought together representatives from corporations and investors along with scholars from faculties of Islamic law to explain that *sukuk* were rooted in Islam, and that they would be directed toward religiously approved, *halal* projects, making a case for why *sukuk* would benefit the economy and citizens more broadly while allowing people to invest ethically.[78] Therefore, with or without a formal Azhari endorsement, the financial instrument—and the

---

74. "Salafis Oppose Saudi Infrastructure Loan, Claiming 'Usury,'" *Egypt Independent* February 12, 2013.

75. Alexandre Goudineau, "Sukuk Law in State of Flux until al-Azhar Review," *Egypt Independent*, April 4, 2013.

76. Interview, AD, Cairo, September 25, 2013.

77. "Majlis al-wuzara' al-masri yuwafiq 'ala qanun al-sukuk wa yahily li-l-shura," *al-Arabiya*, February 27, 2013; Muhammad al-Samkuri, "Qayadi al-Ikhwani: Al-sukuk 'mawlud islami' wa satustakhdim fi-l-mashari' al-halal," *al-Masry al-Youm*, May 1, 2013.

78. Muhammad al-Samkuri, "Qayadi al-Ikhwani: Al-sukuk 'mawlud islami' wa satustakhdim fi-l-mashari' al-halal," *al-Masry al-Youm*, May 1, 2013.

policies promoting it—represented, in the movement's view, an example of using the power of the state to work for Islam.

The MB's focus on Islamic policymaking as a kind of righteous action was also evident in its approach to using the institutions of state to support *zakat*, or religiously obliged tithing: it pushed for the institutions of state to encourage individual righteous action and to create the conditions under which religious law and righteousness could flourish, but preferred to use state policy and power to create a more "just" society than to enforce the letter of religious law. Evoking a caliphal term from Islamic history, the FJP's election platform proposed a *bayt al-mal* (house of wealth) to collect money paid annually as *zakat* by Muslims, which would be voluntary but would also serve as a pillar of social justice by reducing inequality and poverty, rather than replacing existing state taxation authority (Mittermaeier 2020, 120–21). When Salafi legislators proposed a bill to establish a state fund into which Muslim citizens could pay their *zakat* while calling to apply the Islamic penal code to various crimes, the FJP-led parliamentary religious affairs committee argued that *zakat* contributions must remain a voluntary religious act and declared that building the right kind of state and creating the conditions under which it might be able to apply sharia rulings—mainly conditions of economic justice—would require several years to achieve.[79]

Confronting the Contradictions of *Shar'iyya*

Popular opposition to the Morsi government and discontent with economic problems increased in late 2012. Despite increasing street protests and non-Islamist anger at the Islamist domination of the constituent assembly, the MB/FJP leadership continued to frame the popular and religious legitimacy (*shar'iyya*) of its mandate as inextricably linked. In public statements, MB activists and their allies positioned themselves as legitimate rulers because they were defenders of the popular will and majority

---

79. Bissan Kassab and Mohammad Khawly, "Egypt: Muslim Brotherhood and al-Azhar Follow Salafi Lead," *al-Akhbar English*, March 23, 2012.

values, pitted against a counterrevolutionary "deep state" whose machinations amounted to a "conspiracy" against the Islamic regime. When the Egyptian judiciary hinted in November 2012 that it might dissolve the constituent assembly for violating constitutional guidelines, Morsi used his power as president to issue constitutional declarations that limited the judiciary's review of the executive, and, while non-Islamists protested this decision as one that threatened democracy and the gains of the January 25 revolution, the MB/FJP leadership insisted that their actions were aimed precisely at protecting popular and democratic legitimacy. They rallied in large numbers to counter protests against Morsi, declaring that "the people" were against "morally corrupt" secularists, wanted the application of God's will, and supported Morsi for protecting the nation against the remains of the old regime (*feloul*) in institutions such as the judiciary.[80]

At a conference of Islamic thinkers, deputy general guide Khairat al-Shater argued that those who wished to aggravate Egypt's economic problems and stall plans for development were driven by foreign interests; another Islamic thinker made the claim that "we have two camps, one with sharia and legitimacy and the other against it."[81] As anti-Morsi protests increased in late 2012, the MB and its allies continued to portray opponents of Morsi's rule as "enemies of religion" and of the will of the majority: provincial and local MB/FJP branches' social media divisions accused American and Christian groups of inciting protests against a legitimate leader, and they blamed media outlets purportedly beholden to old regime interests for spreading unflattering news about the Morsi regime's achievements.[82] MB leaders used religious and democratic frames of legitimate rule interchangeably in opposing those who threatened to overthrow the Morsi government and eventually succeeded in getting the

---

80. Heba Afify and Magdy Samaan, "Morsy's Men: Sharia as an Ambition, Stability as an End," *Egypt Independent*, December 3, 2012.

81. Nouran el-Behairy, "We Are the People, We Are the Majority," *Daily News Egypt*, December 8, 2012.

82. For articles and social media posts about the MB from FJP and MB websites translated in English, see https://mbinenglish.wordpress.com/category/2012/page/2/ (accessed April 29, 2023).

military to do so in the summer of 2013. In speeches preceding the coup of June 30, MB leaders called on Egyptians to come together in the interest of the nation, insisted that the Morsi-led government represented the legitimate will of the majority of Egyptians that would be overturned with new elections, and argued that the MB wanted to bring people together for the good (*salih*) of the nation.[83]

Leaders and supporters of the MB who addressed a large crowd at the Rabaʻa al-ʻAdaweyya square sit-in to protest the military's planned coup alternated between positioning the MB as defenders of the revolution and democracy against those who wished to undo its gains and declaring that the MB had the support of God and worked for His will. Nationalist imagery and national flags accompanied speeches about the responsibility of all gathered to defend the revolution: banners near the main stage showed pictures of MB "martyrs" of the revolution with text stating that they had been killed by "thugs" belonging to Mubarak's ruling party as well as by the newly formed National Salvation Front of non-Islamist opposition parties that had called for a military intervention to overthrow Morsi. The crowd chanted that "they have thugs (*baltageyya*), we protect legitimacy (*sharʻiyya*)," and religious preachers, including the popular televangelist Safwat el-Hegazy, declared from the stage that supporters of Morsi were the "real revolutionaries."[84] Slogans on banners and in signs held up by Brothers declared that the MB were only interested in applying the will of the nation, while opposition groups did not wish to respect the ballot. Some speakers forecasted that Morsi would win again by millions of votes, while warning that oppressors would use thugs to ensure that the people would never win power.

Slogans printed on banners and chanted by the crowd also asserted that the "people wanted the application of sharia," and that there was "no

---

83. "President Mohammed Morsi's Address to the Nation," MENASource, Atlantic Council, June 28, 2013, https://www.atlanticcouncil.org/blogs/menasource/translation-president-mohamed-morsi-s-address-to-the-nation/; Mohammed al-Beltagy, speech at Rabaʻa al-ʻAdaweyya square, June 21, 2013, https://web.archive.org/web/20130623125249/https://www.youtube.com/watch?v=FWR8_K4vbWo.

84. Field notes, Rabaʻa al-ʻAdaweyya square, June 28, 2013.

shar'iyya (legitimacy) without sharia." One chant called out to all "preachers" (*du'at*) of different Islamic groups to "make it [politics] Egyptian and legitimate," echoing a slogan repeated at many pro-sharia rallies over the previous year and centering Islamic activists as responsible for upholding political and religious legitimacy in Egypt. Chants of "God is great" accompanied "Long live Egypt," and "Yes to *shar'iyya*, no to secularism and liberalism" were chanted alongside calls to "finish the project" of revolution (*thawar, ahrar, hankammil al-mishwar*). A speaker who claimed to be a member of the Gama'a Islamiyya argued that those gathered in the square were there to apply *shar'iyya* and the "will of the nation." The occasional speaker in Azhari religious clothing also went on the stage to announce that al-Azhar was with the Brothers, while insisting that opposition *shaykhs* were "fake" and did not speak for al-Azhar.[85]

When Morsi was overthrown in a military coup in early July 2013, images and discourse at the Raba'a al-'Adaweyya sit-in framed Islamists as martyrs for nation and faith, promising to "give our blood for sharia and *shar'iyya*." People said prayers for those who, they claimed, had been shot by security forces "while saying Ramadan prayers." Banners and slogans in both English and Arabic around the stage pitted "people power" against the "military coup" and affirmed support for "continuity" over the "unknown." Old election posters with Morsi's image were put up in the square alongside Egyptian flags and slogans calling for the "purification" of the judiciary. Religious scholars giving sermons from the stage on one Friday reminded those gathered of the religious purpose and rewards of their actions: citing the story of Moses, one proclaimed that the faithful would prevail even if under siege at the moment, and that believers must try to protect their rights even as Pharaoh tried to take them away.[86] The MB's social media and YouTube channels similarly depicted the movement's "martyrs," killed by security forces who sought to remove them from the square, as men who had sacrificed themselves for their country's freedom, in contrast with shadowy state forces and a dictator who quelled

---

85. Field notes, Raba'a al-'Adaweyya square, June 28, 2013.
86. Field notes, Raba'a al-'Adaweyya square, July 12, 2013.

images of popular demonstrations, and spoke poor Arabic (Cornet 2021, 16–17; Koa 2018, 589–90). Other movement media portrayed the movement's righteous activists as ordinary sons of the soil who had fought for popular freedom and dignity, humble and reliable democratic champions, true believers fighting oppression just like famous figures from Islamic history (Koa 2018, 588–90). They compared field marshal Abdel Fattah al-Sisi, who had launched a coup against Morsi, to Pharaoh, and his coup to the Mongol sack of Baghdad and faulted the new regime for its exacerbation of popular economic problems, once again fusing religious and democratic frames of legitimacy (588).

The Religious Value of Political Work after the Coup

Activists from the MB and its leadership took different lessons from the failure of its first experiment with governance. Some maintained that the movement's political strategy had failed to adequately follow and promote religious values. Others argued that an investment in governance had been premature and hurt the *da'wa* through its failures, and still others thought that the movement should have invested more in political outreach and learning in order to fulfill its religious obligations through governance. Arguments that the movement should withdraw from electoral politics altogether as a result of political failure were, however, quite rare, and most of those who voiced criticism of the movement leadership's strategy believed that better political strategy could have served the Islamic mission well.

One argument voiced by student activists who were committed to the movement and had also participated in political activity, without actually joining the FJP, was that although the MB had done good work in government, this work did not speak for itself, and the movement should have built the expertise and skill necessary to publicize its work and persuade people of the value of Islamic rule and to undermine those who worked against it as part of the "deep state."[87] Morsi had been patriotic and eco-

---

87. Interview, AS and YS, Cairo, September 29, 2013.

nomically capable and had not been corrupt, my interviewees said, and his administration, along with the government of prime minister Hisham Kandil, had much to show for its brief time in power. Citing examples of economic and political success such as wheat self-sufficiency and the manufacture and availability of global brands of electronic products in Egypt and security in Sinai as instances of good governance that should have persuaded people of the effectiveness of Islamic rule, activists pointed to the new constitution, and the freedoms and forms of leadership accountability it guaranteed, as positive achievements for Islamic rule, lauding the *sukuk* initiative as one that could help achieve a "renaissance" as it had in Malaysia.[88] Activists contended that the MB-run government was undermined by a hostile media, an excessive focus on achieving political consensus, and a timid approach to bureaucratic reform that limited the reach of what the administration could do, because those who ultimately ran the state's institutions were not cooperative. Women sympathetic to the MB who led Quranic reading groups in a mosque in a lower-middle-class Cairo neighborhood at the time of the coup similarly defended Morsi's position as a "democratically elected" president and framed opposition to his rule as serving the interests of the elite against those of the people (Mustonen 2020, 96–97). One preacher described the opposition to controversial constitutional articles associated with Islamists, such as article 219, as driven by elite interests, because elites did not want to give up the gains from corruption that sharia would make illegal (99).

These activists drew the lesson that political work had to be more bold in order to do good and make that good visible and to achieve the promise of Islamic governance. One activist opined that the MB should have been more revolutionary and asserted its right to make policy independently of the military council sooner, for quicker political success, claiming that "the biggest factor that makes people love or hate the Islamic project is political work, and success."[89] Another activist made the case that the fail-

---

88. Interview, AS and YS, Cairo, September 29, 2013.
89. Interview, YS, Cairo, September 29, 2013.

ure of a first attempt at establishing Islamic government was a sign that the movement had pursued an Islamic state prematurely, without first having prepared society to accept Islam, but that this was not cause to believe that governance was bad for Islam.[90] Another argued that the Islamic project had been somewhat discredited by its premature reliance on the state, and that the movement should not have overinvested in—and allowed itself to be excessively occupied with—party work, but rather should have pursued politics in equal measure, as a parallel road, to *tarbiya* and the building of good Muslims and the Muslim society. Yet he framed his critique of politics in terms of its disproportionate influence and did not reject the utility of politics for the Islamic mission in fundamental terms.[91]

Lessons about the futility of certain tactics abounded in MB discourse after the coup. In a shift from older directive discourse that urged members to tap all potential sources of social influence to spread God's word, multiple student activists said that the movement had learned not to make pragmatic alliances with televangelists, despite their social influence and their ability to connect emotionally with people to persuade them to be better Muslims, because they had discredited the Islamic project with their political positions.[92] Some argued that Morsi's "battle to reform the state" had been misguided, insisting that the Brothers should instead "wage the battle to break up the institutions of state."[93] Others offered the opinion that Morsi should have been more brutal in ridding Egypt of members of its old political elite, including al-Azhar, who had failed to stand up for the people.[94] Critics acknowledged that mistakes would be part of a learning process in politics, and that the MB would pay for its mistakes, but insisted that this did not mean that they were "going to give

---

90. Interview, AS, Cairo, September 29, 2013.

91. Interview, AK, Cairo, May 8, 2013.

92. Interview, AB, Cairo, September 24, 2013; interview, AS and YS, Cairo, September 29, 2013.

93. Tom Perry and Abdelrahman Youssef, "In Egypt, Ideas of a Radical Islamist Make Comeback," Reuters, December 2, 2013.

94. Interview, AS and YS, Cairo, September 29, 2013.

up now and say it's all over"—rather, they had to prove their responsibility and perform their role, as youth leaders, as they always had.[95] Similarly, after the coup, one *daʿiyya* in an Islamist women's group argued that "we" (i.e., Islamists, as well as representatives of the people) had to hold on to the belief that Islam and politics were the same, and instead of listening to those who said there could be no democracy or elections, or even the army, or a president, or religious scholars, one should listen to God; yet she also noted that it was important to think for oneself instead of being swept away by a crowd protesting in a square (Mustonen 2020, 98–99). Her language of a "just society" remained imbued with democratic norms (101).

As far as these activists were concerned, the Islamic mission was not irrevocably yoked to politics and would not fail with politics' (temporary) failure. Even those Brothers who railed against the institutions of state such as the judiciary and army that had, in their view, betrayed the nation, remained committed to seeing themselves as the nation's representatives. There were some who became disillusioned with democracy, like one young Morsi supporter who insisted that "if ballot boxes don't bring righteousness, we will all go back to demanding a caliphate."[96] But, for the most part, the movement continued to accept electoral politics as a legitimate option for achieving its goals. Some MB activists who believed they had lost faith in democracy as a path to achieve their goals said that their skepticism was due more to their experience with military intervention and repression as a barrier to real democratization than due to a loss of faith in politics and democracy altogether; they argued that the movement should keep its options open for rebuilding, pressuring the regime, and working for its goals, whether through peer preaching and transnational networks, or revolutionary action.[97]

The MB leadership similarly continued to accept electoral politics as part of its mission after the coup. In a statement from the FJP in 2014,

---

95. Interview, AB, Cairo, September 24, 2013.
96. Robert Worth, "A Familiar Role for Muslim Brotherhood: Opposition," *New York Times*, July 28, 2013.
97. Mohamed Adam, "Waiting for God's Victory," *Mada Masr*, April 13, 2014.

the leadership affirmed its commitment to democracy and to addressing the people with wisdom and with "God's truth." They also called on the army to return to the barracks, asserting that the sovereignty of the people (*sha'b*) must be restored, and that the state must represent the land and bring justice to the people who lived on it as a matter of religious duty.[98] MB leaders continued to call for a "reinstatement of democratic life" in rebuking the coup regime and to appeal to "honorable citizens" to refuse to participate in a constitutional referendum proposed by a military-led transitional government after the 2013 coup, on the grounds of being both antidemocratic and potentially threatening Egypt's Muslim identity by removing articles that mandated more concrete sharia compliance for legislation.[99] One influential leader, from the Muslim Sisters wing, stated that the movement had not lost its faith in politics as part of the comprehensive mission of Islam or changed its mind about the necessity of political participation as a result of repression, and that the movement had always believed that "in order to practice religion correctly, we must practice politics a little."[100] Politics was essential to fighting tyranny, she continued, and, if the MB wished to survive, it must challenge the overthrow of its elected president. She insisted, however, that the MB must always see themselves as "God's soldiers on earth" rather than worrying about administrative positions and noted that Muslim Sisters who had been active in the FJP had never ceased their spiritual cultivation activities, which had also been crucial for public service.[101] Some members who had resented the way electoral work had dominated the time, energy, and resources of the movement were glad to have a balance restored and said that they felt the lesson that religion and politics could not be separated

---

98. Freedom and Justice Party, "Al-ikhwan yuqaddamun khata 'ajala li-tashih al-wada' al-maqluba fi Misr," IkhwanOnline, May 9, 2014.

99. "Pro-Morsi Alliance Criticises Constitutional Amendments," *Ahram Online*, August 27, 2013, https://english.ahram.org.eg/NewsContentP/1/80065/Egypt/ProMorsi-alliance-criticises-constitutional-amendm.aspx; "Persisting Brothers," *Mada Masr*, September 6, 2013.

100. Interview, HAM, Cairo, November 23, 2013.

101. Interview, HAM, Cairo, November 23, 2013.

had been reaffirmed for them.¹⁰² Student activists agreed that the coup had been "educational" in teaching them about the values of endurance and reinforcing what their movement elders had taught them: regardless of short-term political results, victory could only come from God, and one must therefore always "work for God."¹⁰³

Political Learning and Righteous Political Action after 2015

As field marshal Abdel Fattah el-Sisi consolidated the coup through new constitutional and electoral rules that allowed him to continue to control executive power as an elected civilian in 2014, the *gama'a* and its party were once again banned. Some of its leaders were jailed while others went into exile in Turkey. With a temporary collapse in structure and no clear sense of its future, the movement clustered into different leadership factions: some, associated with the old guard, who sought to keep the movement alive by going underground again; some who tried to set up a new leadership structure overseas, with support from sympathetic Islamist groups in Turkey and elsewhere; some that decided to explore revolutionary options; and some that focused on introspection to consider what they had learned from political experience. Two of these factions, each claiming to represent the authentic leadership of the movement, put out statements in the years to follow that were widely circulated and influential, reframing the movement's historical narrative about the religious merits of engaging and disengaging from electoral politics. In 2015, a group that called itself a sharia committee under the tutelage of MB leader Mohamed Kamal put out a document titled "The Jurisprudence of Popular Resistance to the Coup" (*Fiqh al-muqawama al-sha'biya li-l-inqilab*) that cited religious authority to propose revolutionary mobilization against the coup regime, and, in 2017, after Kamal was killed by security forces, a more cautious leadership group staked its position as the true inheritor of the *gama'a*'s mission, putting out a document titled

---

102. Omayma Abdel-Latif, "Back to Basics," *al-Ahram Weekly*, April 30, 2013; interview, AK, Cairo, May 8, 2013.

103. Interviews, AS and YS, Cairo, September 29, 2013.

"Vision 28" to lay out lessons from the MB's political experience that should guide its future.[104]

The different factions emerging from the postcoup period disagreed starkly on the best strategy for achieving God's will in the new political environment, but upheld the principles that political power—and the outcomes of political work more generally—were critical for the *da'wa*'s success, and that righteous action had to be tailored for specific political environments. Where the revolutionary Jurisprudence of Popular Resistance camp argued that the existing Egyptian political order was too flawed to accommodate godly political work, and the MB had done all they could to work for God through democratic means, the pragmatic Vision 28 leadership that took over after Mohamed Kamal was assassinated contended that the MB needed to focus more on the skills and methods needed to achieve the political empowerment that would help them work for God.

The "Jurisprudence of Popular Resistance" text's authors argued that revolutionary action and resistance were necessary to oppose what they defined as an infidel regime. The statement argued that a jihad of armed resistance was justified against those who had overthrown Morsi, because the violent overthrow of a ruler who had wished to rule by sharia and to establish an Islamic state was wrong, and because Morsi had clearly sought rule not to assert his own power, but, as a good Muslim, to do his duty, and had been nominated by others for it (Awad 2017, 11).

Sisi, by contrast, had fought God's revealed truths and did not seek to rule by sharia himself. While setting up a Qutbist contrast between apostate and godly political orders, the revolutionary wing acknowledged *shura* and popular election as key to the legitimacy of an Islamic regime, too, and a reason why its overthrow was religiously illegitimate: Morsi had become an imam by gaining the people's allegiance (*baya'*) through elections, and a military coup did not establish the same kind of legitimate

---

104. Abu al-Izz Dhia-addin Asad, "Fiqh al-muqawama al-sha'biya li-l-inqilab," https://www.scribd.com/doc/305775800/كتاب-فقه-المقاومة-الشعبية-للإنقلاب (accessed April 29, 2023); Society of Muslim Brothers, "Vision 28," https://issuu.com/madamasr/docs/ikhwanvi28-compressed.pdf.

bayaʿ for a new regime (Awad 2017, 10). The text also presented the rights and freedoms of Muslim citizens as a central goal of righteous political work, and defended armed struggle as a tool for restoring these rights and freedoms against state terror, emergency laws, and oppression.[105] Popular legitimacy and support remained important even for armed jihad: activists were urged to pursue a media jihad alongside armed resistance and warned against labeling their opponents infidels, so as to win "domestic and international sympathy" for their work (14–15).

Addressing rhetorical questions about what had changed for the movement to now seek a return to armed resistance, the text also asserted that Muslim activists (*al-ahrar*, or the free) had taken the path of democracy and constitutional struggle as far as possible, achieving through constitutional means what older established parties had never been able to; and because the ostensible proponents of democracy had revealed their faithlessness in overturning it through force and without concern for rules, the Brothers had the right to undo these changes through their own, sound means (*al-dimuqratiyya allati kafar biha ashabuha, fahaqq al-ahrar an yiltamisu al-tagheer binilyat*).[106] The text made a more forceful argument for violent jihad than MB texts had in the years of electoral participation, but it affirmed that jihad required multiple kinds of work simultaneously, with spiritual preparation required to do all kinds well. The text cited Banna's discussion of the power of faith, unity, and finally armed force, just as MB leaders had to justify engaging in electoral politics, but emphasized that the time had come for revolutionary power, and that activists could carry out their spiritual preparation through practice, rather than waiting to complete spiritual preparation before moving on to violent jihad (Awad 2017, 13–14).

After Kamal's assassination, a more cautious movement leadership took over that focused on rebuilding the organization and bringing more politically radical members back into the fold. This new leadership undertook a self-assessment process through workshops and consultations to

---

105. Asad, *Fiqh al-muqawama*, 44.
106. Asad, 40.

set the organization on a new path in time for its upcoming ninety-year anniversary and produced a document titled "Vision 28," laying out lessons from the *gama'a*'s unsuccessful political experiment (Willi 2021, 368). This document affirmed the Jurisprudence of Popular Resistance position that Banna's vision for Muslim politics had been a revolutionary one, and that the *gama'a* was committed to political engagement in order to achieve its eventual goal of an Islamic state: "In an attempt to study the lessons we need to learn for our revolution to continue; to benefit from our experience; avoid our mistakes and pause in front of the important points that we should not lose track of in the dust of the ongoing revolution's battle."[107] The document asserted that the Islamic project needed political power, and that the MB had been right to prioritize participation in any process that allowed them to use existing political mechanisms to achieve their goals.[108]

One lesson that the document's writers emphasized was that the *gama'a* had not embraced politics fully enough, but had worked "under the ceiling imposed by the state, [with] no attempt to raise that ceiling," in part because its leadership was focused on survival and organizational unity.[109] However, they argued, political success required political specialization, for politics could not be a mere extension of *da'wa*. If people were to be persuaded to believe in the Islamic political project, they had to be shown that it could deliver material and moral welfare. Pursuing public support through *khayriyya* (charitable) outreach, while also seeing this outreach as a moral mission, had not worked, because people were not persuaded by ethical behavior alone, and different social sectors required different approaches. Moreover, selecting leaders (*rumuz*) for the political party from—and based on their achievements in—the *da'wa* sector, had made it less likely that these leaders would develop the skills needed for political success. Nor had the *gama'a* worked seriously enough to train members in political skills and to pursue opportunities to work in public institutions.[110] Requiring electoral politics to serve the *da'wa* mission had been

---

107. Society of Muslim Brothers, "Vision 28," 22.
108. Society of Muslim Brothers, 8.
109. Society of Muslim Brothers, 8, 23.
110. Society of Muslim Brothers, 4, 12–13.

a mistake, too: the movement had entered parliamentary politics to gain political cover for social service work, but instead should have focused on using parliamentary politics to cement political gains and form alliances with others.[111] Further, a party that had the *gama'a* as its social sponsor could have succeeded, but its dependence on the *gama'a* made the group's core mission more vulnerable to political backlash, and public concerns about the "Brotherhoodization" of the state.[112] The writers assessed lessons from the movement's failed experience with party formation in 2006 and its attempt to build a party after the 2011 uprising that would fall under the authority of the *gama'a*, and concluded that a party independent from the *da'wa* structure of the *gama'a* was essential.[113]

The writers argued that the MB must let go of its historical suspicion of parties as forces of division and embrace an independent political party in order to correct these errors and achieve its goals.[114] The professional overlap between the goals of the party and of the *da'wa* structure of the MB had failed, and a party must have one task—competing for power—rather than taking responsibility for all the goals and aspirations of the movement for individual and social cultivation.[115] With this approach, the MB could, the document contended, embrace the revolutionary spirit that had always been at the heart of their mission and Banna's thought, rather than remaining cautious and reformist out of a concern with self-preservation, and build relationships with other revolutionary parties.[116] This required promoting and making the most of the movement's more revolutionary activists and icons, instead of allowing movement loyalists to always represent the group, without worrying about whether political leaders would stray from the movement's *minhaj*.[117] According to the document,

---

111. Society of Muslim Brothers, 6–7.
112. Society of Muslim Brothers, 19–20.
113. Society of Muslim Brothers, 16–17.
114. Society of Muslim Brothers, 15.
115. Society of Muslim Brothers, 28, 17.
116. Society of Muslim Brothers, 22–23.
117. Society of Muslim Brothers, 25.

elections, revolutionary methods, and a variety of political tools were all useful for the *gama'a*'s long-term mission. Politics was not to take over the entire mission, and was not the only tool in the movement's arsenal, but it was an important one that deserved to be treated on its own terms, and not as a positive byproduct of expanding social piety.

Where the training curricula of the 2011–13 period insisted on the convertibility of preaching and political outreach skills, the post-2015 self-assessment concluded that the two different kinds of work must be separated, even as they were both spiritually valuable. The document specifically challenged older *khayriyya* norms of using success in public service—for instance, in distributing bread or launching cleaning campaigns—as a path to political *da'wa* in that such an approach overly burdened political activists and left them liable to excessive critiques and expectations.[118] Rather than seeing political success and failure as the will of God, which the movement could only accept patiently, movement leaders should have tried harder to win over public opinion through civil and legal action and political pressure.[119] The writers argued that the MB's writings and own *da'wa* and internal debates had not adequately cultivated or prioritized political leadership and should have used the lessons learned from on-the-ground interactions to inform political strategy more effectively.[120]

Its *tarbiya* programs, similarly, had focused on spiritual character building, but not intellectual issues that offered activists a broader perspective on politics, economics, and administration, or even on the political nature of Islam and its jurisprudence, which would have been necessary to succeed in political work.[121] The group had focused on winning elections in the short term, but not enough on developing party leaders and cadres. As a result, when the MB tried to do many things at once (e.g., running social services, competing to control parliament, the

---

118. Society of Muslim Brothers, 17–19.
119. Society of Muslim Brothers, 13.
120. Society of Muslim Brothers, 6–7.
121. Society of Muslim Brothers, 11–12.

constituent assembly, unions), it did so ineffectively and increased popular discontent, making others see its *da'wa* figures as "the state" and blaming them for state failures.[122]

The movement's factions differed dramatically on the utility of violence for its new political mission, as well as on the practical implications of seeking political revolution, but used the same frames of righteous action through politics to make their case. Both of the above positions echoed the belief that the MB must seek to represent a believing nation, and that the state, and political work, were legitimate forms of righteous action for Islam that must be judged according to the norms of individual piety and a just Islamic society. Both argued that the comprehensive Islamic mission required an Islamic state and winning over public opinion, in addition to spiritual conversion and preaching. Both embraced *tamkin* or empowerment through a variety of tools as a path to a more godly polity, without making clear ethical distinctions between revolutionary and participatory political work. As in older episodes of reframing, internal organizational struggles over strategies for new challenges produced different interpretations of what Islamic political work would look like in practice, and what its short-term priorities must be. But, as the movement continued to struggle to define its operational priorities in a new era, its frames of righteous action in pursuit of an Islamic state accommodated a range of tools that made it difficult to say with any certainty that the movement had turned either definitely revolutionary or definitely anti-statist as a result of its experience of political failure.

---

122. Society of Muslim Brothers, 17–19.

Conclusion

When members and observers of Islamist movements alike claim that "working for God" drives what Islamists do in the public sphere, they present religious motivation and piety as fairly stable and agreed-upon concepts. They generally understand what people must do in order to follow God's will in the world and to attain salvation as defined broadly by scriptural rules and jurisprudence around what is religiously meritorious. For Islamists like the Muslim Brothers, norms of ethical action are justified with reference to fixed conceptions of what defines a pious Muslim: a person who tries to please God in their everyday actions in addition to following all religious rules for worship. Yet the path from piety to action is not clear cut: over time, Islamic activists have interpreted "working for God" to justify different forms of activism and have made different strategic choices about how best to perform piety and spread God's message in different political contexts. What enables Islamists like the Muslim Brothers to understand their ever-changing forms of activism as mobilizing people for religious salvation according to clear religious rules and goals?

As the preceding chapters have shown, Banna's founding goal of bringing modern young Muslims "back" to God and changing society by cultivating ethical individuals remained a constant focus of the Brothers' activism. Personal choices and accountability to God's will were key principles for the movement, both for individual and collective salvation: pious activists were expected to think about how all aspects of personal, familial, social, economic, and political life served or undermined God's will, because true Islam, according to the MB, did not recognize any part of life that was outside the scope of Islam and rejected any separation between faith and behavior. Godly behavior both depended on and helped to produce a sociopolitical context that would please God. The MB's mobilizational discourse framed the goal of Islamic education and activism as guiding and enabling individuals to make the right choices about ethical conduct in different contexts, both for their own spiritual progress toward salvation, and with an eye to how their choices would help build a social order that allowed the largest number of people to live good Muslim lives.

Like all social movements with normative goals, the MB framed possible activist choices both in terms of their alignment with the foundational and long-term socioreligious goals of Islamism, and in terms of what was most feasible and likely to work in current circumstances. Thus, when MB leaders considered pious individual practice as key to producing social justice, and just societies as those that required—and would further cultivate—individual piety, they saw one of the movement's jobs as defining and elaborating the kinds of pious practice that would earn individuals religious merits in different contexts, and allow them to enact a more Islamic social order. Activists were reminded that "working for God" required exercising sound spiritual judgment and making contingent, often pragmatic, choices about how to perform Islamic ethics in everyday life, while working toward the ultimate goal of a comprehensive Islamic order, and that the movement leadership would guide them in making the right choices.

The movement leadership's guidance framed political participation and nonparticipation as spiritually valuable in different ways over time. In previous contexts, Islamist thinkers had argued that the superiority of Islamic norms of governance and justice over those of the hegemonic Western and secular sociopolitical orders meant that good Muslims must build alternatives to the institutions of secular sociopolitical orders, primarily by building a pious society from the bottom up, one individual at a time. From the 1980s onward, however, MB leadership contended that existing institutions could offer sites and resources for Muslims to cultivate their own ethical conduct and to carry out social *tarbiya* by modeling good Muslimhood for others, or allow for the empowerment or *tamkin* of Islam by applying state resources toward Islamic goals. In addition to making the case for how political participation could enable sound ethical conduct, the MB leadership also made the case that participating in, and improving, electoral politics and state institutions would serve as a kind of advertisement for Islamic justice to less committed Muslim citizens, and therefore constitute a kind of *da'wa*.

The imperative of demonstrating how Islam and good Muslim individuals could offer uniquely just and effective governance pushed MB leaders to reframe the ethical value of work needed to achieve these outcomes as well. Where initial arguments for the value of electoral participation in the movement's directive discourse emphasized doing individual good acts as key to convincing others to be more committed Muslims, as well as important tools for activists to cultivate their own ethical conduct, later movement discourse formulated political work that achieved just outcomes—along with work that elevated and empowered good Muslims in politics—as spiritually valuable. Thus, training in political skills, as long as these skills were oriented toward working for a more godly political order, came to be perceived as a kind of *tarbiya* and valued for how it could help the individual Muslim and those they served to advance spiritually. The movement leadership evaluated a range of potential political strategies as helpful for promoting the cause of Islam over the course of two decades of political liberalization and framed their value in terms of spiritual as well as instrumental utility. In the early years of their engagement in electoral politics, the MB leadership presented the Islamic activist's role as one of *nasiha* or moral advice to rulers and exhortation to follow Islamic laws, evoking the classical role of the religious scholar in ensuring that rulers followed God's will. The movement's goal for bringing about a more Islamic state, as it entered electoral politics, was to cultivate good Muslim activists via *tarbiya* and good Muslim citizens who would support a more Islamic polity via *da'wa*. Political success and state control were not short or medium-term goals; as MB leaders highlighted, it was a Muslim's duty to work for God, and God would decide when they were rewarded with power. To the extent that a Muslim activist could apply God's will (*tatbiq al-shari'a*), or command the right (*al-amr bi-l-ma'ruf*), they were expected to do so in their own lives while waiting for society to be gradually Islamized through *da'wa* and therefore prepared for Islamic rule. To the extent that *tamkin* or empowerment was possible for the MB, it would happen as the movement expanded its membership and cells in Egyptian society.

As its leaders embraced electoral politics and opportunities over the next two decades, they changed the sequence in which committed Muslims could pursue these goals, with different strategies still framed as righteous action and worship. Notably, they argued that *tamkin* or state power, in whatever piecemeal form possible through partial electoral success, could sustain the *daʿwa* because state power, via laws and administrative and educational institutions, helped to protect and enable, or potentially restrict, the free practice of Islam, whether through preaching and sound religious education, or through the resources with which the state could implement or undermine social justice. MB activists were increasingly directed to pursue *tamkin* at any site in which they could exercise authority, whether in everyday social institutions or in bureaucratic and electoral positions, and to use their social or political influence or resources to spread God's word, enact Islamic justice or elevate and empower pious people, all of which would draw others closer to God. For instance, applying Islamic justice through social service programs might be helped by access to institutional or economic resources, which could, in turn, expand the movement's social implantation by drawing in new members impressed by the exemplary work of Muslims in power. Work toward *tamkin* was therefore spiritually valuable because it helped both to establish Islamic justice and to persuade more people to become committed Muslims.

Similarly, the leadership defended electoral opportunities from the mid-1980s onward as allowing Muslims to access not only more resources for *daʿwa* but also legislative and institutional influence that could enable good Muslims to ensure that Islam was defended as a value in public education and law, and that state action remained within the bounds of sharia. The *tamkin* offered by electoral politics and state influence could be used to bring people justice and instill in them Islamic values, thereby allowing the state to be an ally of the *daʿwa* and support the bottom-up work of preaching and cultivation. Additionally, the movement leadership expanded its advocacy for applying (*tatbiq*) or implementing (*tanfidh*) the rules and norms of the sharia in everyday life, from arguing that this was the obligation of individual Muslims in their own lives, homes, and movement *usar* (families, or cells) but that only an Islamic state could ultimately apply sharia in the public sphere, to urging these individual Muslims to apply and enforce these norms in any sphere in which they could use their influence. They elaborated this argument over years of justifying participation in electoral politics that was not likely to allow Islamists to attain real power in government, but that allowed for incremental gains in social influence, perceiving new opportunities to work for God as worth taking advantage of, in line with Banna's exhortation to apply Islam in all possible spheres of one's life. Movement leaders also reframed sharia implementation to extend to using whatever tools were available to good Muslims—including those offered by the state and elected positions—to solve the problems of citizens and work for a more just society.

All of these new ways of working for God required skills that had to be reconciled with the movement's understanding of *tarbiya* or spiritual cultivation, particularly as the MB increased its investment in electoral work in the 2000s, and as the movement faced divisions over whether or not political specialization would detract from the *da'wa*. After the 1990s, movement educational materials framed the skills and capacity necessary to use public institutions and elected positions effectively and ethically, for the material and moral betterment of the nation, as interchangeable with the skills needed to work for God within movement organizational circles. Movement leaders emphasized that public outreach and activism could both cultivate an individual activist's spiritual growth and serve as a kind of *tarbiya* for others. This "social *tarbiya*" (*tarbiya ijtima'iyya*) actively depended on dealings with the world outside the movement. The MB had historically approached such dealings (*ta'mul*) strategically, either as a way of ensuring the movement's survival, or as a way of spreading the *da'wa*. By the mid-2000s, however, the movement's directive discourse represented dealings with others, whether through electoral outreach, constituent service, or social welfare work through public institutions, as religiously meritorious acts in themselves, insofar as they were motivated by a desire to please God. Drawing people to Islam and cultivating the public support needed for projects of Islamic governance to succeed, even in hostile and corrupt settings, was a kind of righteous action. Doing good for others in social and economic interactions and acting with an eye to religious perfection (*ihsan*) in interpersonal relations had long been encouraged as marketers of spiritual growth in the movement. A range of political and social activities, such as making decisions according to the norms of *shura*, in movement or electoral work, were included in metrics of religious growth for movement activists by the time the MB formed an official political party in 2011. Similarly, acts like speaking truth to power, in the process of electoral campaigning or parliamentary debate, holding government accountable to believing citizens and to God, and other forms of work that contributed to building a more Islamic and just political order were held up as forms of individual ethical cultivation and as religious obligations in *tarbiya* materials by 2011. The social nature of such work was key: engaging others in righteous action, by urging them to vote by their conscience, to support godly candidates, or to work for the positive reform (*islah*) of the nation, building support for Islamic norms of justice and opposing all that violated God's will, were all religiously meritorious acts for both for the preacher-activist and the recipient of their message.

Because these forms of work were aimed at the public good, they were also considered collective religious duties (*al-furud al-kifaya*) that required cooperation and organization. A "just" society was key to the comprehensive mission of Islam, for Banna, who framed an Islamic order that respected and cultivated upright Muslims in contradistinction to the tyranny of immoral rulers and those who supported the oppression of Islam, either directly or through un-Islamic institutions and laws. The MB's directive discourse in its *tarbiya* materials by 2011 expanded the definition of an "Islamic" order to include multiple kinds of concrete and worldly efforts to do good for people and to achieve everyday social justice, from the distribution of subsidized bread to preventing corrupt merchants from claiming popular subsidies, with legal support from a state that was guided by sharia. Training materials for advanced activists argued that the jihad needed to uphold the Islamic order against those who sought to weaken it included training and sacrifice for political work, and not just war against the foreign enemies of Islam.

Possibilities and Limits of Reframing

What lessons can we draw from the MB's evolution about how and why Islamist "mission talk" evolves, and what remains constant, as movements participate in electoral politics? Political opportunities matter in pushing Islamist leaders to rethink their operational and strategic priorities in working for more Islamic societies. State repression or the opening of new possibilities for influence triggered rethinking for the MB, just as leadership transitions did. Yet movement responses to these opportunities were not only instrumental but also expressive and performative: leaders strategically framed these opportunities in terms of their ability to serve movement success, which they defined in terms of the *da'wa* mission as much as electoral gains. Political learning and adaptation followed an identity-upholding logic alongside an electoral one. Supporting what Schwedler (2006) and Pfeifer (2019) observe for Islamist movements in Yemen and Jordan, and Tunisia, respectively, I find that MB leaders regularly engaged in internal debates about what politics meant for the movement's overall commitments to preaching and cultivation, making considerable efforts to persuade members to rethink what could constitute "justifiable" action for Islam, and that these debates were important in producing lasting changes in the movement's directive discourse.

I also find, following Schmidt (2008, 309), that "institutionalized ideas," or those that are incorporated into formal organizational norms and practices, such as training programs, are likely to constrain future decisions and to allow members to embrace new forms of activism. Throughout different stages of political experimentation, the MB leadership emphasized the continuity of its goals, and the identity of its members, and the movement's primary focus on building the righteous individual and society, for their salvation. Political work was always represented as upholding, not undermining, this mission: a just social and political order was valuable for individual and collective salvation, and for doing God's will on earth, more than for the worldly outcomes that it helped to achieve, which, activists were reminded, were for God, not humans, to decide. This insistence on the religious grounding of political work, and the religious merits that the movement leadership assigned to social outreach, helped motivate activists in the absence of concrete political successes. Leaders also considered some strategic options and alliances desirable because they enabled activists to live up to their Islamic values and uphold their identities: for instance, building oases of justice and doing good in everyday life, rather than withdrawing from public life and letting injustice and corruption dominate in society or in parliament. Potential voters and supporters mattered as Muslims whose righteousness could be cultivated and expressed through outreach, and parliament mattered as a site for ethical conduct and commanding the right.

Identity-affirming strategic choices were shaped by the movement's role and position in a wider political and religious field, as well as within the political discourse of Egyptian "national Islam." Implementing sharia was a goal that it shared with the Azhari religious establishment and, later, with newly politicized Salafi parties, and this enabled the MB to present its mission as one that aimed to uphold rather than overturn the existing national consensus on the need for Islam-infused law and education. It also pushed the movement to define its mission for social Islamization in distinction to the statist Azhari mission, notably in emphasizing the need for the Azhari establishment to serve the nation rather than the political elite and applying sharia through popular accountability. When the MB faced the choice, after 2011, of competing or allying with the newly politicized Salafis, or working with non-Islamist democratic parties, its leadership chose to uphold its Islamic identity, disciplining those who thought that the new FJP must formally separate from the MB as a base movement. Yet it also presented itself as the most reliable Islamic party not because of its more puritanical approach to Islamic law and willingness to apply the penal code of sharia, but because of its experience in service and its skills in working for the good of Muslims.

Tying religious obligation so closely to political work was not uncontroversial in the MB, given the movement's continuing commitment to seeing politics as only one part of a broader mission of social Islamization, and its historical aversion to partisanship. The movement's directive discourse, particularly its educational materials, reaffirmed that politics must remain in the service of *da'wa* and could not replace it, and that those active in politics must continue to cultivate their spiritual discipline to be sure that they remained guided by God's will in whatever they did. Yet this discourse expanded the scope of righteous and religiously meritorious action and concepts like commanding the right and applying sharia to include governance and social service, such that *da'wa* no longer occupied a clear space outside politics. At the same time, it continued to affirm that, while political achievements helped people gain religious merits, political success was not to be pursued for itself: activists still worked for God and depended on divine approval for positive outcomes. Electoral majority-seeking after the 2011 uprising brought the tensions inherent in this framing into relief. Activists who argued that *ta'mul* with those outside the movement for the goal of establishing a godly political order required building coalitions with a wide range of actors to support a democratic state, and that those with strong political skills were best suited to the task of building a more Islamic state, found themselves at odds with a leadership that continued to prioritize religious cultivation and piety as metrics of advancement within the new political party and to be wary of any political strategy that was not clearly justified as advancing religious training and goals. After the movement's political ambitions were thwarted by a military-led coup, supported by a substantial popular movement, that overthrew Mohammed Morsi, many Brothers who had been wary of a political strategy, and many who had been convinced that the movement would not fail politically as long as it had God's favor, challenged the idea that politics could help achieve the goals of the *da'wa*.

Some activists argued that supporting amoral political strategy and elevating political goals over those of serving God had been a mistake, and that the failure of the MB's first experiment in governance was because they had not prioritized religious cultivation first. This group contended that pursuing state power before ensuring that society was thoroughly Islamized had been a mistake, and that the movement must now return to its missionizing work and put off the political project. Others thought that making the legitimacy of an Islamic order and God's will contingent on political outcomes controlled by mere humans, was a religious mistake, one that risked demeaning religion in the eyes of the people rather than elevating it. While some in this category argued that this required rejecting political work altogether, others made the case that the lessons of 2013 were that political work should be clearly separated from—and pursued independently of—the *da'wa* mission, even as it continued to be guided by Islamic values, so as to avoid discrediting God by presenting flawed humans as His agents. Some of these critics argued that the lesson of the coup was that the MB had not invested adequately in cultivating political skills and could and should do better at winning elections. Yet others asserted that the coup had shown Islamists that, while political power was important for the Islamic project, the Egyptian state would always find a way to undermine Islamist electoral victories, and that the movement should have taken a more revolutionary approach to overhauling the state right away, rather than focusing on using limited state capacities for moral oversight and cultivation. In the various self-critique statements and proposal for organizational rehauling that emerged from competing movement factions in the next two years, the main lines of division centered on different strategies and short- and medium-term priorities for achieving an Islamic political order, rather than on "organization-first" versus "politics-first" lines.

Framing political work as guided by divine truth did, however, raise the stakes of political dissent within the movement, fragmenting its unity, as the Brothers became increasingly invested in politics from the mid-2000s onward. Studies by Vannetzel (2014) and Menshawy (2021) of MB members who were alienated from the movement show how disagreement over political choices could quickly escalate into accusations of insufficient religious commitment within movement ranks. Because members were supposed to devote their lives and subsume their individual views and preferences to those of the *gama'a*, in order to follow its guidance on how best to serve God in every sphere of life, those who resisted the hierarchical decision-making or strategic choices of the movement leadership were frequently ostracized as insufficiently moral (Vannetzel 2014). The master frame of *rabaniyya*, or how to arrange one's relationship with God, that Menshawy (2021, 7) highlights as key to how Brothers understand their place in the movement and in the world, and the equation of "satisfying God" with "satisfying the movement," with its insistence on the importance of the *gama'a*'s solidarity and group support for living as a good Muslim, made it easy to frame dissidents as being insufficiently pious, or even as having rejected religion itself. Further, movement members who had been trained to see political and social work as guided by a strong—even utopian—ethical vision, could quickly become disillusioned with strategic choices that the leadership made for political gain or self-preservation, again weakening unity and commitment within movement ranks (12–13).

Comparative Lessons

As the "mother movement" for many Arab Islamist movements, the MB is frequently held up as an example for Islamist evolution in other contexts. And, like the MB, Islamist movements in countries like Morocco and Tunisia are also understood to change mainly in response to political incentives from the state, or democratization processes, with the background assumption that all Islamist movements ultimately seek political power and will adapt operationally and, eventually, ideologically, in order to maximize their public influence. Movements like the Movement for Unity and Reform (MUR) in Morocco and Ennahda in Tunisia did encounter political opportunities that presented them with choices between electoral success and fidelity to their *da'wa* mission, and the different economies of religious and political competition that they faced did influence their strategies. As with the MB, tensions between mother movements and the political parties that their leaders formed from the early 2000s onward resulted, to some extent, from organizational divisions of labor and priorities, and the ideological compromises that would be necessary for further political success (see, e.g., Brown 2012a; Wolf 2017; Spiegel 2015). However, in most of these movements, their ideational rethinking and ultimate choices regarding electoral strategy also depended on internal movement reframing of political strategies in terms of concepts of ethical and godly action, and individual and collective salvation. Some of these choices, such as the Moroccan Adl wa Ihsan's decision not to engage in electoral politics despite accepting politics and the state as important players in the quest for Islamic justice, and the Tunisian Ennahda's decision to separate party work from preaching, despite a commitment to seeing politics as bound to apply Islamic notions of justice, cannot be sufficiently understood as direct responses to opportunities for power, but require tracing how movement leaders persuasively presented some political strategies as more faithful to core notions of righteous action than others. The trajectories of these movements show similar processes of adaptation to politics as we have seen in the case of the MB and also demonstrate that it is difficult to predict how an Islamist movement will adapt to electoral politics as a function of its theological principles of action, or the political opportunities it faces. Framing righteous action in terms of religious obligation mattered in defining changing operational priorities for these movements over time, and even in whether or not they chose to separate preaching from electoral work, but we see substantial contingency in how this reframing helped justify different political strategies.

The Moroccan Islamist social movement sector offers an example of how movements with similar goals and political incentives formulated their strategies in response to new political opportunities in terms of different concepts of righteous action. The two main Islamist movements in Morocco, the Movement for Unity and Reform (MUR), with its offshoot Justice and Development Party (PJD), and the Adl wa Ihsan, or Justice and Charity movement (AWI), both promoted *tarbiya* and *da'wa* to help people live according to God's will, and, like the MB, both held that the moral renewal of the citizenry was an essential prerequisite for social reform and justice. Both movements arose out of different social and historical contexts—the MUR from student *jama'at* in the 1980s, and the AWI around a charismatic, anti-monarchist, former Sufi leader in the late 1970s. Both used a similar bottom-up approach to cultivating young people's Islamic ethics and organizing them through religious study groups and family cells (*usar*) to be better Muslims and spread the *da'wa*, working on the assumption that existing state institutions and public education were inadequate for religious cultivation, even with a state that formally accepted the king as "commander of the faithful." By the late 1990s and early oughts, the Moroccan state establishment, which allowed multipartyism while placing security restrictions on parties deemed threatening to the monarchy, offered Islamist movements the opportunity to form legal political parties, and the MUR formed a party, the PJD, while the AWI refused to, even though it developed a political bureau or "circle." The two movements justified their choices in terms of similar concepts of religious activism, while diverging on what role the state could productively play in promoting social Islamization.

The founder of AWI, Abdelsalam Yassine, was similar to Banna in centering individual spiritual growth and salvation as the ultimate goal of all activism, whether social or political. Like Banna, he believed that *tarbiya* and individual transformation were the starting point of all social change, and that righteous companionship (*suhba*) and regular religious practice enabled believers to act righteously in their lives; like Banna, he also emphasized a believer's obligation to work for social Islamization, by commanding the right, exhorting others to follow Muslim norms, and offering advice (*nasiha*) to those in power (Yafout 2017; Houston 2017, 155–59). Yassine urged Muslim activists to act for Islam in various spheres of life, but warned against action without proper spiritual preparation: correcting the outward manifestations of spiritual decay, such as un-Islamic behavior, separately from the spiritual decay that caused it, was akin to focusing on removing rotten fruit rather than the diseased branches that produced them (Houston 2017, 159).

Yassine evoked the same hadith about commanding the right through the hand, the heart, and the tongue that Banna and later Brothers had done and evoked Mawdudi and Qutb in arguing that an Islamic society needed a vanguard to act as "soldiers of God" and lead people out of ignorance, but prioritized a different process for social Islamization (Houston 2017, 159). In his foundational text, *Al-minhaj al-nabawi* (The Prophetic Method), he asserted that pious Muslims had a collective obligation (*fard kifaya*) to serve people, which required acquiring relevant knowledge and using organization and solidarity to help others be more pious (Motouakal 2014, 240). Piety required practical, righteous action: individuals in the AWI movement were urged to cultivate their spirituality through *dhikr,* to fill their days with prayer, *da'wa* and useful work rather than idleness, and to incorporate faith into their everyday routines and economic and social dealings, in order to enact and embody faith in their everyday lives (Motaouakal 2014, 203; Yafout 2017). For Yassine as for Banna, *tarbiya* was both a prerequisite for carrying out social Islamization obligations, and something that could be furthered through social and political outreach. Echoing the MB concept of practical *tarbiya*, the AWI's *minhaj* focused on cultivating virtuous, moral activists inspired by historical Islamic figures who constantly strove to improve their Islamic ethics and could model good Muslimhood for others, while helping them in their economic, social, and moral endeavors (Yafout 2017, 24). The movement exhorted activists to value community action as a way of reducing social injustice, but community work that allowed an activist to be among the people and close to their problems was also meant to awaken their conscience and change their own spiritual practice (24). Contemporary activists affirmed that a good Muslim, in the *gama'a*'s view, had to be an upright citizen (*muwatin salih*) and to love doing good for people.[1] The AWI formed a political division in 1998 to create bridges with other organizations and to explore different methods to pursue its goals, and, as a result, its *tarbiya* expanded to include building political and economic knowledge. It began to publish reports on health care, education, and the economy, with the leader of its political wing declaring that "we are working, we are trying to do our jobs, preparing ourselves ... waiting for the opportunity when it is possible to really participate" (Yildirim 2016, 197).

Yet even those who worked in youth and political sections in the movement insisted that their main goal was salvation: you could not succeed in this world without preparing for the afterlife, and any political work the movement might engage in was intended for *da'wa*.[2] While the ultimate goal of Islamic activism, per Yassine's writings, was to achieve an Islamic state that would have *da'wa* officials be responsible for the spiritual and educational development of believers, this work needed people who had attained a certain level of *tarbiya* and had first developed virtues like faith, sacrifice, moderation, and, ultimately, *ihsan* or goodness and excellence in all behavior (Motaouakal 2014, 237–40). An individual Muslim could not behave well with others, in the AWI approach, until

---

1. Interview, MBM, Casablanca, July 7, 2016.
2. Interview, ML, Rabat, June 23, 2016; interview, MB, Casablanca, June 17, 2016.

they achieved individual *ihsan* or excellence in their behavior and corrected their own relationship with God; therefore, they must first work on cultivating their own good behavior (*suluk*), ethics (*akhlaq*), and relations with family members.³ *Tarbiya* was intended to infuse all aspects of the movement's work, rather than having a place only in the preparatory stages of activism, or in one section of the movement's overall work: one member noted that Abdelsalam Yassine had defined *tarbiya* as something that happened "before, during, and after [any other work], meaning that *tarbiyya* is foundational, we don't say 'the *tarbiyya* side," even when there were separate divisions for economics and politics (Khanani 2021, 117).

Justice (*'adl*) was one of two parts of the movement's mission, and Adlists believed that a good Muslim life is not possible without justice.⁴ When educating others about "real Islam," Adlist activists emphasized that Islam required justice and that their activism required showing people that they cared about social problems and that Islam had answers for these problems.⁵ The movement's aim in society was to radically transform all social, economic, political, and cultural relations and to replace a Western order with one that was based on Islamic reason and spiritual values (Cavatorta 2007, 389). Activists argued that justice was the defining feature of the ideal Islamic order, and that it entailed equity and fair distribution among people. Citing Yassine and repeating similar framings in MB discourse, they contended that the disappearance of the Islamic political regime had been a reason for the decline of Islam in people's lives and beliefs.⁶ Echoing religious sayings cited by the MB, and similar examples from the lives of the early caliphs, Adlists argued that fighting poverty and hunger were important prerequisites for spreading support for Islam socially, because justice was the central value of Islam, and because a hungry person could not hear the word of God.⁷ In Adlist thought, a good

3. Interviews, ML, Rabat, June 23, 2016, Four Adlists, Sale, Morocco, August 13, 2018.
4. Interview, HB, Rabat, June 22, 2016.
5. Interview, MB, Casablanca, June 17, 2016.
6. Interview, MB, Casablanca, June 17, 2016.
7. Interview, CG, Ain Sebaa, August 18, 2018.

Muslim had to be a righteous citizen (*muwatin salih*) and to love doing good for people.⁸

Like Muslim Brothers, Adlists repeated the claim that Islam could not be separated from any aspect of public life.⁹ Yet the movement refused to define a vision of an Islamic state or Islamic governance, or even to engage in electoral politics in the near term, framing Islamic rule (*hukm*) only in terms of democracy and justice. They believed that individual values and social mentalities had to change in order for such a state to be possible, and that the only Islamic government was that which people would choose after they had been properly educated about Islam and allowed to work freely for justice.¹⁰ Social outreach and charity work, whether in the form of medical assistance or help for the poor, was driven by a desire for justice as well as preaching and framed as freeing people from their bonds of slavery to others, empowering them, and helping them recover their confidence (Motaouakal 2014, 208). But godly rule (*hukm*), for Yassine, could be achieved by applying *shura* and working for greater political freedom rather than potentially empowering a morally illegitimate monarchical state (Macias-Amoretti 2015, 341).

Yassine cited Abul Ala Mawdudi's failed project for an Islamic state in Pakistan as a negative example of how inadequate preparation through *tarbiya* would sink efforts at Islamic state-building (Houston 2017, 160–61). Movement activists were also taught that Yassine had learned from the Chinese Cultural Revolution that social mentalities were more important to change than the political structures of a regime.¹¹ Rather than envision a sequence in which a properly educated vanguard would progressively build influence in the state and use its resources to apply sharia or Islamize society more effectively, Adlist activists argued that the corrupt, nominally Muslim Moroccan regime was bound to collapse due to its own

---

8. Interview, MBM, Casablanca, July 7, 2016.
9. Interview, MB, Casablanca, June 17, 2016.
10. Interview, CG, Ain Sebaa, August 18, 2018; interview, MB, Casablanca, June 17, 2016.
11. Interview, HB, Rabat, June 22, 2016.

failures, and that their own mission was to build support for true Islam via *daʿwa* and education, so that people would abide by sharia and learn to love God.¹² A leader of the political circle asserted that freedom and democracy were good because they helped restore the dignity and freedom of Muslims and allowed them to work for the good, by calling to God with gentleness (*rifq*) and offsetting that which was evil with that which was good (Motouakal 2014, 203). Similarly, democracy was good because it allowed Muslims to be better Muslims: it promoted egalitarianism, valued by Islam, and elevated and helped people cultivate and practice *shura*, which was equal to other worshipful practices like prayer and *zakat* in faith (Khanani 2021, 63). It also protected the conditions that made worship possible, and upheld the faith of the majority (202, 204). The good that one could do in political and social activity, by working for a moral, egalitarian distribution of resources and assisting people in attaining bread and dignity, or helping the rich purify their wealth through *zakat*, made such work a form of worship (Khanani 2014, 150–58, 193).

Applying sharia through the state was not, however, a goal that the Adlists identified as part of their mission: instead, they argued, people should be educated so that they chose to apply sharia in their own lives, or in public, whether or not they participated in politics. As one activist stated, bars could be open, but Muslims should be taught not to go to them.¹³ Working for freedom and justice in cooperation with others was a better way to establish sharia, a contemporary leader of the political circle maintained, than to establish a state that applied the letter of Islamic law while neglecting its spirit, as Saudi Arabia and Sudan had done.¹⁴

Despite approaching political work and democratic endeavors in very similar ways, as forms of righteous action, aimed at bringing people individually and collectively closer to God, Adlists, Muslim Brothers, and MUR/PJD activists approached empowerment or *tamkin* via politics very differently. *Tamkin* was something that Adlists believed should be done

---

12. Interview, HB, Rabat, June 22, 2016; interview, ML, Rabat, June 23, 2016.
13. Interview, ML, Rabat, June 23, 2016.
14. Interview, HB, Rabat, June 22, 2016.

at the grassroots level of society and through *daʿwa*, rather than via seats in parliament or portfolios in government (Motaouakal 2014, 206–7). Building organizational strength and wealth were perceived as kinds of jihad by Yassine, and his argument that giving money to a cause was a good way to convert pious intentions into tangible results resembled the MB approach to organization building as well (Bienert 2007, 22–24). Like the MB, Adlists thought that organizations were not valuable in and of themselves, but for the purpose they could serve: those without good principles were "bodies without souls," and they placed national political parties in this category, because they cooperated with and upheld a corrupt regime (Bienert 2007, 22–24). They encouraged members to be active in student and professional associations; undertook social service, literacy, and job training projects; and developed new sections for students, civil servants, and women, because these kinds of institutions enabled people to cooperate in the service of justice, do *daʿwa* by transmitting correct ethics through their work, and make progress toward salvation by living just lives and serving people.[15] These were all the more necessary for serving God and justice, as the state generally restricted Adlists from working in recognized mosques, as "oppositional" religious actors, and because they offered Muslims a chance to be empowered and free of their position as "consumers, importers, and debtors" in everyday social and economic life (Yafout 2017; Yildirim 2016, 196).

The AWI built enough popular support from its social and religious activism that it was able to turn out large numbers of people for protests against government policies and, as such, could have leveraged the social capital it had built for power-seeking, had it chosen to.[16] Yet the movement leadership saw its strength as reduced, not increased, by political participation. Nadia Yassine, the daughter of the founder and his successor, stated that "we prefer to keep our strength; our strength is on the confidence of our people, their trust; we don't want to be puppets in the government" (Yildirim 2016, 196). The MUR/PJD also framed its mission of

---

15. Interview, ML, Rabat, June 23, 2016.
16. Interview, HB, Rabat, June 22, 2016.

working for Islam in terms of cultivating individuals through proper *tarbiya*, and for Islamic values of equity and *shura*; however, they reacted to new political opportunities differently, arguing that political engagement did allow for Islamic work. The MUR had shared the MB's skepticism of politics, and Ahmad Raysuni, its intellectual leader in the late 1990s and early 2000s, had openly criticized Banna's vision of an eventual Islamic state for privileging the wrong kind of activism and allowing the state to monopolize the definition of the common good, arguing that it was better to cultivate a community of pious citizens that would be vigilant in working for the common good and would apply God's will in society (Zeghal 2008, 190–92). In later years, however, the PJD accepted elections as valuable for the Islamic mission, as long as candidates agreed to serve God and not be personally ambitious, because elections could help to work out how to apply God's will and achieve the interest (*maslaha*) of believers in a given set of circumstances (Khanani 2014, 242–44; Willis 2007, 47; Zeghal 2008, 187–91).

Where AWI leaders perceived the monarchical political order as a fundamental violation of Islam and were content with acts of righteous resistance to a corrupt state, PJD leaders acted on the incentives offered by the Moroccan regime to build their own institutional resources and to ensure that their organizational flourished (Spiegel 2015b). They framed the benefits of participation, particularly through *shura*, as accruing to both pious individuals and society, because it allowed people to carry out righteous work that was broadly beneficial (*'amal salih mufid*) and was a way of working for the betterment of the nation and ensuring that its powerful institutions defended Islam rather than weakening it (Macias-Amoretti 2015, 340). Further, they argued that elections were an important tool for cultivating *shura* and even if the outcomes of electoral processes and decisions were less than ideally Islamic, they were helpful in revealing public opinion and showing activists where they needed to work harder in educating people to be better Muslims (Zeghal 2008, 196–97). When the PJD finally recognized the monarchy and pledged allegiance to the new king in 1999, it positioned itself as a defender of the nation's Islamic identity, pushing the state to make sharia the main source of legislation and working for Islamic reform within the framework of the constitutional monarchy (Zeghal 2008, 196–97). In part, this reframing was rooted in the MUR's predecessor organizations' older commitment to implementing sharia and working for cultural renaissance and Muslim unity in addition to raising the educational and moral level of the people (Yildirim 2016, 199). The MUR put out a paper explaining its rationale for supporting more political participation in the 1980s that emphasized the utility of politics for protecting *da'wa* and in pushing back against the power of secularists in the public sphere, and it also increasingly argued that "by working on social justice, economic development, we are working to implement in principle what Islam is calling for" (Yildirim 2016, 199, 205).

The PJD's decision to accept the opportunity offered to it by the regime to contest elections and accept formal recognition was a choice presented in terms of what might help it achieve its goals of social Islamization. Survival and organizational resources were valuable to the PJD, and it saw value in being recognized and protected by the state, and benefited from the "spoils of inclusion" (Spiegel 2015, chapter 2). But, in order to justify this choice, it had to first acknowledge the Moroccan regime as fundamentally Islamic rather than fundamentally unjust, as the AWI did, so that working with the state could be a help rather than a hindrance to the religious mission: the argument of *maslaha* or pursuing the public good was possible if the political order was not framed in terms of *mafsada* or corruption (Macias-Amoretti 2015, 337). The PJD's party platforms in 2002 and 2007 defined its goal as "find[ing] solutions to the daily problems of citizens," and the party increasingly emphasized that public affairs and corruption were as important to address as questions of Islamic identity and morals, for Islamic justice (Yildirim 2016, 200–202). Party leader Saadeddine el-Othmani declared that "our party wants to prioritize the economic and social development of the country, not sharia" (Yildirim 2016, 204, 206). While PJD representatives in parliament tried to ensure that state power and resources were used to promote Arab and Islamic education and raised issues like limiting new alcohol licenses, opposing immoral tourism and banking and microcredit programs that used what they considered un-Islamic usury, they generally did not refer to sharia as a body of laws, but as a set of guiding principles (Yildirim 2016, 206; Willis 2007, 66–67). In later years, the PJD came to justify some interest-bearing loans as acceptable if they brought about economic efficiency that would be good for public welfare (Yildirim 2016, 213). During debates about the reform of the Islamic family law code (*moudawana*), the PJD also came to justify legislative outcomes that led to the dilution of sharia codes because the *shura* process that had produced these outcomes was religiously valuable and legitimate, and *dimuqratiyya* or democracy was a valuable way to give people the rights they were due as Muslims (Khanani 2021, 131–36). This was despite the fact that, when the reforms were first proposed, PJD activists had marched alongside those of the AWI to protest it and called for any revisions to be made in conformity with Islam (Zeghal 2008, 244–55).

Where the PJD's activists saw state power as important in defending the holy, AWI members rejected any role for a state in this regard because it was driven by a flawed belief in the monarch's sacredness (Khanani 2014, 270–71). They did not see the state as a potential ally for *daʿwa* as the MB had come to do, even with increased opportunities for electoral power. The AWI focused on the spiritual implications of *shura* primarily for Muslim individuals and framed political participation and voting as activities that could not be spiritually edifying; voting was actually a polluting rather than an ennobling exercise in a corrupt regime, even though democracy was itself a desirable Islamic goal, because it risked getting Islamists "imprisoned in the vicious circle of carrying out instructions from the higher echelons of power" and becoming part of the establishment (*makhzen*) (Cavatorta 2007, 392–93). The PJD, by contrast, conceived of political work as enabling people to change their own lives and those of others for the better, through the skills and social reputation they could gain in the process (Spiegel 2015, 94–96). Reputation and resources were valuable for the PJD in enabling them to offer what they thought were better Islamic cultural alternatives for youth, such as Islamic art, drama, and music events, and Spiegel (2015, chapters 6 and 7) argues that their public visibility and ability to win elections helped recruit young people who were pious and wanted to make a difference, as well as those who wanted more "clean" leadership in politics. While the party formally separated from the MUR movement, and PJD activists distanced their goals from the more narrowly religious ones of enforcing social morality over time, religious activities and movement study sessions remained appealing for party activists and religious ethics remained valuable for their progress in the party (180–90). PJD leaders declared, in 2008, that there could be no "policy without morality," and that their mission continued to be to instill good values in young people and to protect families and morals while seeking renewal according to the teachings of Islam, citing a hadith that said that faith was in the heart but verified by action (Spiegel 2015, 187–88). Where their rivals in the AWI saw the inseparability of faith from all aspects of life as requiring the faithful to stay away from electoral politics, the PJD framed a two-track commitment to preaching and electoral politics, each spearheaded by different organizational leaders, but guided by the same values, as the best way to honor the unity of faith and action.

The Islamist Ennahda movement in Tunisia trod a more similar path to the MB in framing democracy as fundamentally grounded in *shura* and in deepening its organizational commitment to electoral participation and state-directed work as ideally suited for achieving the goals of justice and the public good that its leaders framed as the heart of sharia. As it expanded its participation in parliament and government after the Tunisian uprising in 2011, Ennahda made a clearer organizational division between its preaching and political party wings than the MB had, forming a political party with a formal commitment to secularist norms, and a separate leadership structure. In 2016, the party officially separated itself from the Ennahda social movement and declared its commitment to "Muslim democracy," with Islam as a normative framework for state and politics, instead of "Islamism," with a goal of founding an Islamic state (Pfeifer 2019, 490–93). But, even with a formal separation of party and movement, Ennahda presented its strategic choices as continuous and coherent with its founding Islamic mission.

The Ennahda Party's political leader, Rached Ghannouchi, was also its historical movement leader, and he led the movement to embrace party politics not only as a pragmatic choice within political constraints but also as part of its mission to build a more Islamic—and more authentically Tunisian—society (Cavatorta and Merone 2015, 32–35). Advocating electoral participation as a way to respect and enact Islamic norms, Ennahda leaders from 2011 onward argued that democracy "reflect[ed] the Islamic principles of consultation, justice, and accountability," and that both Islam and democracy were, in their best forms, guided by a shared concern for consensus and opposition to tyranny. As such, Islam could and should provide a normative framework for democracy, particularly in embodying the norms of *shura* by translating Islam's values into law through public deliberation (Pfeifer 2019, 490–91).

When they won a plurality in early elections to the first freely elected legislature following Ben Ali's overthrow in 2011, which prioritized writing a new constitution, Ennahda leaders resisted pressure from conservative Salafi activists to use their access to state power to enforce respect for religion—for instance, by punishing media or public expression that attacked Islamic belief and sacred symbols. They argued that one could apply sharia more effectively by working for justice and following sharia as a set of values and teachings rather than textual prescriptions, which were in any event already established in Tunisian law (Pfeifer 2019, 492). Ennahda's leaders debated the question of whether a new constitution required a formal acceptance of sharia to be Islamic, and Ghannouchi contended that the *shari'i* goals of justice and liberty that could be attained through democracy mattered more than the formal trappings of an Islamic state. Most Ennahda leaders believed that working for Islam in politics meant pursuing the goals (*maqasid*) of sharia, solving everyday problems through *ijtihad*, and inculcating good Islamic values in everyday citizens and their political representatives so as to allow individuals to work for justice (Cavatorta and Merone 2015, 33–37).

For Ennadha, electoral participation and campaigning were forms of working for justice, as long as they were guided by the goals of Islam, and this left room open for other forms of activism to complement electoral activism, and for other ideological entrepreneurs, notably Salafis, to assert their own strategies as more effective in attaining these Islamic goals (Cavatorta and Merone 2015, 38). Even within the broader Ennahda movement, politically engaged activists did not give up preaching and charitable work for electoral work and, by some accounts, even expanded their commitment to charitable work after 2016 (Sigillo 2020, 2–3). This activity was seen as complementing political work for Ennahda activists, rather than being a stage prior to it, and many of them started new *zakat* and *sadaqa*-driven charities in response to the new opportunities offered by political liberalization and access to outside (often Gulf Arab) sources of support, and in response to more social demand for dignity and freedom for Tunisians, and reduced dependence on state clientelism. In charity work as in politics, Ennahda activists echoed the MB norm that all of life must be based on Islamic values, claiming that "we do it for God," out of religious obligation, and not for self-interest or nonreligious forms of social obligation (Sigillo 2020, 8). They cooperated with political activists for different goals and saw *da'wa* and political work as a division of labor for the same task: the spiritual and material reconstruction of society that would solve people's problems and help them be better Muslims (8). Indeed, some asserted, "*da'wa* is the true politics. It's crucial to develop it from below, from the associative field" (17). In some instances, Ennahda social activists even collaborated with Salafi and other Islamic associations to protest artistic productions they deemed anti-Islamic, or to push for more references to religious law in the constitutions (11). Many of their new religious charities were also as comfortable using the language of capacity building, transparency, good governance, and human development as ways of working for the good as they were talking about more conventionally religious forms of public piety (12). While acknowledging that some of their colleagues believed that politics could serve Islamic goals, they also saw value in creating networks to "resist the aggression of the state" and to preserve pious life worlds that allowed people to live modern, yet religiously lawful, lives (13). Therefore, many strategies for social Islamization and for *tamkin* via state and nonstate institutions coexisted and presented feasible options for working for Islam in the Tunisian Islamist movement.

Like Islamist movements rooted in MB thought, Salafi movements in both Egypt and Tunisia developed new interpretations of religious obligation to justify participating in electoral politics after 2011, although their theological starting points differed, and their arguments for the kind of work that counted as godly in the electoral sphere led them to different ends. Like the MB, the PJD and AWI, and Ennahda, Salafi movements varied in how they interpreted similar obligations to spread God's word and work for an Islamic sociopolitical order in a context of political liberalization. Karagiannis (2019, 210–14) argues that Salafis across the Arab world accepted the "master frame" of democracy as compatible, in principle, with Islam, after the 2011 uprisings, and recognized that any goal of establishing an Islamic political order required working pragmatically with the existing political system. Egyptian Salafi movements, notably the Dawa Salafiyya, formed political parties and decided to participate in parliamentary elections in 2011, on the grounds that the religious obligation to ensure that Islam permeated all aspects of a Muslim's life extended to the political sphere (213-14). Yet the Nour Party, the most prominent and successful of the Egyptian Salafi parties, did not consider majority-seeking and control over the state the ultimate goal of its political participation and took a more pragmatic approach to cooperating strategically with different political groups to achieve short-term policy goals that its leaders believed would allow for more Islamic governance. They cooperated with socialists in opposing an IMF loan with terms they deemed usurious, even as the MB argued that its importance for the public good and its low interest rates made it compatible with Islam, and they worked together with the MB to establish stronger constitutional provisions requiring sharia conformity for new legislation (Utvik 2014, 16-21).

Egyptian and Tunisian Salafis alike embraced democracy and citizen empowerment as helpful for increasing the social influence of Islam and, like Ennahda and the MB, framed individual rights as an important foundation to allow citizens to build a more Muslim political order (Karagiannis 2019, 216-17). They retained their skepticism of party politics as a potential deviation from *tawhid* and force for divisive partisanship while accepting elections as a useful first step to bringing those who supported Islam together to work for its political success (Hamming 2013). The various Salafi parties that formed in Tunisia, Egypt, and in other parts of the Arab world added institutional political work to their traditional repertoire of cultivating individual piety and Islamic lifestyles, but defined very different goals for that work (Cavatorta and Resta 2020). Tunisian Salafis were divided among those that remained quietist, those that chose to work outside the formal political order because they viewed electoral politics as rooted in something other than Islam, and those that embraced politics, the latter mostly drawn to the potential for controlling the state and the constitution-writing process so that the political order could be guided by God's law and no other (Blanc 2021, 4-7). This group saw *daʿwa* and religious associations as part of their mission, but argued that "those who possess the reins of affairs to change the country . . . are the parties, and not the associations" (Blanc 2021, 11).

Some political Salafis favored economic policies and tools that could be used to work for the goals of social justice and wealth purification or redistribution that undergirded *zakat*, while others framed Islamic economic goals as requiring national economic independence, and Salafi groups who agreed that political engagement was necessary to act for Islamic norms of economic justice nevertheless disagreed about whether private enterprise and military enterprise were useful or harmful in upholding these norms (Cavatorta and Resta 2020, 11–14). Salafis were broadly committed to individual religious education and moral reform as the root of a better society, but their operational priorities for political activism, and their policy and strategic positions were flexible. For the Nour Party, religious education and oversight to ensure that politicians, bureaucrats, and businessmen acted according to correct religious precepts was important, as was activism to make sure that Islam rather than secularism governed the political system, but, unlike the MB in their time in parliament, Salafi politicians did not consider specific policies or modes of representation and governance to be embodiments of key Islamic values. Yet Egyptian and other Salafi parties continued to move beyond their older suspicion of working with a morally imperfect political order, and Salafis in Kuwait who had more experience with parliamentary participation increasingly legitimized different elements of electoral politics in terms of sharia as well as national welfare (Utvik 2014, 11–15). A Kuwaiti Salafi thinker with broad influence across the eastern Arab states has also highlighted freedom and the right of believers to choose those in power over them and to participate in decision making as central to rule by sharia (Utvik 2014, 20–22).

Rethinking the religious acceptability of politics broadly did not suffice to push Salafis into electoral participation; Islamist movement leaders and thinkers also made different choices based on their interpretation of the possibility of religiously ethical activism and political outcomes within specific local political circumstances. Kuwait Salafi parties held back from electoral participation despite increasingly sympathetic statements from associated thinkers because, like the Moroccan Adl wa Ihsan, they thought that the political opportunities available would not allow them to work for a godly state (Utvik 2014). Tunisian Salafis similarly interpreted available political opportunities as allowing legitimate or illegitimate activism differently, leading some Salafi groups to embrace politics as useful for serving the country, and others to reject the existing Tunisian political order as one that did not allow Tunisia to operate as a land where *da'wa* was possible. These factions disagreed on finer distinctions between situations and activism that were merely religiously permissible versus desirable, and whether participation in a given election could serve the *maslaha* (interest) of the religious community (Utvik 2014; Blanc 2021, 6–9, 12).

Implications and Questions for Further Research

Islamist movements evolve in responding to political opportunities and by reframing what it means to act for God, but rarely along a single or irreversible pathway. They do not differ substantially from social movements more broadly in interpreting political opportunities in terms of founding ideals and in being able to justify a wide range of strategies in terms of these ideals. The radically different adaptive strategies—participation, abstention, and opposition to electoral politics—that have been considered suitable for working for God and cultivating good Muslim activists by movements with similar theological frameworks show that it is difficult to predict how Islamist movements will change in response to new political opportunities. Arab Islamist movements have shown that they are quite capable of renewing commitments to preaching and charitable while investing in electoral party building. Further, movement leaders and thinkers may accept electoral work as compatible with the values of individual spiritual cultivation without necessarily deepening their commitment to principles of individual freedom or political pluralism for their own sake, or accepting all aspects of democracy as compatible with Islamic values and goals.

The lessons of Egyptian and other Arab Islamisms suggest that some framings of activism as kinds of *da'wa*, or forms of empowerment as godly, enable further commitment to activism that can serve goals that are less clearly tied to Islamic principles, but that help cement movement commitment to working through state and political institutions. As such, commitments at one point in political time can pave the way for a wider movement commitment to politics. The ability of organizations to retool their operational priorities and directive discourse to frame electoral politics as supportive of ethical action for godly political outcomes helps determine which Islamic movements will participate in democratic politics. It is, however, less clear how starting ideas and principles lend themselves to particular kinds of political reframing, as evidenced by the divergent paths of MB-inspired movements, and similarities between MB and Salafi movements in the kinds of accommodation with electoral politics that they made. Founding ideals of what counts as Islamic activism limit the possibilities of evolution but do not necessarily direct it, and groups that participate in electoral politics may do so tentatively and instrumentally rather than out of democratic conviction. As such, coding movements as radical or moderate based on founding ideals is less helpful than identifying the key junctures in their responses to political opportunities or their internal evolution where they may choose to embrace electoral and democratic participation or not.

While this research suggests that tensions between organization-first and electoral factions of Islamist movements are less critical than previous research indicated for determining which movements invest in electoral politics and when, it does confirm that Islamist movements themselves see a potential tension between *da'wa* and political work in their operational and organizational priorities and seek to limit this tension. What internal organizational politics shape Islamist movement leaders' choices to embrace or downgrade electoral politics as part of their mission is not within the scope of this analysis. As Islamist movements like the MB become less unified and disciplined, however, it will be important to know who has the authority and credibility within movements to shape directive discourse about righteous political action, and what political pressures they face. We do not yet know who within the MB might push for reinterpretations of religious practice in politics, and what might make one interpretation hegemonic in a movement that no longer has a clear authority governing *tarbiya*. As political failures for Islamist movements and parties pile up, and electoral space shrinks once again in the Arab world, Islamists who supported participation because it could lead to what they saw as more Islamic political outcomes, such as sharia-governed policies and successful *da'wa*, and those who embrace participation for its role in cultivating good Islamic traits in activists, may disagree on the further utility of participation. The ways that movements frame political activism as performing and cultivating piety, will, however, continue to matter in shaping any further evolution of Islamist activism.

Glossary

Bibliography

Index

Glossary

Adab: etiquette, refined manners (also: literature)

'Adl: justice

Amana: trustworthiness

Al-amr bi-l-ma'ruf wa-l-nahy 'an al-munkar: commanding the right and forbidding the evil, an obligation for those with authority in Muslim societies, mentioned in the Quran

Akhlaq: morals; sing. *Khalq* or creation

'Aqida: belief; refers to creed, articles of faith

Bashariyya: humankind

Baya': allegiance or loyalty, pledged to a leader

Din: religion

Dawla: the state; *Islam din wa dawla* (Islam is religion and state) is a phrase used by Islamists to argue that true Islam cannot be limited to mere worship, but rather requires enacting its political model in order to truly apply in a society

Da'i/du'a: preacher/preachers

Da'wa: the invitation to Islam; preaching

Fard al-'ayn: religious obligation for individuals

Fard al-kifaya: religious obligation for the collectivity; pl. *furud al-kifaya*

Fitna: conflict or dissension in the Muslim community, often referring to sectarian conflict, or conflict arising from a lack of popular acceptance of political leadership

Fiqh: religious jurisprudence

Gama'a: literally "group" or "society," and the way that Brothers refer to the Muslim Brotherhood (*gama'at al-ikhwan al-muslimin*); an Egyptian colloquial rendering of *jama'a* or "society" in modern standard Arabic

Gama'iyya: self-help or mutual aid voluntary association in working-class Egyptian neighborhoods

Al-Gama'a al-Islamiyya: the Islamic Group, a student movement that developed on 1970s Egyptian college campuses and that later advocated the violent overthrow of the state

Hadith: sayings of the Prophet Muhammad, as communicated through more or less reliable interlocutors and used as secondary sources of religious law

Hakimiyyat allah: God's sovereignty, term used by Sayyid Qutb, inspired by Ibn Taymiyya, to challenge claims by human leaders to have ultimate sovereignty over Muslim societies and to justify the right of the pious to overthrow rulers deemed to have overstepped divine limits

Haraka/haraki: movement, related to movements

Al-hal al-islami: the Islamic solution (and the argument that Islam always has solutions to real-world problems)

Haqq: rights, truth; pl. *huquq*

Haya' 'amma: public or social authority

Hisba: principle allowing individuals to sue or ask for accountability for individuals or businesses violating the law, used in some high-profile cases to punish perceived violations of Islamic law in Egypt

Hizb: political party or faction

Hizbiyya: partisanship or factionalism

Hukm (ahkam, tahkim): rule (rules of Islamic law, enforcing the rule thereof)

'Ibada/'ibadat: prayer or worship, the realm of worship

Ihsan: perfection that all believers should strive for; behaving as though God were always watching

Ikhlas: sincerity (of faith)

Ikhwa/ukhuwa: brotherhood, fraternal bonds

Imam: literally a prayer leader; also used to refer to a leader of the community chosen for religious rectitude

'Iman: faith

Insha' al-nufus: constructing (good) selves or individual souls

Irada/iradat al-sha'b: the will of the people

Irshad: guidance, implicitly determined by religious qualification

Islah: reform that seeks to improve and turn people and society toward what is righteous

Jahiliyya: pre-Islamic ignorance; also used by Qutb to refer to societies with un-Islamic governments, with the argument that a society really be Muslim without an Islamic government

Jamahir: masses, public

Jihad: efforts, struggle
Khayr: the good
Khayriyya: charitable work, doing good
Khidma: service, usually to society, as a way of serving God
Khilafa/mustakhallifun: vice-regency, regents of God on earth
Mabda'/mabadi': principle(s)
Madhhab/madhahib: schools of religious law, with different approaches to jurisprudence and, occasionally, worship practices
Ma'iya: togetherness and mutual aid, usually in supporting each other's spiritual growth
Marja'iyya: reference, ideal to be measured against
Maqsad/maqasid: ultimate goal(s) or intent(s)
Maslah/masalih: interests, something that is good for someone or a group of people
Maslaha 'amma: the public interest
Minbar: pulpit in a mosque, from which the Friday sermon is given
Minhaj tarbawi/al-Islam: method, path, or system; applies both to the MB's method in teaching young people to be good Muslims and to the broader Islamist belief that the Quran and *sunna* offer practical guidelines for modelling individual, social and political life along an Islamic path to produce a "good" society
Mu'amalat: worldly dealings, often paired with worship as a concern for Islamic ethics and teachings, and law; Islamists consider them subject to the guidance of religious revelation, even if others do not consider them essential matters of faith
Mu'ayyid: supporter, second rung of membership in the MB
Mu'ashara: coexistence; coexisting harmoniously with others and treating the according to Islamic ethics is part of a good Muslim's duty for the MB
Muhib: sympathizer, first rung of informal membership in the Society of Muslim Brothers
Muntasib: full member of the MB, required to pay dues and take leadership roles in movement outreach and activities
Muwatina: citizenship; MB leaders frame "good citizenship" for Muslims in terms of acting according to religious ethics to work for a better society and nation
Nafs/nufus: individuals or souls; individual-level spiritual and ethical transformation is foundational to the MB's mission of social change

Nahda: awakening or renaissance; in Arabic writing, often refers to nationalist cultural and literary revival in the late nineteenth to early twentieth century; for Islamists, it usually refers to an ongoing Islamic revival that started in the 1980s

Nasiha: advice; often used to refer to the counsel that religious scholars and intellectuals are supposed to offer the rule in order to enable him to rule according to Islam

Nizam/nizam kamil wa shamil: system; the idea that Islam offers a "perfect and comprehensive system" for human life, that Islamic activists must strive to enact in modern societies

Qadi/Quda': judge(s), traditionally those trained in Islamic jurisprudence and qualified to offer a judicial opinion or judgement on matters of law based in this jurisprudence; used to refer to the rule-enforcing part of Islam in the MB phrase that they are "preachers, not judges," because the movement long argued that Islamic rules would only apply when people were persuaded of the correctness and comprehensive scope of Islam

Quran: the holy book of Islam, believed to have been sent to the Prophet Muhammad by divine inspiration, recited by him and recorded first through an oral tradition and then written down

Quwa: power or strength

Rasid: stock; often used to refer to the stock of credibility and goodwill that those who do good in society (e.g., Islamists doing welfare and charity work that can allow them to persuade others of the value of the Islamic project)

Riba': usury, making money through unproductive means, considered to violate Islamic rules for legitimate financial gain

Riqabah: oversight, stewardship; used to refer to the MB's goal of moral oversight of parliament in the 1980s

Risala: the message of Islam

Sadqa: virtue; also used to refer to noncompulsory charitable contributions or acts by Muslims that are points in their favor on the path to salvation

Salafi: pious Muslim who believes in strictly following the practices of the companions of the Prophet in everyday life; Salafi movements aimed to cultivate and enforce adherence to such practices and to the letter of Islamic law, with less scope for flexible interpretation

Salih/'amal salih: upright, righteous; righteous work is a guiding principle of MB thought, with the goal of ensuring that people follow God's will in all that they do in worldly life

Sha'b/sha'bi: the people; popular, in the sense of echoing working class and "authentic" national values.

Sharia: God's law, generally used to refer to the rules and the path laid down by the prophetic revelation and traditions and sayings of the Prophet Muhammad, in Islam, to tell believers what is permissible and not, in matters of faith, worship, marriage, inheritance, and many kinds of social transactions

Shar'iyya: legitimacy; when applied to political authority, dependent on fidelity to both electoral and religious principles, for MB leaders

Shura: consultation; used, in Islamic jurisprudence, to refer to the ruler's duty to consult with religious scholars and men of law to ensure ruling according to God's will and the good of the people; applied more broadly to popular and legislative consultation in modern times

Suluk: behavior and practices; believed to be important to cultivate in accordance with Islamic ethics, for Islamist activists

Sulta/sultan: power and authority of rulers.

Sulta 'amma: public authority

Sunna: traditions of the Prophet, based on records and retellings of his practices as a community leader and model Muslim, used as a reference to guide contemporary Muslims' choices, but not considered the word of God

Ta'lim: education, particularly written education

Ta'ssub: extremism and rigidity

Tafahum: mutual understanding; incumbent on Brothers in cultivating bonds with those on the same path of spiritual growth as them

Ta'ruf/ta'rif: getting to know, become familiar with, others; incumbent on Brothers in cultivating bonds with those on the same path of spiritual growth as them

Ta'mul: dealings with others, often outside the sphere of the movement; one is required to be honest in such dealings and show kindness to others as part of being a good Muslim, in the MB's view of ethical cultivation

Tabligh: preaching the divine message to others

Takaful: solidarity, generally cultivated through required emotional, financial, and spiritual support within the *usra*, and later to be extended to all Muslims, in the MB view

Takfir: declaring a person, a regime, or a ruler that is nominally Muslim to be an apostate because they do not act in an adequately Islamic manner as judged by Islamists; a strategy pioneered by Qutb and used by radical Islamist societies in the 1970s to justify killing political leaders

Takwin: formation, often referring to organizational structuring

Tanfidh al-shari'a: implementation or execution of sharia; in MB discourse, this may happen at the individual or social level, in addition to application by public institutions

Tanzim: the organization; refers, within the MB, to the organizational leadership, and those loyal to its hierarchy, often in contrast to those who are dissidents, or prefer more coordination with other political forces and revision of core movement goals.

Taqwa: piety

Tarbiya: Individual upbringing and education, or cultivation; contains a strong moral component, and for the MB, is central to the mission of the movement, which believes that the properly brought up Muslim individual, with a correct sense of how Islam requires him to act in the world, is key to a just and truly Muslim society

Tarbiya ijtima'iyya: social education; used in MB discourse to refer to the education that an individual may receive by working in society, or that the individual may impart to society through social institutions and work in them

Tatbiq al-shari'a: application of sharia, used in MB discourse to refer to the use of institutions and social authority to ensure that sharia is adhered to and applied in laws and other modes of institutional power

Thawab **(sometimes written** *sawab***):** merits toward religious salvation

'Ulama: scholars of Islam who use their knowledge of its religious texts and jurisprudence to rule on matters of law as well as to teach; in the Egyptian context, since the mid-twentieth century, authorized scholars have been licensed by institutions taken over by the state and are not authorized to preach without state approval

Usra: the "family" or cell that is the first structure of the MB as an organization, generally containing fewer than ten members, of varying levels of seniority, and headed by a naqib or leader, who is a full member and is responsible for their education; mutual aid, emotional, and spiritual support, as well as enacting solidarity and applying God's will, are supposed to be practiced first within the usra

Usul: "fundamentals," "principles," or "basics," used in Islamic instruction to refer to the basics of the faith, which are not open to much debate or interpretation

Umma: the community of believers, in classical Islamic usage; used to refer to the nation or community of Muslims in modern usage

Ustadhiyya: educational leadership, used to refer to the MB's goal of ultimately establishing its role as a universal spiritual and educational authority; sometimes used by nonmovement members to refer to the movement's hegemonic ambitions in the world

***Watan*:** the nation

***Wasatiyya*:** moderation, the middle path; a term often applied, and self chosen, by religious scholars and intellectuals seen as mentors or fellow travelers for the MB in the 1990s, who argued that social and political engagement, and flexibility on doctrine, would be good for the movement's future

***Wilaya*:** governorship or ruling; used to refer to temporal political authority

***Zakat*:** religious obligation to donate a small percentage of one's wealth annually to charitable causes, one of the five pillars of Islam

***Zulm*:** oppression or injustice, generally carried out by those with worldly power

Bibliography

Primary Sources

Abdel-Hamid, Chaimaa. 2013. "Hamdi Hassan: La confrérie a des cadres capables d'occuper des postes importants." *Ahram Hebdo*, no. 963 (2013).
Abdel-Latif, Omayma. 2012. "Unholy Alliance." *Al-Ahram Weekly*, December 27, 2012.
———. 2013. "Back to Basics." *Al-Ahram Weekly*, April 30, 2013.
Abdel-Quddus, Muhammad. 1984. "Awlad al-balad." *Al-Wafd*, June 14, 1984.
———. 1984. "Al-Ikhwan al-muslimin wa tatbiq al-shari'a." *Al-Wafd*, June 28, 1984.
Abou Rayyah, Mahmoud. 2006. *Fi Nur al-Islam*. Dar al-Tawzi' wa-l-Nashr al-Islamiyya, Egypt.
Abul Nasr, Hamid. 1987. "Risala min al-Ikhwan al-Muslimin li-l-ra'is Hosni Mubarak." *Al-Sha'b*, February 17, 1987.
Adam, Mohamed. 2014. "Waiting for God's Victory." *Mada Masr*, April 13, 2014.
Afify, Heba, and Magdy Samaan. 2012. "Morsy's Men: Sharia as an Ambition, Stability as an End." *Egypt Independent*, December 3, 2012.
Al-Ahali. 1992. "A'lan al-barnamij al-intikhabi li-murashihi al-Ikhwan fi niqabat al-muhamin." September 2, 1992.
Ahmed, Yasmine Moataz. 2012. "Who Do Egypt's Villagers Vote For? And Why?" *Egypt Independent*, April 10, 2012.
Al-Ahram. 1985. "Majlis al-Shaab: Ittifaq al-mu'aradah wa-l-aghlabiyya 'ala dirasah al-muta'niya li-l-shari'a al-islamiyya." February 12, 1985.
———. 1987a. "Al-aghlabiya wa-l-mu'arada tatanafisun amam Majlis al-Shaab fi-l-radd 'ala bayan al-hukuma." June 22, 1987.
———. 1987b. "Munaqasha hawl tatbiq al-shari'a al-islamiyya, tashtariq fiha al-aghlabiya wa-l-mu'arada." June 24, 1987.

Ahram Online. 2012. "Constituent Assembly to Vote on Sharia in Egyptian Constitution." August 28, 2012. https://english.ahram.org.eg/NewsContent/1/0/51484/Egypt/0/Constituent-Assembly-to-vote-on-sharia-in-Egyptian.aspx.

———. 2013. "Pro-Morsi Alliance Criticises Constitutional Amendments." August 27, 2013. https://english.ahram.org.eg/NewsContent/1/64/80065/Egypt/Politics-/Aboutus.aspx.

Al-Ahrar. 1984a. "Wa min al-intima' ma' qatl." January 30, 1984.

———. 1984b. "Al-barnamij al-intikhabi li-qa'imat al-tahaluf hizb al-Amal." March 23, 1987.

———. 1984c. "Umar al-Tilmissany yaqul: Al-Ikhwan al-Muslimin laysu intihaziyin." May 7, 1984.

———. 1986. "Al-tayar al-islami yasa'y li-l-husul 'ala al-aghlabiya wa ba'd bi-l-tasaddy li-l-fasad." April 7, 1986.

———. 1987. "Bayan al-tahaluf: madha qaddam nuwab al-tahaluf?" August 3, 1987.

Al-Akhbar. 1985. "Fadilat al-imam al-kabir: Tatbiq al-shari'a laysa bi sha'rat talassuq 'ala al-murakkabat: Wa 'ala kul fard an yatbuq al-shari'a fi manziluhu qabl al-dawla." July 13, 1985.

Akher Sa'a. 1984. "Hiwar ma' al-duktur Wahid Rafa'at." March 21, 1984.

Al-Arabiya. 2013. "Majlis al-wuzara' al-masri yuwafiq 'ala qanun al-sukuk wa yahily li-l-shura." February 27, 2013.

Asad, Abu al-Izz Dhia-addin. 2015. "Fiqh al-muqawama al-sha'biya li-l-inqilab." Accessed March 29, 2023. https://www.scribd.com/doc/305775800/كتاب-فقه-المقاومة-الشعبية-للإنقلاب/.

al-Ashmawy, Muhammad Said. 1985. "Haqiqat sha'r al-Islam huwa al-hall." *Al-Akhbar*, July 13, 1985.

Atlantic Council. 2013. "President Mohammed Morsi's Address to the Nation." Atlantic Council MENASource, June 28, 2013. https://www.atlanticcouncil.org/blogs/menasource/translation-president-mohamed-morsi-s-address-to-the-nation/.

el-Behairy, Nouran. 2013. "We Are the People, We Are the Majority." *Daily News Egypt*, December 8, 2012.

al-Beltagy, Mohammed. Speech at Raba'a al-'Adaweyya square, June 21, 2013. https://www.youtube.com/watch?v=FWR8_K4vbWo (no longer available).

al-Buhayri, Ahmad. 2012. "Al-Azhar Insists on Keeping Sharia Law in the Constitution." *Al-Masry al-Youm*, July 11, 2012. Translated by Naria Tanoukhi,

Al-Monitor, July 12, 2012. https://www.al-monitor.com/politics/2012/07/al-azhars-sheikh-we-insist-on-pr.htm.

Chick, Kristen. 2012. "Egypt Pursues Blasphemy Cases as Morsi Defends Ban at UN." *Christian Science Monitor*, September 27, 2012.

Egypt Independent. 2012. "Islamist MPs Attack Family Laws and National Council for Women." March 13, 2012.

———. 2013a. "Independent Teachers' Syndicate: Ministry Is Brotherhoodizing Education." January 7, 2013.

———. 2013b. "Salafis Oppose Saudi Infrastructure Loan, Claiming 'Usury.'" February 12, 2013.

Elmeshad, Mohamed. 2012. "Shater Faces Early Hiccups on Campaign Trail." *Al-Masry al-Youm*, April 11, 2012.

el-Erian, Essam. 1992. "Niqabat al-atba' wa hissar al-aghlabiya al-samita." *Al-Sha'b*, September 15, 1992.

———. 2007. "Al-Ikhwan al-Muslimin wa mafhum al-dawla." Fikercenter. Accessed June 15, 2010. Personal copy.

Fadel, Abdel Sabour. 1988. "Afwan ya qanun, inta mutaham." *Al-Nur*, December 14, 1988.

"Fann al-ta'mul ma' al-mujtama'." 2011. Accessed March 29, 2023. https://www.ikhwanwiki.com/index.php?title=العمل_الجماعي.

Feteha, Ahmed. 2012. "Egypt Tourism Officials Expect Little Change under Morsi—for Now." Ahram Online, June 27, 2012. https://english.ahram.org.eg/NewsPrint/46334.aspx.

Freedom and Justice Party. 2012a. "Dr. Morsi's Electoral Program—General Features of the Nahda Project." April 28, 2012. https://ikhwanweb.com/dr-morsis-electoral-program/.

———. 2012b. "Muslim Brotherhood Statement on Islamic Law and National Identity." November 4, 2012. https://ikhwanweb.com/muslim-brotherhood-statement-0-27/.

———. 2013. "Ready for Parliamentary Elections, Condemning Violence." Ikhwanweb, February 17, 2013. https://ikhwanweb.com/freedom-and-justice-party-conf/.

———. 2014. "Al-ikhwan yuqaddamun khata 'ajalah li-tashih al-wada' al-maqluba fi Misr." Ikhwanonline, May 9, 2014.

Goudineau, Alexandre. 2013. "Sukuk Law in State of Flux until al-Azhar Review." *Egypt Independent*, April 4, 2013.

al-Guindi, Anwar. 1987. "Manshur intikhabi rakm 1." *Al-Sha'b*, March 24, 1987.

Al-Gumhuriyya. 1987. "Dr. Muhammad Ali Mahgoub: 90% min qawaninuna la tata'rid al-shari'a: al-hukuma multazima bi-'adam isdar qanun mukhalif." July 12, 1987.

———. 1988. "Kayf tahawalat al-shari'a al-islamiyya ila sha'r siyasi?" November 13, 1988.

Habib, Rafiq. 2006. "Al-ikhwan wa marhalat al-tamkin." *IkhwanOnline*, March 28, 2006. https://www.ikhwanonline.com/article/19081.

Hanna, Fouad. 1988. "Ayn al-aqbat fi-intikhabat al-niqabat al-mihniyya?" *Al-Sha'b*, December 8, 1988.

Hashim, Mustafa. 2012. "Burhamy li-l-Shorouk: Itafaqna ma' al-ikhwan 'ala hadhaf kalimat 'mabadi' min nass al-shari'a fi-l-dustur." *Al-Shorouk*, June 30, 2012.

el-Hennawy, Noha. 2011. "Political Freedom, Competition Drives Rifts between Muslim Brotherhood Factions." *Egypt Independent*, March 24, 2011.

———. 2012. "Morsy Campaign Discovers Religion's Potency in Politics." *Al-Masry al-Youm*, May 3, 2012.

Heshmat, Gamal. 2012. "The 2nd Article in Egypt's Constitution Is Supported by Most Egyptians." Ikhwanweb, August 4, 2012. https://ikhwanweb.com/gamal-heshmat%3a-the-2nd-article/.

Hussein, Adil. 1989. "Ahbatna al-fitna . . . wa lina arba' mulahizat." *Al-Sha'b*, January 24, 1989.

IkhwanOnline. 2011. "Al-ikhwan al-muslimin . . . Man nahnu? Wa mada nurid?" April 2011. Accessed May 19, 2023. https://www.ikhwanonline.com/article/237677.

IkhwanWiki. 2005. "Al-barnamij al-intikhabi li-l-ikhwan al-muslimin." Accessed March 29, 2023. https://www.ikhwanwiki.com/index.php?title=2005_البرنامج‌الانتخابي_للإخوان_المسلمين.

———. 2023. "Al-tarbiya fi fikr jama'at al-Ikhwan al-Muslimin." Accessed March 29, 2023. https://www.ikhwanwiki.com/index.php?title=جماعة_فكر_في_التربية_الإخوان_المسلمين.

Kassab, Bissan, and Mohammad Khawly. 2012. "Egypt: Muslim Brotherhood and al-Azhar Follow Salafi Lead." *Al-Akhbar English*, March 23, 2012.

al-Kenany, Abd al-Halim. 1993. *Hadith al-Da'wa: Kitabat al-ustadh al-murshid bi-magallat al-Da'wa: al-Ustadh Umar al-Tilmissany*. Tanta: Dar al-Bashir lil-Thaqafah wa-al-'Ulum al-Islamiyya.

Khazbak, Rana. 2012. "New Presidential Team Hints at Brotherhood-Salafi Rapprochement." *Egypt Independent*, August 30, 2012.
Kroum, Hassanein. 1985. "Yakhty' man yaqul an al-Wafd 'ilmani." *Al-Ahrar*, April 8, 1985.
Al-Liwa' al-Islami. 1992. "Al-'alam al-Islami yata'aradh li-l-mu'amirat wa-l-'amal ma'qud 'ala wihda al-muslimin." September 17, 1992.
Mada Masr. 2013. "Persisting Brothers." September 6, 2013.
Mahmoud, Ali Abd al-Halim. 1989. *Wasa'il al-tarbiya 'aind al-ikhwan al-muslimin: Dirasa tahlili tarikhi*. Mansoura: Dar al-Wafa' li-l-Taba'a wa al-Nashr wa-l Tawzi'.
Marroushi, Nadine. 2012. "Renaissance Man: Gehad El Haddad Works as the Islamist Project's Pragmatist." *Egypt Independent*, July 31, 2012.
Mashour, Mustafa. 1987. "Kharij al-majlis." *Al-Sha'b*, May 5, 1987.
———. 1989. *Qadaya asasiya fi-tariq al-da'wa*. Cairo: Dar al-Tawzi' wa-la-Nashr al-Islamiyya.
Al-Masry al-Youm. 2007. "Barnamij hizb 'Al-Ikhwan al-Muslimin': Mabadi'." August 10–11, 2007.
———. 2011a. "Al-bab al-awwal min barnamij hizb al-Hurriya wa-l-'Adala." April 5, 2011.
———. 2011b. "With Nour Party, Salafis Attempt to Tap into Party Politics." May 19, 2011.
———. 2011c. "Na'ib al-murshid: al-mashru' al-islami alladi tahmiluhu al-jama'a 'taklif allah'." June 20, 2011.
———. 2012. "Egypt Salafists Propose Constitutional Ban on Prophet Insults." July 19, 2012.
Mayo. 1988a. "Hiwar ma'a al-imam al-kabir Shaykh al-jama'at al-Azhar: al-dimuqratiyya fi-l-Islam a'maq athran min dimuqratiyyat al-gharb." May 16, 1988.
———. 1988b. "Shaykh al-Azhar yaqul li-Mayo: Al-hal . . . an na'awd ila al-Islam." May 26, 1988.
Al-Mesreyoon. 2012. "Al-Azhar yanjah fi naza' fatil azmah al-mada al-thaniya bayn al-ikhwan wa-l-salafiyun." July 6, 2012.
Michael, Maggie. 2012. "Egypt Brotherhood Hopeful Promises Clerics a Role." Associated Press, April 4, 2012.
Mushtahry, Abd al-Latif. 1987. "Bayan kubar al-'ulama al-jami'yya al-shar'iyya hawl intikhabat majlis al-sha'b al-masri al-rahina." *Al-'Itisam*, April 1987.

Mustafa, Magdy. 1987. "Al-'ulama yusahahun khata' ra'is Majlis al-Sha'b: al-qurud al-rabawiya la tadakhal dimn al-masalih al-mursala wa-l-badil mawjud." *Al-Nur*, May 6, 1987.

Noh, Mokhtar. 1985. "Al-Islam: Ghany bi-hall al-mushkilat jami'an." *Al-Akhbar*, August 24, 1985.

Al-Nur. 1987. "Zu'ama al-mu'arada fi Majlis al-Sha'b: kayf yuqawadhha al-islamiyyun?" April 29, 1987.

———. 1989. "Al-ittijah al-Islami athbat jadaratuhu fi qiyadat al-niqabat al-mihniya." February 1, 1989.

———. 1992. "Dr. Muhammad Ali Bishr yatahaddath bi-l-Nur: "1/2 million guineah min niqabat al-muhandisin . . . li-dahaya al-zalzal; 200,000 muhandis yu'ainun al-misakin . . . majanan." October 28, 1992.

Oktobar. 1987a. "Fi awwal hadith li-l-murshid al-'am li-l-Ikhwan al-Muslimin ba'd al-intikhabat: tatbiq al-shari'a al-islamiyya yakun bi-l-tadrij." April 19, 1987.

———. 1987b. "Ibrahim Shukry, za'im al-mu'arada al-jadid fi Majlis al-Sha'b: Al-dawla al-diniyya la tatafaq ma' al-din." April 26, 1987.

Owais, Ahmed. 2012. "Al-Ikhwan yaftahun al-nar 'ala al-'ilamiyin wa yasfunuhum bi kadhbat faraon." *Al-Shorouk*, May 14, 2012.

Perry, Tom. 2012. "Egypt's Mursi Frees Islamists Jailed by Mubarak." *Reuters*, July 31, 2012.

Perry, Tom, and Abdel Rahman Youssef. 2013a. "Egypt's Brotherhood Turns to Flour Power." Reuters, June 13, 2013.

———. 2013b. "In Egypt, Ideas of a Radical Islamist Make Comeback." Reuters, December 2, 2013.

Perry, Tom, and Tamim Elyan. 2012. "In Power, Egypt's Brotherhood Seeks Balance on Islamic Law." Reuters, July 25, 2012.

Rabie, Dalia. 2013. "Egypt's Imams Fight for Their Mosques' Independence." *Egypt Independent*, April 7, 2013.

Rady, Mohsen. 1990. *Al-Ikhwan al-Muslimun taht Qubbat al-Barlaman*. Cairo: Dar al-Tawzi' wal Nashr al-Islamiyya.

Radwan, Fathi. 1984. "Al-'ilmaniyya wa tahaluf al-Wafd wa-l-Ikhwan." *Al-Sha'b*, March 20, 1984.

Ramadan, Abdel Azim. 1984. "Al-Wafd wal-l-Ikhwan al-Muslimin: lam kul hada al-zub'ah?" *Al-Wafd*, March 22, 1984.

———. 1989. "Ahlam al-haraka al-islamiya al-mu'asira . . . wa ihzanuha." *Oktobar*, October 19, 1989.

Rizk, Ahmed. 1987. "Al-ijtima' alladi lam mutahadiruhi al-mala'ika." *Al-'Itisam*, March 1987.

Rose el-Youssef. 1984. "Al-Sheikh al-Tilmissany: Al-'ilmaniyya laysat al-ilhad." May 14, 1984.

al-Samkuri, Muhammad. 2013. "Qayadi al-Ikhwani: Al-sukuk 'mawlud islami' wa satustakhdim fi-l-mashari' al-halal." *Al-Masry al-Youm*, May 1, 2013.

Al-Sha'b. 1984a. "Fi muhadirat 'an tatbiq al-shari'a al-islamiyya, al-muhandis Ibrahim Shukry: Innahum yumtihanun al-insan fi qism al-shurta wa yuman'aun tatbiq al-shari'a al-islamiyya" June 12, 1984.

———. 1984b. "Al-Amin al-'am li-l-majlis al-'ali li shuy'un al-islamiyya: Tatbiq al-shari'a matlab dini wa sha'bi." October 16, 1984.

———. 1987. "Al-qissa al-haqiqiya li ma dar fi-l-jalsa . . . wa asbab insihab al-mu'arada; bayan al-tahaluf al-islami raddan 'ala bayan al-hukuma bi Majlis al-Shaab." June 22, 1987.

———. 1988. "Al-mu'tamir al-thani li-l-'ajaz al-tibbi fi-l-Quran wa-l-sunna yu'akkid: Dharurat tatbiq al-shari'a al-islamiyya." November 29, 1988.

———. 1989. "Madha ba'd taza'id al-batala bayn al-muhandisin?" January 17, 1989.

———. 1992a. "Al-niqabat al-fara'iya fi-l-Iskandriya wa Tanta wa Beni Sueif wa Aswan: ta'yid wasi' li-l-murashihin al-islamiyin bi-niqabat al-muhamin." August 28, 1992.

———. 1992b. "Al-youm, 12 murashihan li-l-tayyar al-Islami yukhawwadun mu'araka niqabat al-muhamin, haqana injaz malmusa fi-l-niqabat al-fara'iya wa nuqaddim barnamijan kamilan li-l-nahud bi-l-niqaba al-'amma." September 11, 1992.

———. 1992c. "Naqd li-l-fikr al-'arabi . . . wa da'wa li-l-ijtihad tuhayyaz li-l-'adl badlan min al-tahayyiz li-l-huwa." October 3, 1992.

Shalaby, Ethar. 2007. "Freedom Ends When It Violates the Freedom of Others, Says MB Deputy Head." *Daily News Egypt*, August 27, 2007.

Al-Sharq al-Awsat. 2007. "Ikhwan Misr yu'atarafun bi-khata' fi barnamijuhum li-l-hizb al-siyasi hawl 'haya' al-'ulama' al-muqtaraha." October 16, 2007.

al-Shater, Khairat. 2011. "Mashru' al-nahda al-islami." YouTube video, 1:32:03, April 24, 2011; translation available at Hudson Institute, Current Trends in Islamist Ideology, vol. 13, April 10, 2011. https://www.hudson.org/national-security-defense/khairat-al-shater-on-the-nahda-project-complete-translation-.

al-Shawy, Tawfiq. 1985a. "Sayyadat al-shari'a al-islamiyya wa sayyadat al-qanun fi Misr." *Al-Sha'b*, October 15, 1985.

———. 1985b. "Mabda' hakimiyya al-shari'a al-islamiyya wa shar'iyya qawanin fi-l-tashri' al-Misri." *Al-Sha'b*, October 22, 1985.

al-Sioufi, Ahmed. 1984. "Bayan al-hukuma tajahil tatbiq al-shari'a al-islamiyya wa lam yuhaddad dawr al-Azhar, wa lam yash'ar ila al-qadaya al-islamiyya." *Al-Sha'b*, October 2, 1984.

Society of Muslim Brothers. "Vision 28." Accessed May 19, 2023. https://issuu.com/madamasr/docs/ikhwanvi28-compressed.pdf.

Al-Tahrir TV. 2012. "Egyptian President-Elect Mohamed Morsi in Victory Speech: I Will Be the President of All Egyptians." June 24, 2012. https://www.memri.org/tv/egyptian-president-elect-mohamed-morsi-victory-speech-i-will-be-president-all-egyptians.

al-Tilmissany, Umar. 1984. "Al-tahaluf al-Wafd wa-l-ikhwan bi-la musawamat wa la shurut." *Al-Wafd*, May 10, 1984.

Al-Wafd. 1984. "Al-mu'araka al-intikhabiyya mutahawilat ila mahzala." May 17, 1984.

———. 1985. "Ra'is al-Wafd yada'w ila iqama mujtama' islami sahih." March 7, 1985.

———. 1987. "Al-tahaluf: nihayat tariq amma bidayat marhala?" April 17, 1987.

al-Wa'i, Tawfiq Yusuf. 2001. *Al-Fikr al-siyasi al-mu'asir 'aind al-Ikhwan al-Muslimin*. Kuwait: Maktabat al-Minar al-Islamiyya.

Wassim, Rime. 2011. "Islamiyya, Islamiyya." July 29, 2011. https://vimeo.com/27130745?fbclid=IwAR00gLp_OuVXuQSD4pKehiulhM9Vmcd3OoJXrH6rDCa2xnS-OA32OrHODns.

Worth, Robert. 2013. "A Familiar Role for Muslim Brotherhood: Opposition." *New York Times*, July 28, 2013.

Yahya, Muhammad. 1984. "Al-haraka al-islamiyya wa qadiya fi sahifat al-Ahram." *Al-Sha'b*, June 19, 1984.

Zakariyya, Fouad. 1987. "Takfir al-tafkir: Radd 'ala al-duktur Yusuf al-Qaradawy." *Al-Sha'b*, June 2, 1987.

Secondary Sources

Abdo, Geneive. 2002. *No God but God: Egypt and the Triumph of Islam*. New York: Oxford Univ. Press.

Adly, Amr. 2016. "Between Social Populism and Pragmatic Conservatism." In *Egypt's Revolutions: Politics, Religion, and Social Movements*, edited

by Bernard Rougier and Lacroix Stéphane, 61–78. Basingstoke: Palgrave Macmillan.
Agrama, Hussein Ali. 2010. "Secularism, Sovereignty, Indeterminacy: Is Egypt a Secular or a Religious State?" *Comparative Studies in Society and History* 52 (3): 495–523.
———. 2012. *Questioning Secularism: Islam, Sovereignty, and the Rule of Law in Modern Egypt*. Chicago: Univ. of Chicago Press.
al-Anani, Khalil. 2009. "The Young Brotherhood in Search of a New Path," Current Trends in Islamist Ideology, Hudson Institute, October 5, 2009. www.hudson.org/national-security-defense/the-young-brotherhood-in-search-of-a-new-path.
———. 2016. *Inside the Muslim Brotherhood: Religion, Identity, and Politics*. New York: Oxford Univ. Press.
al-Anani, Khalil, and Maszlee Malik. 2013. "Pious Way to Politics: The Rise of Political Salafism in Post-Mubarak Egypt." *Digest of Middle East Studies* 22 (1): 57–73.
Al-Arian, Abdullah A. 2014. *Answering the Call: Popular Islamic Activism in Sadat's Egypt*. Oxford: Oxford Univ. Press.
Ardovini, Lucia. 2021. "Re-thinking the Tanzim: Tensions between Individual Identities and Organizational Structures in the Muslim Brotherhood after 2013." *Middle East Law and Governance* 13 (2021): 130–49.
Asad, Talal. 1986. "The Idea of an Anthropology of Islam." Occasional Paper, Center for Contemporary Arab Studies, Georgetown Univ.
Awad, Mokhtar. 2017. "The Rise of the Violent Muslim Brotherhood." Current Trends in Islamist Ideology, Hudson Institute, July 27, 2017. https://www.hudson.org/national-security-defense/the-rise-of-the-violent-muslim-brotherhood.
al-Awadi, Hisham. 2004. *In Pursuit of Legitimacy: The Muslim Brothers and Mubarak, 1982–2000*. New York: I. B. Tauris.
Bayat, Asef. 2005. "Islamism and Social Movement Theory." *Third World Quarterly* 26 (6): 891–908.
Baker, Raymond W. 2003. *Islam without Fear: Egypt and the New Islamists*. Cambridge, MA: Harvard Univ. Press.
Berman, Sheri. 2001. "Review Article—Ideas, Norms, and Culture in Political Analysis." *Comparative Politics* 33 (2): 231.
Bienert, David. 2007. "The Concept of *Jihad* in the Writings of Abdessalam Yassine." M. Phil thesis, Worcester College, Oxford Univ.

Billig, Michael. 1995. "Rhetorical Psychology, Ideological Thinking, and Imagining Nationhood." In *Social Movements and Culture*, edited by Hank Johnston and Bert Klandermans, 64–82. Minneapolis: Univ. of Minnesota Press.

al-Bishri, Tariq. 1985. "La question juridique entre Shari'a Islamique et Droit Positif." Translated by Bernard Botiveau. *Dossiers du CEDEJ*, no. 3. "Les intellectuels et le pouvoir: Syrie, Egypte, Tunisie, Algerie."

Blanc, Theo. 2021. "Opportunity, Ideology, and Salafi Pathways of Political Activism in Tunisia." *Third World Thematics: A TWQ Journal* 5 (3–6): 276–95.

Brooke, Steven. 2017. "From Medicine to Mobilization: Social Service Provision and the Islamist Reputational Advantage." *Perspectives on Politics* 15 (1): 42–61.

Brooke, Steven. 2019. *Winning Hearts and Votes: Social Services and the Islamist Political Advantage*. Ithaca, NY: Cornell Univ. Press.

Brown, Nathan J. 1997. "Shari'a and State in the Modern Muslim Middle East." *International Journal of Middle East Studies* 29 (3): 359–76.

———. 2012a. *When Victory Is Not an Option: Islamist Movements in Arab Politics*. Ithaca, NY: Cornell Univ. Press.

———. 2012b. "When Victory Becomes an Option: Egypt's Muslim Brotherhood Confronts Success." Carnegie Papers, January 2012. https://www.jstor.org/stable/resrep12815.

Brown, Nathan J., and Adel Omar Sherif. 2004. "Inscribing the Islamic Shari'a in Arab Constitutional Law." In *Islamic Law and the Challenges of Modernity*, edited by Yvonne Yazbeck Haddad and Barbara Freyer Stowasser, 55–80. Lanham, MD: Rowman & Littlefield.

Brownlee, Jason. 2010. "The Muslim Brothers: Egypt's Most Influential Pressure Group." *History Compass* 8 (5): 419–30.

Cavatorta, Francesco. 2007. "Neither Participation nor Revolution: The Strategy of the Moroccan Jamiat al-Adl wal-Ihsan." *Mediterranean Politics* 12 (3): 381–97.

Cavatorta, Francesco, and Fabio Merone. 2015. "Post-Islamism, Ideological Evolution, and 'la tunisianité' of the Tunisian Islamist Party al-Nahda." *Journal of Political Ideologies* 20 (1): 27–42.

Cavatorta, Francesco, and Valeria Resta. 2020. "Beyond Quietism: Party Institutionalisation, Salafism, and the Economy." *Politics and Religion* 13 (2020): 796–817.

Clark, Janine. 2003. *Islam, Charity, and Activism: Middle-Class Networks and Social Welfare in Egypt, Jordan, and Yemen*. Indianapolis: Indiana Univ. Press.

Cook, Michael. 2003. *Forbidding Wrong in Islam: An Introduction*. New York: Cambridge Univ. Press.

Cornet, Catherine. 2021. "The Cinema of the Young Muslim Brothers: Claiming a Space in Egyptian Pop Culture." *British Journal of Middle East Studies* 48 (1): 59–77.

Donati, Paulo R. 1992. "Political Discourse Analysis." In *Studying Collective Action*, edited by Mario Diani and Ron Eyerman, 136–67. London: Sage.

Dupret, Bauduoin. 1993. "La problématique du nationalisme dans la pensée islamique contemporaine." *Égypte-Monde Arabe* 15–16: 377–88.

——— 2000. *Au nom de quel droit: répertoires juridiques et réference religieuse dans la société égyptienne musulmane contemporaine*. Paris: Maison des Sciences de l'Homme.

——— 2003. "A Return to the Shariah? Egyptian Judges and Referring to Islam." In *Modernizing Islam: Religion in the Public Sphere in the Middle East and Europe*, edited by Francois Burgat and John Esposito, 125–43. New Brunswick, NJ: Rutgers Univ. Press.

Eickelman, Dale, and Jon Anderson. 2003. *New Media in the Muslim World: The Emerging Public Sphere*. Indianapolis: Indiana Univ. Press.

Field, Nathan and Ahmed Hamam. 2009. "Salafi Satellite TV in Egypt." *Arab Media and Society* (Spring 2009): 1–11.

Fine, Gary. 2005. "Public Narration and Group Culture: Discerning Discourse in Social Movements." In *Social Movements and Culture*, edited by Hank Johnston and and Bert Klandermans, 127–43. Vol. 4 of *Social Movements, Protest, and Contention*. Minneapolis: Univ. of Minnesota Press.

Finnemore, Martha, and Kathryn Sikkink. 1998. "International Norm Dynamics and Political Change." *International Organization* 52 (4): 887–917.

Gamblin, Sandrine. 2015. "International Tourism in Post-Revolution Egypt: Value Conflict and Economic Pragmatism." In *The Political Economy of the New Egyptian Republic*, edited by Nicholas S. Hopkins, 134–52. Cairo: American Univ. in Cairo Press.

Gamson, William. 1988. "Political Discourse and Collective Action." *International Social Movement Research* (1): 219–44.

Ghanem, Ibrahim. 1994. *The West in the Eyes of the Egyptian Islamic Movement*. Cairo: Ummah Press Service.

el-Ghobashy, Mona. 2005. "The Metamorphosis of the Egyptian Muslim Brothers." *International Journal of Middle East Studies* 37 (3): 373–95.

Haenni, Patrick. 2016. "The Reasons for the Muslim Brotherhood's Failure in Power." In *Egypt's Revolutions: Politics, Religion, and Social Movements*, edited by Bernard Rougier and Lacroix Stéphane, 19–39. Basingstoke: Palgrave Macmillan.

Hamid, Shadi. 2014. *Temptations of Power: Islamists and Illiberal Democracy in a New Middle East*. Oxford: Oxford Univ. Press.

Hamming, Tore. 2013. "Politicization of the Salafi Movement: The Emergence and Influence of Political Salafism in Egypt." *International Affairs Review* 22 (1): 2–18.

Henry, Clement. 2015. "Islamic Finance in the New Egypt." In *The Political Economy of the New Egyptian Republic*, edited by Nicholas S. Hopkins, 194–216. Cairo: American Univ. in Cairo Press.

Hirschkind, Charles. 2001. "Civic Virtue and Religious Reason: An Islamic Counterpublic." *Cultural Anthropology* 16 (1): 3–34.

Houston, Sam. 2017. "Sufism and Islamist Activism in Morocco: An Examination of the Tradition of 'Commanding Right and Forbidding Wrong' in the Thought of 'Abd al-Salam Yassine." *Middle Eastern Studies* 53 (2): 153–65.

Hudson Institute. 2012. "Khairat al-Shater on the Nahda Project." Complete translation. Current Trends in Islamist Ideology, April 10, 2012. https://www.hudson.org/national-security-defense/khairat-al-shater-on-the-nahda-project-complete-translation-.

Ibrahim, Hasanayn Tawfiq, and Huda Raghib 'Awaḍ, eds. 1996. *Al-Dawr al-siyasi li-Jama'at al-Ikhwan al-Muslimin fi dhill al-ta'dudiya al-siyasiya al-muqayyada fi Misr: dirasa fi al-mumarasa al-siyasiya 1984–1990*. Cairo: Al-Mahrousa.

International Crisis Group. 2008. "Egypt's Muslim Brothers: Confrontation or Integration?" *Middle East/North Africa Report* no. 76 (June 18): 1–26.

Ismail, Salwa. 1998. "Confronting the Other: Identity, Culture, Politics, and Conservative Islamism in Egypt." *International Journal of Middle East Studies* (30): 199–225.

——— 2003. *Rethinking Islamist Politics: Culture, the State, and Islamism*. London: I. B. Tauris.

Jadaane, Fahmy. 1990. "Notions of the State in Arab-Islamic Writings." In *The Arab State*, edited by Giacomo Luciani, 247–83. Berkeley: Univ. of California Press.

Johnston, Hank. 1995. "A Methodology for Frame Analysis: From Discourse to Cognitive Schemata." In *Social Movements and Culture*, edited by Hank Johnston and Bert Klandermans, 217–46. Minneapolis: Univ. of Minnesota Press.

Kandil, Hazem. 2015. *Inside the Brotherhood*. Malden, MA: Polity.

Karagiannis, Emmanuel. 2019. "The Rise of Electoral Salafism in Egypt and Tunisia: The Use of Democracy as a Master Frame." *Journal of North African Studies* 24 (2): 207–25.

Ketchley, Neil. 2013. "The Muslim Brothers Take to the Streets." *Middle East Report* 269 (Winter 2013): 12–17.

Khanani, Ahmed. 2014. "Islamism and the Language of Democracy in Morocco." PhD diss., Indiana Univ.

——— 2021. *All Politics Are God's Politics: Moroccan Islamism and the Sacralization of Democracy*. New Brunswick, NJ: Rutgers Univ. Press.

Koa, Moeen. 2018. "Techniques of Strategic Political Communication: The Egyptian Muslim Brotherhood's Persuasive Devices." *International Journal of Strategic Communication* 12 (5): 571–98.

Krämer, Gudrun. 2010. *Hasan Al-Banna*. Oxford: Oneworld.

———. 2015. "Making Modern Muslims: Islamic Reform, Hasan al-Banna, and the Egyptian Muslim Brotherhood." In *Delimiting Modernities: Conceptual Challenges and Regional Responses*, edited by Sven Trakulhun and Ralph Weber, 197–214. Lanham, MD: Lexington.

Kratochwil, Friedrich. 1987. "Rules, Norms, Values, and the Limits of 'Rationality.'" *Archives for Philosophy of Law and Social Philosophy* 73 (3): 301–29.

Kratochwil, Friedrich, and John Gerard Ruggie. 1986. "International Organization: A State of the Art on an Art of the State." *International Organization* 40 (4): 753–75.

Lauziere, Henri. 2012. "The Religious Dimension of Islamism: Sufism, Salafism, and Politics in Morocco." In *Islamist Politics in the Middle East: Movements and Change*, edited by Samer Shehata, 88–106. Abingdon: Routledge.

Lia, Brynjar. 1998. *The Society of the Muslim Brothers in Egypt: The Rise of an Islamic Mass Movement*. Ithaca, NY: Cornell Univ. Press.

Lombardi, Clark. 2001. "State Law as Islamic Law in Modern Egypt: The Amendment of Article 2 of the Egyptian Constitution and the Article 2 Jurisprudence of the Supreme Constitutional Court of Egypt." PhD diss, Columbia Univ.

Lombardi, Clark B., and Connie J. Cannon. 2016. "Transformations in Muslim Views about 'Forbidding Wrong': The Rise and Fall of Islamist Litigation in Egypt." In *Shari'a Law and Modern Muslim Ethics*, edited by Robert W. Hefner, 135–57. Bloomington: Indiana Univ. Press.

Macias-Amoretti, Juan. 2015. "Seeking an 'Other' Desperately: The Dialectical Opposition of Political Islam in Morocco." *Journal of North African Studies* 20 (3): 336–48.

Mahmood, Saba. 2005. *Politics of Piety: The Islamic Revival and the Feminist Subject.* Princeton, NJ: Princeton Univ. Press.

Malik, J. 2018. "Fiqh Al-Daʿwa: The Emerging Standardization of Islamic Proselytism." *Welt Des Islams* 58 (2): 206–43.

March, Andrew F. 2013. "Genealogies of Sovereignty in Islamic Political Theology." *Social Research: An International Quarterly* 80, no. 1 (2013): 293–320. doi:10.1353/sor.2013.0011.

Martini, Jeffrey, Dalia Dassa Kaye, Erin York, and the Rand Corporation. 2012. *The Muslim Brotherhood, Its Youth, and Implications for U.S. Engagement.* Santa Monica, CA: Rand.

Masoud, Tarek E. 2014. *Counting Islam: Religion, Class, and Elections in Egypt.* New York: Cambridge Univ. Press.

Masoud, Tarek, and Amaney Jamal. 2012. "Who Votes Islamist and Why? Preliminary Evidence from Egypt and Tunisia." Paper presented at Midwestern Political Science Association meeting, April 13, 2012, Chicago, IL.

McLarney, Ellen Anne. 2015. *Soft Force: Women in Egypt's Islamic Awakening.* Princeton Studies in Muslim Politics. Princeton, NJ: Princeton Univ. Press.

Mellor, Noha. 2018. *Voice of the Muslim Brotherhood: Daʿwa, Discourse, and Political Communication.* Abingdon: Routledge.

Menchik, Jeremy. 2016. *Islam and Democracy in Indonesia: Tolerance Without Liberalism.* New York: Cambridge Univ. Press.

Meijer, Roel. 1997. *From al-Daʿwa to al-Hizbiyya: Mainstream Islamic Movements in Egypt, Jordan and Palestine in the 1990s.* Amsterdam: Research Center for International Political Economy and Foreign Policy Analysis.

Menshawy, Mustafa. 2021. "The Ideology Factor and Individual Disengagements from the Muslim Brotherhood." *Religions* 12: 198.

Mitchell, Richard P. 1969. *The Society of the Muslim Brothers.* Oxford: Oxford Univ. Press.

Mittermaeier, Amira. 2020. "Islamic Charity as (Non)Political in Contemporary Egypt." *Islamic Law and Society* 27 (2020): 111–31.

Motaouakal, Abdelouahad. 2014. "Al-Adl wa-l-Ahsan: An Explanation of Its Rise and Its Strategy for Social and Political Reform in Egypt." PhD diss., Univ. of Exeter.

Moustafa, Tamir. 2007. *The Struggle for Constitutional Power: Law, Politics, and Economic Development in Egypt.* Cambridge: Cambridge Univ. Press.

———. 2010. "The Islamist Trend in Egyptian Law." *Politics and Religion* 3 (3): 610–30.

Mustonen, Liina. 2020. "The Mosque and Women's Resistance: Rethinking the Summer of 2013 in Cairo." In "Women and Islam: Beyond Activism," special issue, *Egypte/Monde Arabe* 21 (3): 89–104.

Naguib, Nefissa. 2015. *Nurturing Masculinities: Men, Food, and Family in Contemporary Egypt*. Austin: Univ. of Texas Press.

Onuf, Nicholas. 2013. *Making Sense, Making Worlds: Constructivism in Social Theory and International Relations*. London: Routledge.

Pepinsky, Thomas B., R. William Liddle, and Saiful Mujani. 2018. *Piety and Public Opinion: Understanding Indonesian Islam*. New York: Oxford Univ. Press.

Peters, Rudolph. 1988. "Divine Law or Man-Made Law?" *Arab Law Quarterly* 3 (3): 231–53.

Pfeifer, Hanna. 2019. "The Normative Power of Secularism: Tunisian Ennahda's Discourse on Religion, Politics, and the State (2011–2016)." *Politics and Religion* 12 (3): 478–500.

Philbrick Yadav, Stacey. 2013. *Islamists and the State: Legitimacy and Institutions in Yemen and Lebanon*. London: I. B. Tauris.

Ranko, Annette. 2015. *The Muslim Brotherhood and Its Quest for Hegemony in Egypt: State-Discourse and Islamist Counter-Discourse*. Wiesbaden: Springer VS.

Risse, Thomas, and Kathryn Sikkink. 1999. *The Power of Human Rights: International Norms and Domestic Change*. New York: Cambridge Univ. Press.

Rock-Singer, Aaron. 2016. "The Salafi Mystique: The Rise of Gender Segregation in 1970s Egypt." *Islamic Law and Society* 23 (3): 279–305.

Rommel, Carl. 2018. "Men in Time: On Masculine Productivity, Corruption, and Youth Football in the Aftermath of the 2011 Egyptian Revolution." *Men and Masculinities*, 21 (3): 341–62.

Rosen, Ehud. 2008. "The Muslim Brotherhood's Concept of Education." Current Trends in Islamist Ideology, Hudson Institute, November 11, 2008. https://www.hudson.org/national-security-defense/the-muslim-brotherhood-s-concept-of-education.

Roy, Olivier. 1994. *The Failure of Political Islam*. Cambridge: Harvard Univ. Press.

Rutherford, Bruce K. 2008. *Egypt after Mubarak: Liberalism, Islam, and Democracy in the Arab World*. Princeton, NJ: Princeton Univ. Press.

Schmidt, Vivien A. 2008. "Discursive Institutionalism: The Explanatory Power of Ideas and Discourse." *Annual Review of Political Science* 11 (1): 303–26.

Schwedler, Jillian. 2006. *Faith in Moderation: Islamist Parties in Jordan and Yemen*. Cambridge: Cambridge Univ. Press.

Schwartz-Shea, Peregrine, and Dvora Yanow. 2012. *Interpretive Research Design: Concepts and Processes*. New York: Routledge.

Scott, Rachel M. 2014. "Managing Religion and Renegotiating the Secular: The Muslim Brotherhood and Defining the Religious Sphere." *Politics and Religion* 7 (1): 51–78.

Shehata, Samer. 2012. "Political Da'wa: Understanding the Muslim Brotherhood's Participation in Semi-authoritarian Elections." In *Islamist Politics in the Middle East: Movements and Change*, edited by Samer Shehata, 120–45. Abingdon: Routledge.

Shehata, Samer, and Joshua Stacher. 2006. "The Brotherhood Goes to Parliament." *Middle East Report* 240: 32–39.

el-Shimy, Yasser. 2015. "The Muslim Brotherhood." In "Egypt after the Spring: Revolt and Reaction," edited by Emile Hokayem with Hebatalla Taha, special issue, *Adelphi Series* 55: 453–54.

Sigillò, Ester. 2020. "Islamism and the Rise of Islamic Charities in Postrevolutionary Tunisia: Claiming Political Islam through Other Means?" *British Journal of Middle Eastern Studies* 49 (5): 811–29.

Singer, Hanna. 1990. "The Socialist Labour Party." Master's thesis, American Univ. in Cairo.

Somers, Margaret R. 1994. "The Narrative Constitution of Identity: A Relational and Network Approach." *Theory and Society* 23 (5): 605–49.

Snow, David A., and Robert D. Benford. 1988. "Ideology, Frame Resonance and Participant Mobilization." *International Social Movement Research* 1: 197–217.

Snow, David A., and Robert D. Benford. 1992. "Master Frames and Cycles of Protest." In *Frontiers in Social Movement Theory*, edited by Aldon Morris and Carol McClurg Mueller, 133–55. New Haven, CT: Yale Univ. Press.

Spiegel, Avi. 2015. *Young Islam: The New Politics of Religion in Morocco and the Arab World*. Princeton, NJ: Princeton Univ. Press.

———. 2015b. "Succeeding by Surviving: Examining the Durability of Political Islam in Morocco." Working paper, Rethinking Political Islam series, Brookings Institution, Washington, DC.

Stacher, Joshua. 2001. "Moderate Political Islamism as a Possible New Social Movement: The Case of Egypt's Wasat (Center) Party." Master's thesis, American Univ. in Cairo.

Swidler, Ann. 2005. "Cultural Power and Social Movements." In *Social Movements and Culture*, edited by Hank Johnston and Bert Klandermans, 25–40. Minneapolis: Univ. of Minnesota Press.

Tabaar, Mohammad Ayatollahi. 2018. *Religious Statecraft: The Politics of Islam in Iran*. New York: Columbia Univ. Press.

Tammam, Hossam. 2010a. *Tasalluf al-ikhwan: Ta'akl al-atruha al-ikhwaniyya wa sa'ud al-salafiyya fi jama'at al-ikhwan al-muslimin*. Bibliotheca Alexandrina, Alexandria, Egypt.

———. 2010b. "Policy Brief: The Political Future of the Muslim Brotherhood in Egypt Following Its Exit from Parliament." Arab Reform Initiative, no. 43, February 2011.

Topol, Sarah. 2012. "Egypt's Salafi Surge." *Foreign Policy*, January 4.

Utvik, Bjorn Olav. 1995. "Filling the Vacant Throne of Nasser: The Economic Discourse of Egypt's Islamist Opposition." *Arab Studies Quarterly* 17 (4): 29-54.

———. 2014. "The Ikhwanization of the Salafis: Piety in the Politics of Egypt and Kuwait." *Middle East Critique* 23 (1): 5-27.

Vannetzel, Marie. 2014. "Affection, désaffection et défection chez deux jeunes Frères musulmans en Égypte." *Critique internationale* 2014 4 (65): 127-47.

———. 2016a. *Les Frères Musulmans égyptiens: enquête sur un secret public*. Paris: Karthala.

———. 2016b. "Confronting the Transition to Legality." In *Egypt's Revolutions: Politics, Religions, and Social Movements*, edited by Bernard Rougier and Stephane Lacroix, 41-59. New York: Palgrave Macmillan.

———. 2017. "The Party, the Gama'a, and the Tanzim: The Organizational Dynamics of the Egyptian Muslim Brotherhood's Post-2011 Failure." *British Journal of Middle Eastern Studies* 44 (2): 211-26.

Vannetzel, Marie, and Dilek Yankaya. 2019. "Crafting a Business Umma? Transnational Networks of 'Islamic Businessmen' after the Arab Spring." *Mediterranean Politics* 24 (3): 290-310.

Volpi Frédéric, and Ewan Stein. 2015. "Islamism and the State after the Arab Uprisings: Between People Power and State Power." *Democratization* 22 (2): 276-93.

Wedeen, Lisa. 2010. "Reflections on Ethnographic Work in Political Science." *Annual Review of Political Science* 13: 255-72.

Wendell, Charles. 1978. *Five Tracts of Hasan al-Banna*. Los Angeles: Univ. of California Press.

Wickham, Carrie Rosefsky. 2002. *Mobilizing Islam: Religion, Activism, and Political Change in Egypt*. New York: Columbia Univ. Press.

———. 2004. "The Path to Moderation: Strategy and Learning in the Formation of Egypt's Wasat Party." *Comparative Politics* 36 (2): 205-28.

———. 2013. *The Muslim Brotherhood: Evolution of an Islamist Movement.* Princeton, NJ: Princeton Univ. Press.

Williams, Rhys H. 1995. "Constructing the Public Good: Social Movements and Cultural Resources." *Social Problems* 42 (1): 124–44.

Willis, Michael. 2007. "Between Alternance and the Makhzen: At-Tawhid wa al-Islah's Entry into Moroccan Politics." *Journal of North African Studies* 4 (3): 45–80.

Wolf, Anne. 2017. *Political Islam in Tunisia: A History of Ennahda.* Oxford: Oxford Univ. Press.

Yafout, Merieme. 2017. "The Activities of Adl Wal Ihsane in the Neighbourhoods: How to Build a 'Non-Legal' Consensus from a 'Tolerated' Conflict." *International Development Policy* (August 2017): 109–35.

Yildirim, A. Kadir. 2016. *Muslim Democratic Parties in the Middle East: Economy and Politics of Islamist Moderation.* Bloomington: Indiana Univ. Press.

Zeghal, Malika. 1999. "Religion and Politics in Egypt: The Ulema of Al-Azhar, Radical Islam and the State (1952–94)." *International Journal of Middle East Studies* 31 (3): 371–99.

———. 2008. *Islamism in Morocco: Religion, Authoritarianism, and Electoral Politics.* Princeton, NJ: Markus Weiner.

Zollner, Barbara H. E. 2007. "Prison Talk: The Muslim Brotherhood's Internal Struggle during Gamal Abdel Nasser's Persecution, 1954 to 1971." *International Journal of Middle East Studies* 39 (3): 411–33.

——— 2009. *The Muslim Brotherhood: Hasan Al-Hudaybi and Ideology.* London: Routledge.

——— 2019. "The Metamorphosis of Social Movements into Political Parties: The Egyptian Muslim Brotherhood and the Tunisian al-Nahda as Cases for a Reflection on Party Institutionalisation Theory." *British Journal of Middle Eastern Studies.* 48 (3): 370–87.

Index

Abdallah Shanab, Lashin Ali, 83, 85
Abd al-Khaliq, Farid, 91
Abdel-Quddus, Muhammad, 55–56, 58–59, 61, 88
Abou el-Fotouh, Abdel Moneim, 156
Abou el-Magd, Kamal, 40
Abu Bakr, caliph, 133, 175
Abu Hurayrah, 138
Abu Ismail, Hazem Salah, 173
Abul Futouh, Abdel Moneim, 119
Abul Nasr, Hamid, 65, 66, 71, 83
Abu Talib, Sufi, 40, 45
accountability, 43, 147; to God's will, 84, 203; holding governments to, 62, 70; holding representatives to, 59, 106; holding rulers to, 35, 44, 48, 68, 70, 71, 98, 150, 178; MB's leadership and, 8; state's religious, 45, 88
action: agentive, 13; collective, 13, 21, 101, 105. *See also* righteous action
activist. *See haraki*
adab (etiquette), 126, 135, 164–65
advice. *See nasiha*
Afghanistan, 66, 120
Agrama, Hussein Ali, 11
Ahrar Party, 65. *See also* Islamic Alliance
Akef, Mahdi, 69–70, 83, 125, 139–40
alcohol, 81, 82, 85, 87, 180, 183, 222
'amal salih. *See* righteous action; working for God

al-amr bi-l-ma'ruf. *See* commanding the right
al-Anani, Khalil, 7, 13
anthropology and ethnography, 9, 11, 141
applying God's law (*tatbiq al-shari'a*). *See* sharia
applying the Islamic mission. *See tanfidh*
apostasy, 39, 79, 197; *takfir*, 37
al-Arian, Abdullah A., 8, 40–42, 44
Asad, Talal, 4, 11, 30
Asala Party, 171
al-Ashmawi, Hasan, 34
al-Ashmawy, Said, 87
assertive discourse, 15; MB and, 18–19, 42, 108. *See also* constructivism
al-Awa, Mohammed Selim, 112
Awad, Louis, 59
awakening (*sahwa*), 67
'Awda, Abdel Qader, 78
AWI (Adl wa Ihsan/Justice and Charity movement, Morocco), 27, 213, 214–20, 226, 229; collective obligation, 215; *da'wa*, 214, 215, 216, 217–18, 220, 223; democracy, 219; electoral politics, 213, 229; empowerment, 219–20; *hukm*, 218; justice (*'adl*), 217, 218; *minhaj*, 216; Moroccan regime and, 221, 223; *nasiha*, 215; political bureau, 215, 216; religion and politics, 224;

261

AWI (Adl wa Ihsan/Justice and Charity movement, Morocco) (*cont.*)
   sharia and, 219; *shura*, 218, 219, 223; *tarbiya*, 214, 215–17, 218. *See also* Yassine, Abdelsalam; Yassine, Nadia
awqaf. *See* endowments
al-Azhar, 66, 190; autonomy of, 63–64, 67, 88, 126, 148, 185; Azhari leadership, 31, 45, 50, 60, 62–63, 89–90, 185; popularly elected council for, 88; sharia and, 45, 80, 185–86, 210
Azhari Scholars Front, 63

Badr, Zaki, 91
Baker, Raymond W., 11, 112
Balkans, the, 120
Banna, Ahmed Seif al-Islam, 84, 85, 92
al-Banna, Hasan: *Bayn amsu wa-l-yawm* (Between Yesterday and Today), 29, 131; on commanding the right, 23, 35; on comprehensiveness of Islam, 31–32, 69, 77, 207, 208; cultivating the "virtuous citizen," 28–29; *Da'watuna* (Our Mission), 29; epistles (*rasa'il*), 20, 29, 32, 35; Europe, importation of laws and legislative systems from, 95; *fikr haraki* or "activist thought," 37; on God's will, 23; on *hukm*, 23, 34–36, 77, 78; on *islah*, 33–34, 35; Islamic reformist tradition and, 29–30; on Islamic state, 77–78; on jihad, 26, 136–37; MB and, 1, 28, 41, 43; MB's *da'wa* and, 31, 32, 35, 53, 78; MB's framing and, 15; MB's *minhaj* and, 30, 34; on morality, 33, 34, 35, 77–79; *Mushkilat fi dhaw al-nizam al-islami*, 77; Muslims as "practical people," 5, 29, 30, 31, 32; on partisanship, 29, 50, 104; politics and religion, 29, 34–36, 50, 77, 129, 130, 199, 203; on public work, 49; *Risalat al-Ta'lim* (Letter of Instructions), 31–32, 78; on social work, 34; state and *da'wa*, 23; "a state of the message" (*dawlat al-risala*), 150; on state power, 77–79; on *tanfidh*, 43, 94; on *tarbiya*, 30, 31–32, 33, 34, 35, 93; twenty principles, 31–32, 40
Bayat, Asef, 6
el-Beltagy, Mohammed, 156
al-Bishri, Tariq, 112
Brown, Nathan, 1, 167

Cairo University, 40, 52, 175
caliphate/caliph, 89, 98, 126, 134, 175, 194, 217; Abu Bakr, caliph, 133, 175; Abdel Qader 'Awda on, 78; Hasan al-Banna on, 36, 77–78; global caliphate, 93; Hasan al-Hudaybi on, 38; "rightly guided" caliphs, 97; Umar ibn Abdel Aziz, caliph, 163; Umar ibn al-Khattab, caliph, 163. *See also* Islamic state
capital: moral, 115, 143, 167; political, 114, 117; *rasid* (stock), 167; religious, 117, 144; social, 25, 114, 139, 143, 167, 220
candidates, 47, 68, 139; independent, 51; Islamist, 113, 117, 121; MB, 48, 58, 115, 118, 125, 140, 141, 143; sharia and, 173; *tarbiya* and, 141–42. *See also* elections; electoral politics
change (Islamist movements), 2–3, 8, 9–10, 213, 229; drivers of, 4; ideational change, 4, 6, 14; internal debates as drivers of, 4, 6; MB and, 1, 2–4, 6–9, 12, 19, 112, 115, 152, 153, 206; MB's change as in membership, 7; of MB's mission, 2, 7, 17–18, 73, 76,

158, 162, 166; religious framing and, 3–4
charity, charitable contribution. *See zakat*
chauvinism (*ta'ssub*), 49, 73, 101
Christianity, 59, 121, 124, 157, 176, 181; Christian-Muslim unity/tolerance, 57, 130; Coptic Christians, 132; missionaries, 28–29, 33
citizenship, 11; righteous citizenship (*muwatina salima*), 66, 67
Clark, Janine, 6
collective religious obligation (*fard kifaya*), 4; AWI (Morocco), 215; commanding the right as, 23; jihad as collective obligation, 137; MB's activism and, 3; MB's framing and, 4, 15, 17, 18, 25; MB's *minhaj* and, 30; MB's political work as, 22, 23, 25, 129, 132, 159, 208; MB's power-seeking and, 76; sharia and, 61, 62; undertaken by state, 149–50
commanding the right (*al-amr bi-l-ma'ruf*), 38; Hasan al-Banna on, 23, 35; as collective religious obligation, 23; MB and power-seeking, 76, 102, 108; MB's activism and, 3, 12; MB's framing and, 8, 15, 17, 35, 98, 205; MB's *minhaj* and, 30
commissive discourse, 15; MB and, 18–19, 22, 23, 24, 42, 56, 87, 125, 133; Wafd leaders and, 56. *See also* constructivism
Companions of the Prophet (*al-salaf al-salih*), 133, 138
constructivism: framing, 12–20; identity-affirming choices, 27; institutionalization of norms, 19; "ontological narratives," 13. *See also* assertive discourse; commissive discourse; directive discourse; speech acts

consultation. *See shura*
corruption, 97, 180, 208; power-seeking and, 104; the West and, 95
coup (2013): political learning, 191–96, 211–12; against President Morsi, 18, 26, 154, 189, 190–91, 211
Court of Cassation, 60
curriculum: Gama'a Islamiyya, 40; method of cultivation (*minhaj tarbawi*), 32. *See also* MB and educational curricula

Dar al-Ifta', 186
da'wa (invitation to Islam, preaching): AWI (Morocco), 214, 215, 216, 217–18, 220, 223; Azhari preachers, 31; *da'wa*/political work tension, 230; Ennahda (Tunisia), 226; framing and, 229–30; Islamist movements, *tarbiya*, and, 11; jihad and, 137; MUR (Morocco) and, 214, 222, 223; politics and, 11; Sayyid Qutb on, 37; Salafi preachers, 171, 172; televangelists/television preachers, 170, 171, 172, 175, 176, 193. *See also* MB's *da'wa*
al-Da'wa (MB's journal), 21, 43–44, 49, 52, 82; critique of Sadat's policies by, 44–45; MB's mission and, 42–43, 50; as oppositional voice, 45. *See also* media
Da'wa Salafiyya, 171, 227
democracy: AWI (Morocco) and, 219; democratization, 25, 126, 150, 194, 213; Ennahda (Tunisia) and, 224–25; Islamist movements and, 6; MB and, 6, 26, 57, 70, 104, 124–25, 146, 147, 154, 185, 189, 195, 198; Salafi movements and, 226–27; *shura* and, 70

directive discourse, 14, 230; MB and, 18–19, 21, 22, 26, 31, 48, 61–62, 71, 77, 108, 110, 113, 142, 143, 146, 148, 149, 150, 205, 207, 208, 210. *See also* constructivism

EBDA (trade association), 177
economy: economic development, 177, 180; economic reform, 50, 63, 80, 85–86, 125–26; FJP/Morsi's economic policy, 177, 185–87, 192; foreign exchange crisis, 80; Islamic banking, 86; Islamic finance, 85–86; Nahda Project, 177; religious restrictions on economic activity, 87; *sukuk* policy, 185–87, 192; usury, 86, 186, 222, 227; Western financing, 86; *zakat* and, 84, 85, 86, 147, 187
education. *See* curriculum; MB and education; MB and educational curricula; *tarbiya*
efforts, struggle. *See* jihad
Egypt: Islamic identity, 45; legislation and sharia, 59–61, 62–64, 75, 77, 79–86, 184; "national Islam," 77, 210. *See also* state
Egypt, 2011 uprising, 152, 153, 227; MB and, 153–54, 161; MB's legalization, 155–57; SCAF-led transition, 153, 167, 183
Egypt, 2013 coup. *See* coup (2013)
Egyptian Constitution: 2011 constitutional referendum, 168–69; 2011 interim constitution, 154; 2012 Constitution, 153, 154, 192; 2013 constitutional referendum, 195; article 2, 56, 59, 60, 66, 80–82, 147, 184; article 4, 185; article 219, 184–85, 192; "implementing sharia" through constitutional regulations and policymaking, 183–87; Salafis and, 183–84
elections: 1984 parliamentary elections, 47, 48, 59; 1987 parliamentary elections, 64–69, 85, 113, 115; 1990s, 6, 16; 1995 parliamentary elections, 125; 2000 parliamentary elections, 125; 2005 parliamentary elections, 139, 140; 2011 parliamentary elections, 167–69, 172–75, 227; 2005 presidential elections, 139; 2012 presidential elections, 169, 175–77; 2014 presidential elections, 196
electoral politics: AWI (Morocco), 213, 229; Ennahda (Tunisia), 224, 225; framing of, 230; independent candidates, 51; Islamist movements and, 2, 6, 214, 229, 230–31; Islamist movements and adaptation to politics, 2, 6, 214; Islamic principles and, 6; jihad, elections as, 118, 136; liberalization, 48–51, 115, 141, 171; multiparty elections, 44, 47, 48–49, 51, 139; MUR (Morocco) and, 221, 222; Nour Party, 171; reform, 44, 47, 48, 51, 67, 113, 115, 139, 145; syndicate elections, 116, 117–18, 122. *See also* candidates; MB and electoral politics
emotions: emotional cultivation of Muslims, 138; MB and emotional connection with people, 33, 35, 102, 137, 172, 192–93; television preachers and, 172. *See also* love
empowerment (*tamkin*): after 2012 MB victory, state tools and, 178–83; after 2015, 202; AWI (Morocco) and, 219–20; of citizens to hold their representatives accountable, 59, 106; Ennahda (Tunisia) and, 225, 226; MB

and, 18, 59–60, 75, 144–45, 150, 151, 169, 204, 206, 219; MB and power-seeking, 76, 92, 93–98, 102–5, 106, 109–10, 154; MB's Empowerment Project (Mashru' al-Tamkin), 122; MUR (Morocco) and, 219; popular, through religion, 59–60; reframing of, 106; sharia and, 24; *tanzimi* leadership and, 115. *See also* MB and power-seeking

endowments (*awqaf*), 126, 148, 182

Ennahda (Islamist movement, Tunisia), 213–14, 224–26, 227; charitable work, 225–26; *da'wa*, 226; democracy, 224–25; electoral politics, 224, 225; empowerment, 225, 226; party work/preaching separation, 213–14, 224; sharia and, 225; *shura*, 224, 225. *See also* Ghannouchi, Rached

el-Erian, Essam, 69, 92, 117, 149, 176

ethical cultivation. *See tarbiya*

etiquette. *See adab*

excellence/religious perfection. *See ihsan*

Ezzat, Mahmoud, 159

Fadhila Party, 171

fard al-'ayn. *See* individual obligation

fard kifaya. *See* collective religious obligation

fasting, 33, 138

fiqh. *See* jurisprudence

FJP (Freedom and Justice Party): 2011 parliamentary elections, 168–70, 172–75; 2011–12 electoral outbidding and new competition, 170–72; 2012 presidential elections, 169, 175–77; FJP leadership, 156, 171, 176; formation of, 25, 155–56, 208, 210; *gama'a* and, 159–60; in government, limited control of policymaking and cabinet appointments, 178; in government, state tools and empowerment, 178–83; Islamic revival, 152; *minhaj*, 157; on morality, 156–57, 173–74, 180; nonexclusionary nature of, 156, 160; organization and structure of, 161; partisanship, 169–70; political training, 160–61; popular opposition to FJP government, 187; religion and politics, 156–57, 160; sharia application and, 173–76, 178, 179, 180, 183–87; *shar'iyya*, 187–91; social Islamization, 157, 181; *tanzimi* leadership and, 153–54, 160. *See also* MB's politics; Morsi, Mohammed

Foda, Farag, 59

framing, 13; electoral politics and, 230; Islamic activism and, 9, 229–30; Islamist movements and, 13–14, 20, 229; master frames, 15; political reframing, 230; reframing, 14, 222, 229; religion and politics, 10, 19–20; "righteous action" framing, 10–11; scripture and, 11; strategic framing, 14, 15, 71. *See also* MB's framing

Free Officers' uprising (1952), 34

Gama'a Islamiyya, 40, 44, 87, 122

Gama'at al-ikhwan al-muslimin. *See* MB as organization

al-Gamal, Hasan, 88

Gami'yya al-Shar'iyya (charitable association), 68, 141, 142, 170, 171, 181, 190

Ghannouchi, Rached, 224, 225

al-Ghazali, Abdel Hamid, 86

el-Ghobashy, Mona, 6, 7, 14

Ghozlan, Mahmoud, 156

God's sovereignty (*hakimiyyat allah*):
Hasan al-Hudaybi on, 36, 39, 79;
Sayyid Qutb on, 23, 28; repressive
state and, 28
God's will, 5, 75, 203; Hasan al-Banna
on, 23; MB and, 70–71, 74, 75, 88, 105,
109, 203, 205, 208; *shura* and, 71; statist and institution-driven approach
to applying God's will, 75
governance: good, 8, 24, 25, 75, 154, 176,
179–80, 192, 205, 226; Islamic, 79,
105, 132, 153, 176, 178, 179, 192–93,
204, 207, 227; MB and, 8, 24, 25, 35,
37, 75, 96, 100, 130–33, 176, 178, 179–
80, 191, 192–93, 205; in MB curricula,
114–15; sharia and, 24, 25, 39, 100
al-Guindi, Anwar, 67–68

Habib, Muhammad, 88, 144, 146
Habib, Rafiq, 120
al-Haddad, Essam, 122
hadith (sayings of the Prophet), 38, 98,
101, 138, 157, 174, 215; MB's education
programs and, 128, 130, 131, 164, 166
hakimiyyat allah. See God's sovereignty
al-hal al-islami. See Islamic solution
al-Haqq, Shaykh al-Azhar Gadd, 90
haraki (activist): *fikr haraki* (activist
thought), 37; Islamic activists as
political entrepreneurs, 14; Islamic
activists' work as *tarbiya*, 11; mobilizational skills, 101; repression against
Islamic activists, 58, 91. *See also*
Islamic activism
Harb, Talaat, 86
Hasan, Muhammad, 171
Hegazy, Safwat, 172, 175, 189
hisba lawsuits, 82

hizbiyya. See partisanship/partyism
el-Hodeiby, Mamoun, 70, 84, 88, 89, 102,
125–26
Howeidy, Fahmi, 112
al-Hudaybi, Hasan, 9, 40; *Du'at la
Quda't* (Preachers, Not Judges), 37,
79, 93; *Dusturna* (Our Constitution),
39; on God's sovereignty, 36, 39, 79;
on *hukm*, 23, 28, 37, 38, 79; MB's
da'wa and, 36; on righteous action,
37–38; on sharia, 38, 39, 79; on *tanfidh*, 38; on *tarbiya*, 36
hukm (rule): AWI (Morocco), 218; Hasan
al-Banna on, 23, 34–36, 77, 78; as
God's judgment, 23, 28; Hasan al-
Hudaybi on, 23, 28, 37, 38, 79; Islamic
government/*hukuma*, 43, 50, 94, 95,
130–33, 193, 218; MB and, 30, 34, 93,
95–96, 106–7, 108; righteous rule, 38,
39; Umar al-Tilmissany on, 50
Husein, Muhammad, 172
Hussein, Adil, 120

'ibada. See worship
Ibn Taymiyya, 131
ideas: ideational change/evolution, 4,
6, 14, 19; ideational/moral entrepreneurs, 14; institutionalization
of norms and, 19. *See also* ideology;
Islamic ideology
identity: Egyptian Islamic, 45; Islamic
mobilization, -affirming choices, 27;
MB and, 2, 3, 7, 12, 13, 210; Muslim,
and adaptation to politics, 6
ideology, 17. *See also* Islamic ideology
ihsan (excellence/religious perfection),
98, 100, 165, 208, 216, 218
Imara, Muhammad, 130, 131–32

IMF (International Monetary Fund), 80, 185, 227
individual obligation (*fard al-'ayn*), 4, 37, 73; jihad as individual obligation, 137; MB's political work as, 129, 132–33
Iran, 8, 180
islah (righteous reform): Hasan al-Banna on, 33–34, 35; MB's framing and, 15, 17, 51, 67; MB's *minhaj* and, 23, 30; self-reform (*islah al-nafs*), 1; *tarbiya* as tool for, 23; Umar al-Tilmissany on, 62
Islah Party: manifesto, 55, 83
Islam: comprehensiveness of, 31–32, 69, 77, 107–8, 162, 203, 207, 208; as "discursive tradition," 4, 11; Egyptian "national Islam," 77, 210; as political project, 68; as "practical ethic," 11; scripture, 6, 10, 11, 33, 96. See also hadith; Quran; *sunna*
Islamic activism, 36, 78, 113, 141; AWI (Morocco), 217–18; framing of, 9, 229–30; mosques and, 102–3; student activism/youth groups, 40, 46, 92. See also *haraki*; MB's activism
Islamic Alliance (Labor Party/Ahrar Party/MB alliance), 65, 66, 69, 71, 85, 89; ban on members from delivering Friday sermons, 91; election manifesto, 66–67; parliamentary achievements, 72
Islamic exceptionalism, 9
Islamic ideology, 2, 4, 5, 9, 35; "purposeful ambiguity" of, 6. See also MB's ideology
Islamic law. See sharia
Islamic mobilization, 9; construction of, 4–6; contingent leadership framing choices, 27; identity-affirming choices, 27; jihad, political mobilization as, 115; outcome-driven vs. identity-driven definitions of Islamic political project, 27. See also Islamic activism; Islamist movements
Islamic solution (*al-hal al-islami*), 62, 66, 72, 76, 80, 107
Islamic state: Hasan al-Banna on, 77–78; as civil state, 149; Hasan al-Hudaybi on, 37; Islamic governance, 79, 105, 132, 153, 176, 178, 179, 192–93, 204, 207, 227; Islamic government/ *hukuma*, 43, 50, 94, 95, 130–33, 193, 218; Islamist movements and, 2; Islamization and, 75–76, 78; MB's framing of, 26–27, 75–76, 86–92, 97, 131, 148, 205, 207; MB's mission and 2, 3; Pakistan, 218
Islamist movements, 1, 203, 229–31; adaptation to politics, 2, 6, 9, 214; Arab Islamist movements, 213, 229; comparative lessons, 213–29; *da'wa*, *tarbiya*, and, 11; democracy and, 6; electoral politics and, 2, 6, 214, 229, 230–31; framing and, 13–14, 20, 229; Islamic state and, 2; "ontological narratives," 13; reframing of political strategies, 213; religion and, 9–12; religious and political missions as separate and incompatible, 1–2; Salafi movements, 226–28, 230; sharia and, 19; social movements and, 229; speech acts and, 16. See also change; Islamic activism; Islamic mobilization
Islamization. See MB and social Islamization
Ismail, Salah Abu, Shaykh, 52, 55–56
Israel, 6, 42, 44, 59

jihad (efforts, struggle), 26, 37, 100, 149; armed, 43, 93, 197, 198, 202; Hasan al-Banna on, 26, 136–37; *da'wa* and, 137; elections as, 118, 136; goals of, 136, 137; as individual and collective obligation, 137; jihad *al-nafs* (jihad of the self), 136; "Jurisprudence of Popular Resistance" text and, 197, 198; MB's education on, 129, 136–39, 208; passive assertion of faith as form of, 43; political mobilization as, 115; political work as, 129, 136; public work as, 52; Quranic verses on, 136, 138
Jordan, 8, 209
jurisprudence (*fiqh*), 32, 77, 96, 119, 201, 203
"Jurisprudence of Popular Resistance," 197; "The Jurisprudence of Popular Resistance to the Coup" (*Fiqh al-muqawama al-sha'biyya li-l-inqilab*), 196, 197–98, 199

Kamal, Mohamed, 196, 198
Kandil, Hazem, 5, 7, 128
Kandil, Hisham, 192
Karagiannis, Emmanuel, 226–27
khalq, akhlaq. See morality/morals
Khanani, Ahmed, 13
khayriyya (charitable work, doing good), 97, 98, 100, 140, 199, 201; MB's education on, 164, 165, 201. See also welfare
Kratochwil, Friedrich, 20
Kuwait, 228–29

Labor Party (Hizb al-'Amal), 65. See also Islamic Alliance
Lebanon, 8

legitimacy. See *shar'iyya*
Lia, Brynjar, 9, 31
love, 216, 217; of God, 99, 219; in MB's *da'wa*, 49; MB's education on, 164. See also emotions

al-Mahgoub, Rifa't, 86
Mahmood, Saba, 5, 11
Mahmoud, 'Ali Abdel Halim, 130; *Wasa'il al-tarbiya*, 94–105, 106
Mahmoud, Mustafa, 40
Malek, Hasan, 177
March, Andrew, 11
Mashour, Mustafa, 40, 41, 54, 125, 134; didactic purpose of election campaigning, 53; on MB's *da'wa*, 53, 72–73, 93–94; on MB's mission, 42–43; on parliamentary work, 70–71; on pluralism, 55; on political participation, 68; on sharia, 89–90; on *tanfidh*, 43; on *tarbiya*, 70, 72–73
maslaha, masalih. See public good
Mawdudi, Abul-Ala, 136, 215, 218
MB and education, 8, 9, 31, 67, 118, 119, 204, 207; 2011-13: updated training, 160–66; internally reframing training, 157–60; on jihad, 129, 136–39, 208; leadership training, 161, 162–63, 201; MB's central educational council (*lignat al-tarbiya al-markaziyya*), 127; MB's educational wing, 25, 161; MB's *minhaj* and, 29; outreach-oriented training, 25, 101, 105–6, 142, 151, 162, 164, 166, 207; political training, 113–14, 127, 128–32, 136, 139, 151, 160, 161, 164, 205; religious education, 12, 128, 162, 163; religious ethics, cultivation of, 101–2; sharia and education, 24; state-led religious education,

24, 34; *takwin salih* (upright formation), 99; training in *da'wa*, 32, 33, 36, 161, 164–65; training programs, 9, 18, 19, 31, 33, 77, 201; training for public activism, 94, 160–61; training in *shura*, 100–101, 129, 133–35; *usra* system and education/training, 93, 99–100, 101, 105, 106, 127, 129, 161, 162, 163; Western topics, 165–66. *See also* MB and educational curricula; *tarbiya*

MB and educational curricula, 20, 25, 113, 114–15, 127–38, 153; 2011–13 period: 161–66, 201; *Fann al-ta'mul ma' al-mujtama* (The Art of Dealing with Society), 161–66; *Fi Nur al-Islam* (In the Light of Islam), 127–35, 139, 142, 147, 157, 162, 163, 165; *Fi Rihab al-Islam* (In the Vastness of Islam), 127–28, 162; *Min Mabadi' al-Islam* (From the Principles of Islam), 127–28, 162; Pillars program (*barnamij al-raka'iz*), 163; Usama Ibn Zayid curriculum, 162–63. *See also* MB and education

MB and electoral politics, 46, 74, 205, 206, 207; 1985–86: mobilizing voices for God's law in Parliament, 59–64; 1987 parliamentary campaign: activating righteous voters, 64–69; 2000s, 113, 150, 154, 207; 2005–10 electoral and service work as religious performance, 139–50; 2011 religious and popular credit: *da'wa* and capacity building, 167–70; 2011–12 electoral outbidding and new competition, 170–72; campaigning, 18, 24, 47, 48, 51–55, 115, 167–70; coalitions, 154; contesting elections, 51–55; *da'wa* and, 24, 48, 55–59, 65, 66, 69, 167–70; 199–200; didactic purpose of election campaigning, 53, 66; electoral outreach, 17, 115, 117, 139, 144, 167; MB candidates, 48, 58, 115, 118, 125, 140, 141, 143; MB's framing and, 24, 25, 47–48, 51–59, 65, 67–69, 71, 209; "middle generation" and, 6, 112, 123; morality and, 17–18, 67–68; neighborhood level, 141–42; parliamentary elections, 48, 122, 167, 169; partisanship, 24, 47, 50, 57, 65, 75, 89, 103, 113, 121–22, 157; political participation, 67–68, 74, 117, 205, 207; righteous action and, 7, 48, 65, 141; syndicate elections, 116, 117–18, 122; *tanzimi* leadership and, 115; *tarbiya* and, 24, 48, 51–55, 65, 69, 153, 205; Wafd/MB joint election manifesto, 57. *See also* electoral politics; MB's politics

MB and power-seeking, 2, 25, 35, 75, 76–77, 105–12, 206; after 2011, 153–54, 167; collective religious obligation, 76; commanding the right and, 76, 102, 108; *da'wa* and, 76, 80, 98, 102–3, 106, 110–11, 145, 206; empowerment and, 76, 92, 93–98, 102–5, 106, 109–10, 154; *hukm*, 93, 95–96, 106–7, 108; Islamic state, 86–92, 97; Islamization of the state, 76, 88, 108, 109; MB's framing and, 25, 92–105, 106; MB as "statist Islamists," 77; righteous action, 92–105, 153; state power and Islamic mission, 76, 92, 94, 154; state power in the MB *minhaj*, 77–79; state as vehicle for sharia application, 77, 79–90, 92, 93, 107–8, 109; taboo against power-seeking, 93–94; *tanfidh* and, 94–96, 97–99, 105, 107, 108; *tarbiya*, 77, 83, 92–105, 110–11. *See also* empowerment

MB and sharia, 24, 206, 210; after 2011, 172–77, 183–87; after 2012 victory, 178, 179, 180; advocacy for, 48, 60, 62, 63, 64, 81, 90, 109, 119, 172–77, 206; commanding the right and, 24; education and sharia, 24; Egyptian legislation and sharia application, 45, 59–61, 66, 75, 108, 126, 147–48; empowerment and, 24; "implementing sharia" through constitutional regulations and policymaking, 183–87; MB's activism and, 3; MB's *da'wa* and, 5–6, 60, 62; MB's framing and, 15, 18, 24, 25–26, 59, 61, 62–63, 76, 78, 89, 108–9, 183; MB's mission and, 18, 210; MB's politics and, 2, 3, 64, 124–25; partisan instrumentalization of sharia, 76; popular opposition to Morsi government and, 189–90; professionals and sharia application, 119; state as vehicle for sharia application, 77, 79–90, 92, 93, 107–8, 109, 154, 173–74, 178, 207; working for sharia, 15, 18. *See also* sharia

MB and social Islamization, 88, 144, 149, 210; FJP, 157, 181; framing of social Islamization, 26; Islamic state and, 75–76, 78; MB and Islamization of the state, 76, 88, 108, 109; MB's activism and, 7, 8, 102; MB's electoral politics and, 3, 7, 26, 66; MB's *minhaj* and, 30; MB's mission and, 4, 6, 7, 17

MB as organization (Gama'at al-Ikhwan al-Muslimin), 7, 98, 146, 154, 155, 156, 212–13; 2015, factions after, 196–202, 212; change/evolution of, 1, 3–4, 6–9, 12, 17, 19, 112, 115, 152, 153, 206; conservative faction, 112–14, 123, 125, 151–52; credentialing strategies, 17, 18, 21–22, 63; criticism of, 199, 200; disagreement and dissent within, 18, 25, 112, 115, 145, 150–51, 156, 158, 159, 196, 207, 212–13; FJP and, 159–60; founding period, 28–39, 203; "*gama'a*"/"the world" distinction, 7; in government, 178–83; hierarchy, 40, 112, 151, 152, 155, 158, 170; Islamic revival, 152; Islamist intellectuals and, 12, 43, 112; as "mother movement," 213; *nahda* and, 158–59; populism, 25; precedence over political parties, 158; Qutbist faction, 112–13, 197; reformist wing of, 150–51; as self-contained organization, 6–7; *shar'iyya*, 18, 154, 187–91; social networks, 7, 140, 141–42; *tanzimi* leadership and, 2, 3, 113–15, 123, 125, 127, 139–50, 151, 153–54, 155, 160; Wasat faction, 112, 113–14, 123–24; youth and, 40–42, 44, 45, 46, 49, 57, 62, 67, 92, 104, 134, 203

MB's activism, 113, 203; 1970s revival of activism, 39–46; collective religious obligation and, 3; commanding the right and, 3, 12; contextual and adaptive approach, 6; debates on, 12; Islamization/social Islamization and, 7, 8, 102; MB's framing and, 9, 204; religion and, 5, 12, 116; righteous action and, 3, 13; sharia and, 3; state-centered activism, 24; *tarbiya* and, 3, 7, 12, 24. *See also* MB's mission; MB's politics; MB's social activism

MB's conferences, 37, 41–42, 120, 124, 155; Third Conference, 30–31; Fifth Conference, 23, 31, 77, 130; Sixth Conference, 50

MB's *da'wa*, 1, 3, 46, 49, 151, 157, 170, 197, 205–6; Hasan al-Banna and, 31, 32, 35, 53, 78; electoral politics and,

24, 48, 55–59, 65, 66, 69, 167–70, 199–200; growing scope of, 73; Hasan al-Hudaybi and, 36; as individual religious duty, 73; Mustafa Mashour on, 53, 72–73, 93–94; mass media and, 23, 28, 42; MB and power-seeking, 76, 80, 98, 102–3, 106, 110–11, 145, 206; MB's framing, 15, 17, 18, 24, 47, 209; MB's *minhaj* and, 29, 30; MB's mission and, 22, 37, 39, 40, 42, 153; MB's politics and, 26, 48, 50, 52, 53–54, 72, 114, 115, 126, 127, 151, 199, 210–12; *nahda* and, 158; Parliament and, 48, 52, 53–54, 59–60, 69; political work as *da'wa*, 47–48; practical application and examples, 32; preaching wing as constraint on innovation, 6; renewed *da'wa*, 39; righteous action and, 5–6; sharia and, 5–6, 60, 62; *tarbiya* and, 32, 207; training in *da'wa*, 32, 33, 36, 161, 164–65. *See also da'wa*

MB's framing, 13–15, 204, 209–10; Hasan al-Banna and, 15; of campaigning, 3; "civil religion," 8; collective religious obligation, 4, 15, 17, 18, 25; commanding the right and, 8, 15, 17, 35, 98, 205; of constituent outreach, 3; *da'wa*, 15, 17, 18, 24, 47, 209; *islah*, 15, 17, 51, 67; Islamic state and, 26–27, 75–76, 86–92, 97, 131, 148, 205, 207; MB and power-seeking, 25; MB's activism and, 9, 204; MB's discursive tradition and, 3–4, 14–18; MB's electoral politics and, 24, 25, 47–48, 51–59, 65, 67–69, 71, 209; MB's mission and, 18, 25, 26, 209; nationalist framing, 8; of political opposition, 26; of political work, 22, 23, 25, 47, 48, 52, 53–54, 59–60, 69–72, 129, 132, 159, 204, 205, 208, 209; of power-seeking, 25, 92–105, 106; of public work, 25, 28; reframing, 18, 26, 27, 92–105, 106, 157–60, 202, 205, 207; reframing, possibilities and limits of, 209–13; religious framing, 3–4, 209–10; "righteous action," 3–4, 5–6, 7, 8–9, 10, 14–16, 17, 18, 24, 26, 38, 50–1, 206; sharia and, 15, 18, 24, 25–26, 59, 61, 62–63, 76, 78, 89, 108–9, 183; of social Islamization, 26; strategic framing, 14, 15, 26, 71; *tarbiya*, 8, 15, 17, 28, 33; working for God, 12, 16, 17, 204. *See also* framing; MB's politics; worship

MB's ideology, 6, 8–9, 28, 146; comprehensiveness of Islam, 31–32, 69, 77, 107–8, 162, 203, 207, 208; ideational production, 7–8, 19, 20, 21, 29, 35, 41, 42, 114; identity and, 2, 3, 7 12, 13, 210; Islamic project, 8, 25, 26, 84, 87, 91, 169, 199; public spheres/discourses, 8, 20–21, 42; religious identity, 2, 12, 13. *See also* Islamic ideology

MB's leadership, 1; after 2015, 196–99; accountability and, 8; as actors committed to religion, 47; Guidance Council, 44; middle-generation leaders, 112, 113, 117, 119, 123, 127; oppositional voice and, 45, 53; religious mission and, 3, 43; Anwar al-Sadat and, 44–45, 49; *shar'iyya* and, 26; structure, 125, 196, 224; *tanzimi* leadership and electoral politics, 115; *tanzimi* leadership and empowerment, 115; *tanzimi* leadership and FJP, 153–54, 160; *tanzimi* leadership and political work, 2, 3, 113–15, 123, 125, 127, 139–50, 151, 153–54, 155, 160;

MB's leadership (*cont.*)
  tanzimi leadership and *tarbiya*, 113, 114, 115. *See also* Abul Nasr, Hamid; al-Banna, Hasan; al-Hudaybi, Hasan; Mashour, Mustafa; al-Shater, Khairat; al-Tilmissany, Umar
MB's membership: influx of conservatives from rural Saudi Arabia and Gulf states, 112; change, 7; promotion within organization, 30–31; *tarbiya* and, 18. *See also* MB and education
MB's "middle generation": MB and electoral politics and, 6, 112, 123; MB's politics and, 6, 46, 112, 114, 117, 123, 148–49, 150; partisanship and, 113
MB's *minhaj*, 23, 25, 43, 46, 200; adaptation to concerns of the day, 44; Hasan al-Banna and, 30, 34; collective religious obligation, 30; commanding the right, 30; *da'wa* and, 29, 30; education and, 29; FJP, 157; future shifts, 27; *hukm*, 30; *islah*, 23, 30; MB mission and, 6, 16, 22, 140, 158; method of cultivation (*minhaj tarbawi*), 32; "mission talk," 13, 16, 17, 31; Prophetic example and, 33; righteous action and, 32; *tarbiya*, 23, 30
MB's mission, 20, 22, 210; change/evolution of, 2, 7, 17–18, 73, 76, 158, 162, 166; *da'wa*, 22, 37, 39, 40, 42, 153; framing of, 18, 25, 26, 209; *insha' al-nufus* and, 28; Islamic state and, 2, 3; Islamization/social Islamization, 4, 6, 7, 17; Mustafa Mashour on, 42–43; *minhaj* and, 6, 16, 22, 140, 158; "mission talk," 13, 16, 17, 31; political activism and religion, 1, 2–3, 28, 156; reframing of, 18; religious mission, 1, 2, 3, 7; sharia and, 18, 210; state and politics in early MB's mission, 34–39; *tarbiya*, 5, 7, 22, 28, 36, 42, 73. *See also* MB's activism

MB's political party: formation of, 2, 18, 54–55, 64, 83, 114, 115, 123, 146–49, 150, 154. *See also* FJP; Islah Party; Shura Party

MB's political professionalization, 55, 140, 153, 159, 199, 207; 1990s political specialization, 115–26; cultivating Muslim workers for political sphere, 160–67

MB's politics, 1, 113; 2000s directive discourse and *tarbiya*, 126–39; 2011 uprising and, 161; 2013 coup, political learning, 191–96, 211–12; 2015, political learning and righteous political action after, 196–202, 212; anticolonial resistance, 23, 28; Hasan al-Banna and, 29, 34–36; *da'wa* and, 26, 48, 50, 52, 53–54, 72, 114, 115, 126, 127, 151, 199, 210–12; democracy, 6, 26, 57, 70, 104, 124–25, 146, 147, 154, 185, 189, 195, 198; on freedoms, 6, 25, 57–60, 63, 66, 67, 68–69, 88, 91–92, 124, 198; God's will and, 70–71, 74; governance, 8, 24, 25, 35, 37, 75, 96, 100, 130–33, 176, 178, 179–80, 191, 192–93, 205; Hasan al-Hudaybi on, 36–37; internally reframing political work, 157–60; Parliament and *da'wa*, 48, 52, 53–54, 59–60, 69; Parliament and *tarbiya*, 48, 69–71; parliamentary work, 3, 24, 50, 52, 53, 64, 71–72, 74, 76, 91, 110, 114, 116; political adaptation, 3, 17, 73, 161, 209; political bureau, 44, 46; political opportunities and, 18, 26, 27, 115–26, 209; political outreach, 25, 46, 93, 139, 151,

166, 168, 201, 216; political pluralism, 6, 22, 25, 46, 55, 70, 73, 124, 140, 185; political strategies, 1, 7, 18, 73, 155, 191, 197, 205, 206, 211; political work and professional syndicates, 114, 116–23; political work as religious, 22, 23, 25, 52, 109, 129, 132, 159, 208; religion and, 1, 2–3, 4–5, 9, 22, 29, 44–45, 54, 98, 110, 124, 125–26, 129, 139–50, 152, 191–96, 203–5, 209, 210–11; righteous action and, 7, 37, 92–105, 119, 128, 153, 196–202, 207–8; sharia and, 2, 3, 64, 124–25; *shura* and, 25, 69–71, 73, 74, 114, 121, 124, 146–47, 154, 159; state-oriented politics and righteous action, 28; state and politics in early MB's mission, 34–39; *tarbiya* and, 2–3, 18, 25, 26, 48, 51, 69–71, 72, 92–105, 114–15, 139, 145, 150, 151, 152; Wafd Party/MB alliance, 51, 55–59, 61, 64–65; welfare and, 54–55, 114, 121–22, 139, 141–43, 147, 151, 152, 170, 176, 178, 180; women's rights and, 124, 140, 181; "working for God" and, 1, 3. *See also* FJP; Islamic Alliance; MB and electoral politics; MB and power-seeking; MB's framing; MB's "middle generation"; MB's political party; MB's political professionalization

MB's social activism, 103, 106, 143–44, 206, 207, 208, 210; 2011 religious and popular credit: *da'wa* and capacity building, 167–70; after 2011, 160–61; after 2012 MB victory, 179, 200; after 2015, 201; Hasan al-Banna on, 34; charitable work, 141, 160, 167, 168, 170; medical service caravans, 144, 168, 169, 179; neighborhood level, 144, 168; "popular committees," 168–69; religion and, 1, 3, 4–5, 8; social reform, 8, 16, 28, 118; social welfare, 8, 34; *tarbiya*, 28, 114; Together We Build Egypt campaign, 179. *See also* MB's activism

MB's *usra* (movement cell or "family"), 23, 31, 93, 96, 207; education and training, 93, 99–100, 101, 105, 106, 127, 129, 161, 162, 163; importance of, 100, 102–3; *naqib* (leader) of, 127–28; *tarbiya* and, 12, 99

McLarney, Ellen Anne, 11

media: *al-Ahram* (state-run newspaper), 58; *al-Ikhwan al-Muslimin* (MB's magazine), 51–52; *al-'Itisam* (journal), 68; *Liwa' al-Islam* (MB-run newspaper), 52, 70; *Mayo* (state-run magazine), 90; MB's *da'wa* and mass media, 23, 28, 42; *Oktobar* (state-owned journal), 71; online media and blogs, 143, 150; Salafi preachers and satellite media, 171; *al-Sha'b* (newspaper), 23, 58, 63, 65, 68, 87; state-dominated media, 42, 58, 71, 90. *See also al-Da'wa*

Menchik, Jeremy, 5

Menshawy, Mustafa, 212

method. *See minhaj*

methodology and theoretical approach: constructivism, 12–20; data and sources, 13, 14, 16, 20–23, 47; framing, 12–20; implications and questions for further research, 229–31; time periods, 18. *See also* constructivism; speech acts

minhaj (method), 5, 75; AWI (Morocco), 216; *minhaj* of Islam, 68. *See also* MB's *minhaj*

Mitchell, Richard P., 9
model/role model: Brothers as positive role models for others, 43, 48, 52, 159, 165, 168, 206; model Muslim citizen, 35, 67, 84, 204, 216; models of leadership, 97, 162–63; Prophet Muhammad as, 57, 73
Mohieddin, Ala'a, 87
morality/morals (*khalq, akhlaq*), 44, 216, 219, 222; Hasan al-Banna on, 33, 34, 35, 77–79; FJP on, 156–57, 173–74, 180; Hasan al-Hudaybi on, 38; 'Ali Abdel Halim Mahmoud on, 95, 99–100, 103–5, 108, 109, 118; MB on, 18, 51, 67, 69, 70, 72, 74, 83–85, 140, 149, 176, 199, 205, 207, 214; MB's educational curricula on, 130, 133, 138, 164, 165, 166; MB's electoral politics and, 17–18, 67–68; moral action, 30, 38; moral capital, 115, 143, 167; moral citizens, 29, 30; moral code, 11, 78, 84; "moral entrepreneurs," 14; moral reform, 33, 157, 176, 228; sharia and, 78, 83–84, 88, 107; social morality, 109, 180, 223–24; Umar al-Tilmissany on, 49, 61, 62; Wafd Party/MB alliance on, 57. *See also tarbiya*
Morocco, 27, 213, 214. *See also* AWI; MUR
Morsi, Mohammed, 1; 2012 presidential elections, 169, 175–76, 177; 2013 coup against, 18, 26, 154, 189, 190–91, 211; Nahda Project, 177; popular opposition to Morsi government, 187, 188–90; Raba'a al-'Adaweyya sit-in, 189–91; victory speech, 178; vindicated by MB activists, 191–92, 197
mosques: activism and, 102–3; charitable social services, 171; free expression in, 52, 58, 63, 85; MB and, 41, 52, 57, 61, 91, 116; state and, 59
mu'amalat. *See under* worldly dealings
Mubarak, Hosni, 49; 1990 Parliament dissolution, 113, 122; 2011 resignation, 25, 152, 153, 154, 155, 171; anti-extremism laws, 113; electoral reform, 47, 51, 113, 139, 145; state repression of MB, 113, 122–23, 124, 145
MUR (Movement for Unity and Reform, Morocco), 213, 214, 220–24, 226; *da'wa*, 214, 222, 223; electoral politics, 221, 222; empowerment, 219; Moroccan regime and, 221–22, 223; PJD (Justice and Development Party), 27, 214, 220–22, 223; reframing, 222; religion/politics division, 223–24; sharia and, 221, 223; *shura*, 221, 223; *tarbiya*, 214, 221. *See also* Raysuni, Ahmad
Muslim Sisters, 195

nahda. *See under* renaissance
nasiha (advice), 48, 52, 53, 76, 101, 108, 205, 215
Nasser, Gamal Abdel, 37, 39, 43, 58
nationalism (*wataniyya*), 129–30
National Salvation Front, 189
nizam kamil wa shamil (perfect order or system), 29, 77, 93, 108, 135
Noh, Mokhtar, 62, 91–92, 117
Nour Party, 170–71, 172, 186, 227, 228; electoral politics, 171; sharia and, 175

Onuf, Nicholas, 15, 21
Ouda, Bassem, 179

Pakistan, 86, 218
Palestine, 36, 43, 45, 66, 72, 120
partisanship/partyism (*hizbiyya*), 227; Hasan al-Banna on, 29, 50, 104; FJP, 169–70; MB and, 24, 47, 50, 57, 65, 75, 89, 103, 113, 121–22, 157; MB's middle generation and, 113; partisan instrumentalization of sharia, 76; as ungodly/not permitted, 28, 29, 35
perfect order or system. *See nizam kamil wa shamil*
piety (*taqwa*), 10, 37, 73, 226; active, 24, 47; being pious as example to others, 52–53, 65; cultivating, 69–71, 114, 115, 204, 227, 231; faith (*'iman*), 42, 60, 72, 85, 104, 108, 215, 224; individual, 202, 204, 227; MB's education on, 135, 138, 163, 164; MB's education on faith, 128, 129–31, 134, 135, 138; political work and, 52–53, 64, 65, 69, 84, 203, 211; righteous action and, 5, 215; ruling officials and, 95–96; *tarbiya* and, 34, 65
pilgrimage, 37, 118
political opportunities, 2, 213, 214, 221, 229, 230; MB and, 18, 26, 27, 115–26, 209
political theory, 9, 11
politics. *See* electoral politics; MB's politics; political opportunities; religion and politics
power, strength. *See quwa*
prayer: AWI (Morocco) and, 215; MB and, 33, 37, 41, 69, 103, 138
preaching. *See da'wa*
Prophet Muhammad, 26, 33, 42, 52, 73, 78, 177, 181; MB's education programs and, 130–31, 162, 165; on *shura*, 134–35. *See also* hadith; *sunna*

public good (*maslaha, masalih*), 57, 222, 224; FJP and, 176, 177, 185–86; MB and, 25, 42, 53, 56, 62, 69, 72, 76, 80, 84, 95, 104, 129, 145, 227; MB's electoral politics and, 68; sharia and, 61, 80, 82; Wafd Party/MB alliance and, 57

al-Qaradawi, Yusuf, 12, 43, 55, 108, 131, 133
Quran, 29, 30, 39, 52, 68, 96, 120, 157; on *hukm*, 35; MB's education programs and, 128, 130, 131, 133, 134, 162, 163; memorization of, 31; recitation of, 33
Quranic verses: 2:251 (*Al-Baqara*), 131; 3:118 (*Al 'Imran*), 130; 4:58 (*Al-Nisa'*), 131; 4:59 (*Al-Nisa'*), 131; 5:49 (*Al-Maida*), 78; 5:54 (*Al-Maida*), 39; 8:27 (*Al-'Anfal*), 131; 60:8 (*Al-Mumtahina*), 130; on jihad, 136, 138; on religious obligation, 133; on *shura*, 134
Qutb, Sayyid, 5, 128, 215; on *da'wa*, 37; on electoral participation, 51; *Fi Zilal al-Qur'an*, 134; on God's sovereignty, 23, 28; un-Islamic rule as apostasy, 79
quwa (power, strength), 100, 149; MB's education on, 129, 130, 134, 138; organizational strength, 159, 220; power of arms, 93, 104, 198; power of faith, 73, 93, 104, 198; power of unity, 93, 104, 198; *quwa amaliyya*, 104

Rady, Mohsen, 53
Ranko, Annette, 116–17
Raysuni, Ahmad, 221
religion: religious determinism, 9; as "strategic construct," 10. *See also* Christianity; Islam

religion and politics, 9–12, 34, 44–45, 84; AWI (Morocco), 224; Hasan al-Banna on, 29, 34–36, 50, 77, 129, 130, 199, 203; *da'wa*/political work tension, 230; Ennahda (Tunisia): party work/preaching separation, 213–14, 224; FJP, 156–57, 160; framing, 10, 19–20; MB's activism and, 5, 12, 116; MB's politics and religion, 1, 2–3, 4–5, 9, 22, 29, 44–45, 54, 98, 110, 124, 125–26, 129, 139–50, 152, 191–96, 203–5, 209, 210–11; MB's social activism and, 1, 3, 4–5, 8; MUR (Morocco), 223–24; Muslim identity and adaptation to politics, 6; politics and *da'wa*, 11; popular empowerment through religion, 59–60; religion as stable reference for political actors, 11, 203; religious framing and Islamist movements change, 3–4; separation of political and religious missions, 1–2, 4. *See also* Islamist movements; worship

renaissance, 23, 35; *nahda*, 158–59, 192; Nahda Project, 159, 177

repression: ban on MB, 45–46, 145, 196; "liberalization/opening" vs. "repression," 115, 159, 209; Hosni Mubarak and state repression of MB, 113, 122–23, 124, 145; state repression and arrests of MB members, 7, 18, 23, 26, 28, 36, 37, 39, 43, 49, 91, 112, 115, 116, 159, 176, 195, 209

revolution, 122; MB and, 43, 104–5, 155, 189, 196, 197–98, 200, 202, 212

righteous action (*'amal salih*): framing, 10–11; ideational change about, 19; MB and power-seeking, 92–105, 153; MB's activism and, 5, 13; MB's *da'wa* and, 5–6; MB's electoral policies and, 7, 48, 65, 141; MB's *minhaj* and, 32; MB's politics and, 7, 28, 37, 92–105, 119, 128, 153, 196–202, 207–8; MB's "righteous action" framing, 3–4, 5–6, 7, 8–9, 10, 14–16, 17, 18, 24, 26, 38, 50–1, 206; purposes of, 5; as religious obligation, 214; required of individual Muslims, 37–38; required of rulers or public authority, 37; as reward, 13; sharia and, 5–6; "trickle up" process of, 5

righteous reform. *See islah*

Ruggie, John Gerard, 20

rule. *See hukm*

rule of law, 44, 90–91, 147

al-Sadat, Anwar: 1970s liberalizing initiative, 39; assassination of, 45–46, 49, 81; Islamic revival and, 40; MB and, 39, 44–45, 60; political and constitutional reforms, 44–45, 48–49, 60, 81; religion and politics, 44–45, 184

sahwa. *See* awakening

al-salaf al-salih. *See* Companions of the Prophet

Salafism, 63, 87, 156; charitable social services, 171; Salafi movements, 226–28, 230; Salafi parties, 27, 170–73, 183, 210, 227, 228–29; Salafi preachers, 171, 172; sharia and, 172–73, 183–84, 210

salvation/afterlife: 97–98, 216, 217; collective, 12, 26, 164, 203, 209, 213; *da'wa* and, 11, 136, 220; individual, 11, 12, 164, 203, 209, 213; jihad and, 136, 137, 138; MB's education on, 164, 166; political work and, 25, 204, 209,

215, 216, 217; *tarbiya* and, 5; *thawab*, 138
Saudi Arabia, 112, 119, 219
SCAF (Supreme Council of the Armed Forces), 153, 167, 168–69, 178, 183; 2012 Parliament dissolution, 181
Schwedler, Jillian, 6, 19, 71, 209
secularism, 15, 56, 71, 120, 130, 182–83, 190, 228
Serageddin, Fouad, 59
el-Serghali, Ragheb, 172
al-Sha'arawi, Mitwalli, Shaykh, 40
sharia (Islamic law): after 2011, 172–73; AWI (Morocco) and, 219; al-Azhar and, 45, 80, 185–86, 210; candidates and, 173; collective religious obligation and, 61, 62; depoliticization of, 76; Egyptian Constitution, article 2, 56, 59, 60, 66, 80–82, 147, 184; Egyptian legislation and, 59–61, 62–64, 75, 77, 79–86, 184; Ennahda (Tunisia) and, 225; FJP and, 173–76, 178, 179, 180, 183–87; governance and, 24, 25, 39, 100; Hasan al-Hudaybi on, 38, 39, 79; Islamist movements and, 19; morality and, 78, 83–84, 88; MUR (Morocco) and, 221, 223; Nour Party and, 175; parties law and, 44; public good and, 61, 80, 82; as *qanun* or state law, 38, 79; righteous action and, 5–6; Salafis and, 172–73, 183–84, 210; "sharia inflation," 82; Abdel Fattah al-Sisi, and, 197; social justice and, 85, 179; state enforcement of, 172–73; Wafd Party and, 63, 64–65; working for God and, 5–6. *See also* MB and sharia
shar'iyya (legitimacy): MB/FJP and, 18, 26, 154, 187–91; tensions between religious and democratic framings of, 26
al-Shater, Khairat, 122, 128, 156, 158–59, 176–77, 188
al-Shawy, Tawfiq, 61, 62
shura (consultation), 37; AWI (Morocco) and, 218, 219, 223; Ennahda (Tunisia) and, 224, 225; God's will and, 71; MB's politics and, 25, 69–71, 73, 74, 114, 121, 124, 146–47, 154, 159; MB's training in *shura*, 100–101, 129, 133–35; MUR (Morocco) and, 221, 223; Prophet Muhammad on, 134–35; Quranic verses on, 134; as religious obligation, 133, 134; state power and, 78–79; training in, 100–101, 129, 133–35; as worship, 25, 134, 219
Shura Party: manifesto, 54–55, 83
el-Sirghaly, Ragheb, 176
al-Sisi, Abdel Fattah, 191, 196; sharia and, 197
socialism, 50, 65, 227
social justice, 80, 222, 228; FJP and, 187; MB and, 8, 31, 36, 172, 174, 204, 206, 208; sharia and, 85, 179
solidarity (*takaful*), 84, 120, 121, 143, 167, 212, 215; Hasan al-Banna on, 33–34; 'Ali Abdel Halim Mahmoud on, 99, 101, 102; MB's education and, 147; MB's *usra* and, 101, 142; social solidarity, 33, 85, 109
Somalia, 120
Somers, Margaret R., 13
sovereignty, 11
speech acts: audience of, 15, 17; framing and, 15, 16; MB speech acts, 14–20; publication site of, 17; "speech situation," 17
Spiegel, Avi, 6, 13, 222, 223

Stacher, Joshua, 112
state: "Brotherhoodization" of, 200; collective religious obligation as undertaken by, 149–50; MB and Islamization of, 76, 88, 108, 109; religious accountability, 45, 88; repression against Islamic activists, 58, 91; repression and arrests of MB members, 7, 18, 23, 26, 28, 36, 37, 39, 43, 49, 91, 112, 115, 116, 159, 176, 195, 209; repressive, and God's sovereignty, 28; *shura* and state power, 78–79; statist and institution-driven approach to applying God's will, 75. *See also* Islamic state; MB and power-seeking
struggle. *See* jihad
students. *See* youth/students
Sudan, 121, 219
Suez Canal, 36, 179
Sultan, Salah, 172
sunna, 29, 128
Sunni Islam, 156, 184
Supreme Constitutional Court, 59, 60, 80, 81, 82, 184
Swidler, Ann, 20
syndicates: Doctors, 116, 119, 120, 121; Engineers, 116, 118, 120, 121; Lawyers, 116, 117, 118, 120; MB: political work and professional, 114, 116–21; elections, 116, 117–18, 122; training in, activism, 161

Tabaar, Mohammad Ayatollahi, 10
Tagammu' (communist party), 71
takaful. *See* solidarity
tamkin. *See* empowerment
Tammam, Hossam, 7, 112
ta'mul. *See under* worldly dealings

tanfidh (applying the Islamic mission): Hasan al-Banna on, 43, 94; Hasan al-Hudaybi on, 38; 'Ali Abdel Halim Mahmoud on, 105; Mustafa Mashour on, 43; MB and, 34, 36, 75, 206–7; MB and power-seeking, 94–96, 97–99, 105, 107, 108; obligation of, 98
tanfidh al-shari'a (applying sharia). *See* sharia
tanzim. *See* MB's leadership; MB as organization
taqwa. *See* piety
tarbiya (ethical cultivation), 1, 8, 18, 207, 230; AWI (Morocco) and, 214, 215–17, 218; Hasan al-Banna on, 30, 31–32, 33, 34, 35, 93; bureau, 161, 162; candidates and, 141–42; Islamic activists' work as, 11; Islamist movements, *da'wa*, and, 11; Mustafa Mashour on, 70, 72–73; MB and power-seeking, 77, 83, 92–105, 110–11; MB's activism and, 3, 7, 12, 24; MB's *da'wa* and, 32, 207; MB's electoral politics and, 24, 48, 51–55, 65, 69, 153, 205; MB's framing and, 8, 15, 17, 28, 33; MB's *minhaj* and, 23, 30; MB's mission and, 5, 7, 22, 28, 36, 42, 73; MB's politics and, 2–3, 18, 25, 26, 48, 51, 69–71, 72, 92–105, 114–15, 139, 145, 150, 151, 152; MB's social activism and, 28, 114; MB's *usra* and, 12, 99; MUR (Morocco) and, 214, 221; through mutual consultation (*tarbiya shuriyya*), 134, 135; Parliament and, 48, 69–71; practical (*al-tarbiya al-'amaliyya*), 98–99, 113, 115, 117, 129, 135, 142, 216; as religious act, 5; social (*tarbiya al-ijtima'iyya*), 77, 95, 114, 115, 117, 139, 141, 151, 152, 204, 207;

tanzimi leadership and, 113, 114, 115; as tool for *islah*, 23
ta'ssub. See chauvinism
tatbiq al-shari'a. See sharia
thawab. See under salvation/afterlife
theocracy, 24, 56, 59, 88, 131
al-Tilmissany, Umar, 40, 41, 44, 45, 54, 65, 88; didactic purpose of election campaigning, 53; on *hukm*, 50; on *islah*, 62; on MB's *da'wa*, 49, 50; on morality, 49, 61, 62; Parliament and *da'wa*, 53–54; on political parties, 55; political work as religious obligation, 52; public work as jihad, 52; on sharia, 61, 62, 82, 90; on Wafd/MB's alliance, 56, 57
tourism, 180, 222; "halal tourism," 180
Tunisia, 209, 213; Tunisian Salafis, 226, 227–28, 229. *See also* Ennahda
Turkey, 85, 177, 196

Umar ibn Abdel Aziz, caliph, 163
Umar ibn al-Khattab, caliph, 163
umma (nation or community of Muslims), 97, 120, 129–32, 135, 137, 175; collective religious obligation of, 52, 132; commanding the right and, 82; electoral politics and, 50; Islamic state and *umma* as its source of authority and accountability, 149; ruler as delegate of the community (*wakil al-umma*), 133; unity of, 50, 57, 132, 159

Vannetzel, Marie, 4, 8, 141–42, 144, 151, 159–60, 170, 212
"Vision 28," 196–97, 199–201

Wafd Party, 52; commissive discourse, 56; MB's alliance with, 51, 55–59, 61, 64–65; sharia and, 63, 64–65
al-Wa'i, Tawfiq Yusuf, 126–27, 129
Wasat faction, 112, 113–14, 123–24
wataniyya. See nationalism
Wedeen, Lisa, 13, 20
welfare, 8, 30; MB's politics and, 54–55, 114, 121–22, 139, 141–43, 147, 151, 152, 170, 176, 178, 180; public, 54, 80, 84, 86, 96, 97, 176, 178, 180, 223; social, 34, 114, 142, 207. *See also khayriyya*
West, the, 68; atheism, 95, 130; corruption and, 95; health issues and, 119; Islamic society/order as opposed to, 68, 71, 79, 95, 120, 130; materialism and, 109, 130; MB's education and Western topics, 165–66; Western financing, 86
Wickham, Carrie Rosefsky, 6, 7, 8, 112, 115–17, 123
wilaya (government, temporal political authority), 87, 97
working for God (*'amal salih*), 14, 203; MB's framing and, 12, 16, 17, 204; MB's politics and, 1, 3; sharia and, 5–6
worldly dealings: MB's education on, 161–62, 164–65; *mu'amalat* (worldly dealings), 31, 39, 164; social *tarbiya* and 207; *ta'mul* (ethical dealings), 97, 143, 207, 217
worship (*'ibada*), 22, 31, 39, 106, 128, 203; correct worship, 32, 128; elections as, 117; political work as, 119, 146, 167, 206, 219; righteous action as, 99, 147; *shura* as, 25, 134, 219

Yacoub, Muhammad, 171
Yassine, Abdelsalam, 215–16, 217, 218, 220; *Al-minhaj al-nabawi* (The Prophetic Method), 215
Yassine, Nadia, 220
Yemen, 8, 209
Yildirim, A. Kadir, 216, 220, 222
youth/students: Islamic youth groups, 40, 43, 44, 45; MB and, 40–42, 44, 45, 46, 49, 57, 62, 67, 92, 104, 149, 203, 220; MB's education and student activists, 161, 162–63; MUR (Morocco) and, 214; radicalization of, 91; student activism/youth groups, 40, 46, 92, 191, 193, 196; networks, 39, 41, 43; summer camps, 40, 41–42, 118, 120, 160
Yusuf, Yusuf Kamal Muhammad, 117–18

al-Zaafarani, Ibrahim, 156
Zakariyya, Fouad, 87
zakat (charity, charitable contribution), 103, 147, 160, 219, 228; economy and, 84, 85, 86, 147, 187; as obligation, 84, 85, 86
Zollner, Barbara H. E., 9

Sumita Pahwa is an associate professor of politics at Scripps College in Claremont, California, where she also teaches in the Middle East and North Africa Studies program. She received her PhD from Johns Hopkins University and a BA from Middlebury College. Her research interests are in religion and politics, social movements, South Asia, and the Middle East. Her current research focuses on Muslim civil society in India.

www.ingramcontent.com/pod-product-compliance
Lightning Source LLC
Chambersburg PA
CBHW051211300426
44116CB00006B/524